Rohinton Mistry

PETER MOREY

Manchester University Press
Manchester and New York

distributed exclusively in the USA by Palgrave

The right of Peter Morey to be identified as the author of this work has been
asserted by him in accordance with the Copyright, Designs and Patents Act 1988.

Published by Manchester University Press
Oxford Road, Manchester M13 9NR, UK
and Room 400, 175 Fifth Avenue, New York, NY 10010, USA
www.manchesteruniversitypress.co.uk

Distributed exclusively in the USA by
Palgrave, 175 Fifth Avenue, New York, NY 10010, USA

Distributed exclusively in Canada by
UBC Press, University of British Columbia, 2029 West Mall,
Vancouver, BC, Canada V6T 1Z2

British Library Cataloguing-in-Publication Data
A catalogue record for this book is available from the British Library

Library of Congress Cataloging-in-Publication Data applied for

ISBN 0 7190 6714 6 *hardback*
EAN 978 0 7190 6714 3
ISBN 0 7190 6715 4 *paperback*
EAN 978 0 7190 6715 0

First published 2004
12 11 10 09 08 07 06 05 04   10 9 8 7 6 5 4 3 2 1

Typeset in Aldus
by Koinonia, Manchester
Printed in Great Britain
by Bell & Bain Ltd, Glasgow

Rohinton Mistry

Published in our
centenary year
04
HESTER
ERSITY
ESS

CONTEMPORARY WORLD WRITERS

SERIES EDITOR   JOHN THIEME

ALREADY PUBLISHED IN THE SERIES
Peter Carey   BRUCE WOODCOCK
Kazuo Ishiguro   BARRY LEWIS
Hanif Kureishi   BART MOORE-GILBERT
Timothy Mo   ELAINE YEE LIN HO
Toni Morrison   JILL MATUS
Alice Munro   CORAL ANN HOWELLS
Les Murray   STEVEN MATTHEWS
Caryl Phillips   BÉNÉDICTE LEDENT
Ngugi wa Thiong'o   PATRICK WILLIAMS
Derek Walcott   JOHN THIEME

For Ami with love

Contents

ACKNOWLEDGEMENTS viii
SERIES EDITOR'S FOREWORD x
LIST OF ABBREVIATIONS xi
CHRONOLOGY xii

1 Contexts and intertexts 1

2 'Throbbing between two lives': the structures
of migration in *Tales from Firozsha Baag* 27

3 Mistry's Hollow Men: language, lies and the crisis
of representation in *Such a Long Journey* 69

4 Thread and circuses: performing in the spaces
of city and nation in *A Fine Balance* 94

5 Running repairs: corruption, community and
duty in *Family Matters* 125

6 Critical overview 152

7 Conclusion — Rohinton Mistry: international
man of stories 171

NOTES 178
SELECT BIBLIOGRAPHY 197
INDEX 205

Acknowledgements

So many people have helped this study on its way that it seems invidious to single out individuals. However, certain colleagues and friends old and new have had a direct impact on what follows. They include Ken Swindell, who first introduced me to the work of Rohinton Mistry, and Roger Bromley, Shirley Chew and Elleke Boehmer who, quite apart from their perennial support, gave their various seals of approval to the project in its early stages. In London, Roberta Garrett and Kate Hodgkin, colleagues from the University of East London, offered practical help by locating some early reviews of *Family Matters* while I was out of the country. Likewise, Angela Atkins furnished material which gave me a head start on that particular novel. Thanks are also owed to William Radice and Narguess Farzad from the School of Oriental and African Studies, University of London: the former for allowing me to refine some of the ideas relating to *Such a Long Journey* in a guest teaching slot on his South Asian Literature course; and the latter for her patient explication of the Iranian literary heritage and its relation to Zoroastrianism (needless to say, any errors of fact or interpretation in the study are entirely my own). I also wish to single out Stacey Gibson, Associate Editor of the University of Toronto Magazine, who was unstintingly helpful on several occasions, particularly in providing a copy of the magazine's interview with Mistry. Unfortunately for her, this courtesy, promptness and efficiency ensured that I returned to her with quite unrelated queries subsequently, which she nevertheless fielded with patience and cheerfulness. (Thanks also to Prem Poddar for giving me this lead in the first place.) I acknowledge with gratitude the assistance of Richard Gasee at McClelland and Stewart for providing additional information to help make the volume complete. Likewise, thanks go to Rohinton Mistry himself for providing details of his education. I wish also to take this opportunity to thank John Thieme, whose help has been invaluable as the project has come together. He has never been too busy to answer enquiries about any number of issues pertaining both to the Contemporary World Writers Series or Mistry more generally. Equally supportive and forthcoming were Matthew Frost and the team at Manchester University Press, without whom, of course ...

At an institutional level, I would like to thank the School of Cultural and Innovation Studies, University of East London, for the sabbatical period which allowed the book to gain momentum, and the Arts and Humanities Research Board (AHRB) for the generous funding which enabled completion.

Part of the chapter on *Family Matters* has previously appeared in the *Journal of Commonwealth Literature*, 38:2 (2003).

Finally, I would like to thank Amina Yaqin for her patience, support and steaming cups of tea.

Series editor's foreword

Contemporary World Writers is an innovative series of authorita-tive introductions to a range of culturally diverse contemporary writers from outside Britain and the United States or from 'minority' backgrounds within Britain or the United States. In addition to providing comprehensive general introductions, books in the series also argue stimulating original theses, often but not always related to contemporary debates in post-colonial studies.

The series locates individual writers within their specific cul-tural contexts, while recognising that such contexts are themselves invariably a complex mixture of hybridised influences. It aims to counter tendencies to appropriate the writers discussed into the canon of English or American literature or to regard them as 'other'.

Each volume includes a chronology of the writer's life, an introductory section on formative contexts and intertexts, discussion of all the writer's major works, a bibliography of primary and sec-ondary works and an index. Issues of racial, national and cultural identity are explored, as are gender and sexuality. Books in the series also examine writers' use of genre, particularly ways in which Western genres are adapted or subverted and 'traditional' local forms are reworked in a contemporary context.

Contemporary World Writers aims to bring together the theoretical impulse which currently dominates post-colonial studies and closely argued readings of particular authors' works, and by so doing to avoid the danger of appropriating the specifics of particular texts into the hegemony of totalising theories.

List of abbreviations

AFB   *A Fine Balance*
FM   *Family Matters*
SLJ   *Such a Long Journey*
TFB   *Tales from Firozsha Baag*

I have used the editions published in the United Kingdom by Faber and Faber. All page numbers refer to these editions.

Chronology

1952	Rohinton Mistry born in Bombay on 3 July, the second of four children.
1955–58	Enrolled at Villa Theresa Primary School, Bombay.
1958–69	Attends St Xavier's High School, Bombay, a Jesuit foundation with an anglicised curriculum.
1969–73	Studies at the University of Bombay for a BSc in Mathematics and Economics.
1970–71	Briefly considers a career as a folk singer, and is described as 'Bombay's Bob Dylan'.
1972	Meets Freny Elavia at music school.
1975	Emigrates to Canada and settles in Toronto. Finds job as a clerk (later customer service supervisor) in the Canadian Imperial Bank of Commerce, Toronto. Marries Freny.
1979–83	Studies part-time at Woodsworth College, University of Toronto, for a BA in English and Philosophy.
1983	Enters and wins the first Hart House Literary Contest with his story 'One Sunday'.
1984	Wins second Hart House Literary Contest with 'Auspicious Occasion'. The short stories that will later comprise *Tales from Firozsha Baag* begin to be anthologised in Canadian journals and publications.
1985	Awarded a Canada Council Grant enabling him to leave his bank job and become a full-time writer. Wins *Canadian Fiction Magazine*'s annual Contributor's Prize.

1987   *Tales from Firozsha Baag* published by Penguin Books, Canada, Faber and Faber in the UK, and by Houghton Mifflin in the USA where it is re-titled *Swimming Lessons and Other Stories from Firozsha Baag.*

1991   *Such a Long Journey* published. Novel wins Governor General's Award for Fiction, Commonwealth Writers Prize, W.H. Smith Prize. Also shortlisted for the Booker Prize.

1995   *A Fine Balance* published. Novel wins Governor General's Award, Giller Prize, Royal Society for Literature's Winifred Holtby Prize, Los Angeles Times Award for Fiction. Again shortlisted for the Booker Prize.

1999   *Such a Long Journey* made into a film by Sturla Gunnarson, starring Om Puri and Roshan Seth. The film wins three Genie Awards.

2001   *A Fine Balance* chosen to feature as a Book of the Month on the Oprah Winfrey Show. The programme is transmitted early in 2002 with Rohinton Mistry as a studio guest. An extra 750,000 copies of the novel are printed, 500,000 of which are sold.

2002   *Family Matters* published. Once more shortlisted for the Booker Prize. In November Mistry cancels the second half of his US promotional tour, citing the 'unbearable humiliation' of the racial profiling to which he is subjected at US airports.

Contexts and intertexts

> It may be that writers in my position, exiles or emigrants
> or expatriates, are haunted by some sense of loss, some
> urge to reclaim, to look back, even at the risk of being
> mutated into pillars of salt. But if we do look back we
> must do so in the knowledge – which gives rise to pro-
> found uncertainties – that our physical alienation from
> India almost inevitably means that we will not be capable
> of reclaiming precisely that thing that was lost, that we
> will, in short, create fictions, not actual cities or villages,
> but invisible ones, imaginary homelands, Indias of the
> mind. (Salman Rushdie, *Imaginary Homelands*, p. 10)

AT the end of the short story, 'Swimming Lessons', the
narrator, a young writer, observes an old man in his Toronto
apartment block staring silently at the flakes of snow falling
outside. He muses:

> What thoughts is he thinking as he watches them? Of
> childhood days, perhaps, and snowmen with hats and pipes,
> and snowball fights, and white Christmases, and Christmas
> trees? What will I think of, old in this country, when I sit
> and watch the snow come down? ... my snowmen and
> snowball fights and Christmas trees are in the pages of
> Enid Blyton's books, dispersed amidst the adventures of
> the Famous Five, and the Five Find-Outers, and the Secret
> Seven. My snowflakes are even less forgettable than the
> old man's, for they never melt. (*TFB*, 244)

This evocative passage captures the poignant enigma of the
exile's imagination, forged in one culture and location but

obliged to grapple in language with the everyday realities of another. It is tempting to see reflected here the position of its author, Rohinton Mistry, born in Bombay, now resident in Canada, but continually raiding the cupboards of memory for the dusty but tangible remnants of the India he has left behind. Yet the last sentence also suggests an increased vividness to the experiences of a childhood distanced by space as well as time: as if the migrant writer is empowered by that very geographical separation to fashion images with the sharpness of cut crystal, which will throw a new, diffused light on the familiarities of 'home', as well as on the peculiarities of elsewhere. Like the travelling journeyman of the Middle Ages, referred to by Walter Benjamin, bringing back tales of far-flung places, Mistry's work as a whole, with its repeated image of journeys of various kinds, combines 'the lore of faraway places, such as a much-traveled man brings home, with the lore of the past, as it best reveals itself to natives of a place'.[1]

Rohinton Mistry was born into the Parsi community of Bombay on 3 July 1952. He was the second of four children, three boys and a girl. (His younger brother, Cyrus, went on to be a respected playwright in Bombay.) Rohinton's father was an advertising account executive, and he recalls his mother, happy in the role of nurturer 'doing the miracle that all mothers perform of making what was barely enough seem like abundance. We didn't have new clothes and shoes as often as we might have liked but we were certainly better off than half the population.'[2] (Perhaps, in this respect, she is the model for some of his later female characters, using their domestic capacities to keep households together and children fed in spite of the impulsive and often destructive tendencies of their husbands.)

He was educated at St Xaviers, a Jesuit-run institution with a heavily anglicised curriculum, having already, like many of his own young creations, been weaned on the children's books of Enid Blyton and Richmal Crompton. In the school library he discovered more English fiction: works by Agatha Christie and Leslie Charteris, stories about the ace aviator Biggles and the detective Bulldog Drummond. The school itself ensured the digestion of reams of canonical English literature, including Shakespeare, Dickens and the Victorian poets. Recollecting the shape of this curriculum years later, Mistry valued its breadth, but also recognised the mismatch of a colonial education in a postcolonial environment: 'Part of the tragedy of the educated middle classes in Bombay was this yearning for something unattainable that came from what they read. Would that sense of a future elsewhere have been avoided if we had concentrated on an Indian literary canon? I don't know.'[3] Essentially, Mistry seems to be describing the same predicament that Salman Rushdie has seen as typical of the Bombay middle class of his generation, everywhere surrounded by images of a 'dream England' that never existed outside the pages of children's adventure novels.[4]

Given the prevalence of such images of a rainbow's end abroad and the equation of emigration with success in the 1960s and 1970s, it is perhaps unsurprising that, having completed a BSc in Mathematics and Economics at Bombay University, Mistry emigrated to Canada in 1975. He was following his soon-to-be wife, Freny Elavia, whom he had met at music school at the beginning of the decade. After a few fruitless applications he secured a job as a clerk in the Canadian Imperial Bank of Commerce in Toronto. However, despite rising to the level of customer service supervisor, Mistry found the work unfulfilling. He and Freny decided to enrol at the University of Toronto. She eventually qualified as a teacher, while he studied for a BA in English and Philosophy, rekindling his early interest in literature and, no doubt, laying the groundwork for the insistent philosophical questions that were to dog his characters, and which they each, in different ways, try to square with the demands of daily life and family commitments.

In one respect, however, it appears that Mistry became a writer almost by accident. Prompted by his wife to enter the first Hart House Literary contest, he took a few days' sick leave from the bank, settled down at the typewriter and, over a long week-end, drafted the story that would prove to be the competition's winning entry, 'One Sunday'. Apart from a few prescribed forays at school, Mistry has asserted that this 'was the first time I'd ever sat down to write, and I think I was fascinated by the process itself – watching the words appear at the typewriter'.[5] (The following year he matched this achievement when 'Auspicious Occasion', which would become the first story in the volume *Tales from Firozsha Baag*, was also chosen as winner of the Hart House prize.) Lionised by the Canadian literary establishment, and anthologised in various journals, Mistry was propelled into a hugely successful career which has seen him publish a collection of short stories, *Tales from Firozsha Baag* (1987), three novels – *Such a Long Journey* (1991), *A Fine Balance* (1995), and *Family Matters* (2002), receive a host of literary prizes, and achieve recognition as one of the most important contemporary writers of postcolonial literature.

Mistry draws his inspiration both from sharply recalled childhood experiences and from the upheavals of migration. However, as always with such intense and apparently personal narratives, the relationship between fiction and autobiography is hard to determine. Certainly there are overlaps between the events and life choices of the writer and some of his characters: Mistry felt pressured into taking his first degree in a science subject rather than the arts, to which he was arguably more suited, just as Sohrab Noble, in *Such a Long Journey*, feels the weight of similar strictures but finally rebels against them; and one of his keenest childhood memories is of being sanctioned by his school principal, Father de Souza, to borrow two books a week instead of one from the St Xavier's library, a boast also shared by the young Jehangir Bulsara in *Tales from Firozsha Baag*. However, a writer and his creations should always be treated as separate entities, and Mistry has firmly refuted any direct autobiographical elements in the migration stories in *Tales from Firozsha Baag*, despite critics' determination to look for them there. His own view is more circumspect: 'Writers write best about what they know ... In the broad sense, as a processing of everything one hears or witnesses, all fiction is autobiographical – imagination ground through the mill of memory. It's impossible to separate the two ingredients.'[6]

Being part of a minority community in India, *and* having subsequently migrated to Canada, Mistry can offer a unique perspective on the multiple accommodations involved in the construction of identities. Indeed, identity forms a key theme in his work and is seen in both personal and national terms. His writing provides a wry, but occasionally tragic perspective on the postcolonial nation of India: a perspective from the margins, so to speak. Likewise, the diverse inheritance he enjoys, both as a postcolonial subject and as a member of an ethnic and religious minority group which historically favoured the British and adopted British cultural values in the days of the Raj, can be seen in the literary influences on his fiction, which include the great works of nineteenth- and twentieth-century European literature, the key texts of Indian literature in English, and the Persian epic storytelling tradition. Moreover, Mistry's life and writing can be seen to interrogate 'the national' as a supposedly adequate signifier of identity on a number of levels. His acquired 'Canadianness', and the setting of the last few stories in *Tales from Firozsha Baag,* make him a chronicler of the experience of migrancy to set alongside Salman Rushdie and Bharati Mukherjee – although his unassuming, carefully crafted prose is a world away from Rushdie's linguistic pyrotechnics and Mukherjee's dark ironies – and situate him within the hesitant and sometimes contradictory project of Canadian multicultural-ism, a project of which Mistry, among others, is avowedly suspicious. On the other hand, his recurring treatment of India, and especially Bombay, in the 1960s and 1970s, makes him a sensitive, compassionate but at times acerbic commentator on the abuses of power associated in particular with Indira Gandhi's administrations. This commentary is played out in novels of rare power and symbolic complexity, which often pit well-intentioned marginal or 'minor' figures against sinister institu-tional forces in a way reminiscent of both the individualistic struggles of the classic modernist subject, and the dutiful Parsi who is required to participate actively in promoting the forces of good and contesting those of evil in the world in the name of *Ahura Mazda,* the Wise Lord.

Indeed, the Zoroastrian faith provides the philosophical mortar with which the lives and choices of many of Mistry's characters are bound together. Zoroastrianism is the world's oldest surviving prophetically revealed religion. As such it has had a profound influence on the development of later belief systems, such as Judaism and Christianity. In fact, the intellectual traditions and moral framework of Zoroastrianism have helped shape much of the western intellectual tradition. The religion was established by the priest and prophet Zarathustra (also known as Zoroaster), who probably came from the north eastern region of modern day Iran. Very little is known about Zarathustra himself. Other than the seventeen *Gathas* or hymns attributed to him, nothing survives to offer a direct link between modern-day Zoroastrians and their prophet. Even dating Zarathustra and his teachings proves difficult. Several western scholars of Zoroastrianism have estimated that Zarathustra was active some time around the fifth or sixth centuries before Christ. However, there is a tradition among the Parsis that suggests that their prophet lived and taught as far back as 5000 to 6000 BC. There is no historical evidence to support what is, on the face of it, an extremely early date, but, as Eckehard Kulke has pointed out, this belief 'is of enormous psychological relevancy because it helps the Parsees [sic] to that feeling of religious exclusivity necessary for the existence and survival of the community'.[7] Majority opinion among contemporary scholars of the religion, however, based on evidence which indicates a linguistic link between Zarathustra's fragments and the later texts of the Hindu Vedic tradition, suggests a date of around 1400 BC.[8] However, such dating remains to a certain extent speculative, not least because an enormous amount of useful evidence – indeed much of the whole tradition – was lost when Alexander's conquering army destroyed the library at Persepolis, home to many of the faith's sacred scriptures, in 331 BC.[9] Nevertheless, it appears that the great Persian kings of the Achaemenian dynasty, Cyrus and Darius, who ruled in the sixth century BC, followed a brand of religion akin to Zoroastrianism, while under their successors, the Sassanians, who ruled between 226 and 651 CE, Zoroastrianism became the official state religion.

Within Zoroastrianism, worship is directed towards the one true God, *Ahura Mazda* (also known in the Pahlavi language as *Ohrmazd*), who was before the beginning of time and shall be when everything has passed away. *Ahura Mazda* stands at the head of a pantheon of spiritual entities called the *Amesha Spentas*, personifications of attributes such as Truth, Righteousness, Good Thoughts, Power, Health and Long Life.[10] Against these manifestations of Light stands the evil spirit, *Angra Mainyu* (or *Ahriman*), who dwells in darkness and is the instigator of all deceit. (The tension between these manifestations of Good and Evil, and the question of the extent to which *Angra Mainyu* came after, and is subordinate to, *Ahura Mazda*, has meant that Zoroastrianism has been understood both as a monotheistic and a dualistic religion, depending on historical context and the intellectual preferences of the times.)[11] What is clear is that the decision to follow the path of righteousness, and thus assist in the cosmic struggle of good against evil, and *Ahura Mazda* against *Angra Mainyu*, must be consciously made by each Zoroastrian. Not to assist proactively the force of good in one's everyday life is tacitly to support the power of evil. This choice is enshrined in the Zoroastrian ethical code, requiring from the believer 'good thoughts, good words and good deeds' (*'manashni, gavashni, kunashni'*).

For the Zoroastrian, then, faith is manifest in a morally informed interaction with the material world, rather than the retreat from it sanctioned by some other religions. Yet there are also physical symbols and rituals that serve to remind the Zoroastrian of his or her faith and its attendant obligations. For example, fire is an object of veneration, not as a deity in itself, but as an earthly symbol of divine righteousness or *Asha*. Rohinton Mistry's writing is imbued with the ancient Zoroastrian faith on every level. Several scenes take place in the Zoroastrian place of worship, the Fire Temple (*Atash Bahram*), particularly in *Family Matters*, where the protagonist Yezad comes to see the slow tranquility of the Fire Temple, with its ancient rituals and ever-burning flame, as a haven from the chaotic and uncontrollable world around him. Mistry also introduces the non-Parsi reader to Zoroastrian funerary rites, especially in the moving description of the subdued procession that accompanies Dinshawji to his final destination in the *Dakhma,* or Tower of Silence, in *Such a Long Journey,* while at the beginning of the same novel, we witness the protagonist, Gustad Noble, at his morning prayers – a ritual that requires the untying and retying of the sacred *kusti* cord worn by all Parsis after their *navjote* ceremony initiating them into the faith.

Great emphasis is placed on purity in Zoroastrian doctrine and practice. One example of this is the way in which the sacred fire is carefully tended and kept free from pollution. Likewise, the fate of the dead, whose corpses are deposited in the Towers of Silence where they are stripped of flesh by vultures – a controversial method of disposal with both advocates and opponents in the modern Parsi community – is designed so that none of the four elements, earth, air, water and especially fire, should be contaminated. This interest in issues of purity and pollution greatly exercises Mistry in his work. The body as a visceral, leaky, malfunctioning and vulnerable entity plays a prominent role in each text, as the author appears fascinated by the impossible demands of inviolability. The requirements of purity take many forms, sometimes being translated by charac-ters into a need to hold themselves aloof from the corrupt and corrupting world around them; a quietism which contravenes the faith's insistence on engagement, and which Mistry appears to view as an understandable but potentially disastrous abroga-tion of basic human fellowship. Sometimes, however, the pure and impure, sacred and profane collide accidentally in moments of grotesque farce: Mrs Mody is forced to travel through the hot plains in the same car as the putrifying body of her husband in 'The Collectors'; and the proud Rustomji finds his spotless ceremonial wear soiled by a chance projectile of betel juice while on the way to the Fire Temple in 'Auspicious Occasion'.

However, because of a declining birth rate, strict laws about intermarriage with other faiths, and a historical interdiction against accepting conversions, the number of Zoroastrians is in slow but steady decline. It has been estimated that, at most, there are only 150,000 Zoroastrians left in the world today.[12] Of the remaining Zoroastrians, the majority lives in India, and it is this community that has become known as the Parsis.

The Parsis are mainly based in and around Bombay. The community is composed of the descendants of a group of Zoroastrians who left Iran some time after its conquest by Muslim Arab invaders and the fall of the Sassanian dynasty. Once more, there are problems in dating this flight. It is known that a group of Zoroastrians left Iran for India some time between the eighth and tenth centuries of the Christian era, although the specific dates advanced – 785 or 936 CE – depend on one's reading of the rather unspecific and sole chronicle of this journey, the *Kisseh-i Sanjan*, written by a Parsi priest, Bahman Kaikobad seven or eight hundred years after the events it describes.[13] Furthermore, the exact reason for the flight from Iran to India has itself become something of a contentious issue among twentieth-century Parsi scholars. The traditional view was that the Persian Zoroastrians who migrated found Muslim rule intolerable and set out to find a place where they could practise their religion undisturbed. However, it has also been suggested that '"the migration of the Parsis to the west coast of India was not so much a flight as a readjustment of commercial patterns which had arisen prior to Islam" wherein Parsi dominance of trade with India had been increasingly challenged by the activities of Arab merchants'.[14] Legend also has it that on their arrival in Gujarat they were met by the local monarch, Jadi Rana, who imposed upon them five conditions for acceptance which have become the identifying coordinates of the Parsi community ever since: their priests would have to explain this unfamiliar religion to the king; the Parsis would have to give up their native language and take on Gujarati; the women should discard their traditional dress and adopt that of the local female population; the men should give up their weapons; and Parsi wedding processions could only take place after dark.[15] (Nilufer Bharucha has suggested that these conditions contributed to that feeling of alienation the new arrivals would already have had and, thus, sowed the seeds of that sense of separateness from India the community has always maintained.)[16]

In any case, the Parsis – taking their name from one of their home provinces in Iran – settled in Gujarat as farmers and traders. They lived quietly until the beginning of the European colonial era when trading posts were established first at Surat and later at Bombay. The more enterprising Parsis saw an opportunity and moved to these burgeoning seaports where – unencumbered by the socio-religious prohibitions to do with caste and occupation that impeded Hindu society – their social flexibility saw them become 'the economic mediating community between Europeans and the Indian hinterland'.[17] The rise to power and wealth of a number of Parsis in the eighteenth and nineteenth century was, perhaps unsurprisingly, accompanied by an increasing cultural and political identification with their British colonial masters, with whom they worked so closely, and in whose imperial grandeur they saw both echoes of their own lost Persian greatness, and a model for the future of their community. However, it would be inaccurate to look upon the Parsis as merely forming part of what in Marxist terms might be called a 'comprador class': '(literally, buyers) who specialised in the handling of foreign goods, produced nothing themselves, and were thus essentially parasitic'.[18] On the contrary, as Kulke has argued, the colonial Parsis can be read, rather, as a 'creative minority', in Toynbee's phrase,[19] who were instrumental in the rise of modern Bombay. Parsis played a dominant role in the creation of wealth in the city and thereby in India as a whole. In the nineteenth century they were at the heart of the development of banking and insurance, of ship-building, cotton and other textiles, jute, chemicals, steel and, later, aviation. Of the many entrepreneurs – several of whom were elevated to the peerage by the sympathetic British – perhaps the most cele- brated was J. N. Tata, whose tentacular business interests made him a millionaire many times over and who established a dynasty whose influence is still felt today. The nineteenth century was also the era when Parsis took the lead in social reform. From the 'Young Bombay' movement of the mid-nineteenth century, liberal thinkers, influenced by the tenets of humanism imbibed with their western-style education, spread out into wider Indian society, reshaping their own community, its structures and practices along the way. Figures such as Dadabhai Naoroji, Sir Jamset Jeejeebhoy, K. R. Cama and D. F. Karaka took the lead over issues such as education, religious reform and political representation, while Behramji Malabari spent much of his life working for the uplift of Indian women. (Indeed, the Parsi community led the way in the education of women, with the writer, lawyer and activist Cornelia Sorabji holding an especially prominent place.) Likewise, philanthropists such as Sir Dinshaw Petit, Sir Cowasjee Readymoney and N. M. Wadia carried the charitable spirit their religion required of them out into the country and beyond. Moreover, despite their general anglophilia, Parsis were also active in the early, moderate phase of the Indian Congess Party. Naoroji, Pherozeshah Mehta and D. E. Wacha highlighted the economic disequilibrium of colonialism and argued for improved British rule or, failing that, Home Rule (*Swaraj*). (In fact, Naoroji was the first Indian politician to call for *Swaraj* in his presidential address to the Congress Party.)[20] However, for all this furious activity, the Parsi community as a whole was still overwhelmingly loyal to the British. Indeed, at the time, the interventions of nationalist politicians such as Naoroji and Mehta – while bestowing a sense of relevance and importance on the community – were often seen as subversive and reprehensible. (Needless to say, in the postcolonial era their role has been revalued and they are now viewed as central to the community's sense of itself in the pre-independence era.)

In postcolonial India the Parsis have seen their prominence decline and their previously disproportionate influence shrink, as Indian society has shaped itself through secular, and latterly, Hindu paradigms. As well as a numerically declining population, there is also a sense of narrowing opportunity for young Parsis in India. The attraction of migration to the west – such as that undergone by Rohinton Mistry – has correspondingly increased.

Nevertheless, at the heart of Parsi group identity are still the same essential elements that have historically given them a feeling of difference from the surrounding cultures: religious uniqueness; ethnic identity; a shared history and a sense of elite status.[21] Buttressing the latter for much of the last three hundred years was the presence of the British. As Tanya Luhrmann has put it, the Parsis identified with the 'symbolic discourse of colonial authority'.[22] They internalised the powerful side of colonial self-representation to create an image of the 'Good Parsi' who, like his British role-model, was 'more truthful, more pure, more charitable, more progressive, more rational and more masculine than the Hindu-of-the-masses'.[23] As with other elite Indians, the Parsis shaped their ideals and aesthetics around British values. However, their sense of self became frozen at a particular moment of communal ascendancy. Now there is a notion among the Parsis that they have themselves become ineffectual and emasculated, overtaken by the majority Hindu population who now manifest the qualities of a dominant group. This Parsi feeling of degeneration is encapsulated in the phrase Luhrmann uses as one of her chapter titles in *The Good Parsi*: 'We are not What we Were'.[24]

It is possible to see the position of the Parsis as a preeminent example of that hybridity diagnosed as characteristic of the colonial encounter by Homi K. Bhabha – himself an Indian-born Parsi who now lives and works in the West. Bhabha describes colonial identity as marked by ambivalence, involving a process of both identification with the colonial Other, and a disavowal of him. Essentially, colonial identity is a site of hybridity that lies *between* coloniser and colonised, and is characterised by both fear and desire. On the part of the colonised – in this case the Parsis – internalisation of colonial paradigms leads to the creation of mimic men and women who eagerly lap up the values of their masters but, for all their efforts, can never erase the difference that exists between them. As Childs and Williams, quoting Bhabha, explain, mimicry is sanctioned by the coloniser, who wishes to produce an approved, revised version of the native:

all the better to exclude and denounce the majority 'bad natives'. Mimicry is ambivalent because it requires a similarity and a dissimilarity: 'a difference that is almost the same, but not quite' ... It relies on resemblance, on the colonized becoming like the colonizer, but always remaining different ... 'to be Anglicised is *emphatically* not to be English'.[25]

Thus, while the Parsis distanced themselves from the Indian cultures around them in the colonial period, they could never hope to be fully accepted by the British. Luhrmann suggests that Parsi ambivalence is therefore a product of the double-edged yearning for, and resentment of, British identity; what she calls the 'knot/not at the centre of the postcolonial encounter'.[26] With the departure of the British a deep-seated estrangement from India and a loss of identity come to the fore.

However, there are entries to be made in the credits column of the colonial ledger when it comes to literature and culture. Specifically, a thousand years of life in India cannot be expected to have left the community's outlook unaltered. Susan Stiles Maneck has made a convincing case for the traceable influence of Hinduism on Parsi social structures, and of Islam in the area of theology.[27] That perennial adaptability that served the community so well during colonialism can be seen as the result of a highly developed instinct to blend in with the general environment dating back to the community's arrival in India. Moreover, perhaps the idea of adopting a kind of protective colouring, of borrowing from surrounding cultures, offers us a clue to the magpie-like qualities in the writing of Rohinton Mistry who, in a sense, enjoys an inheritance that borrows from western, Persian and South Asian traditions. The legacy of colonial mimicry is less a debilitating hangover for Mistry than a deep well of literary styles from which he can freely draw. Mistry's various intertexts are not so much Barthesian 'quotations drawn from the innumerable centres of culture',[28] as quotations drawn from various cultures. Linda Hutcheon has remarked on how Salman Rushdie's intertexts are 'doubled' – composed of both Indian and western references and allusions.[29]

Of Mistry it could be said that his texts are governed by a hybridity that operates on three levels: the hybridity of an Iranian cultural tradition transposed, via India, to Canada, and the variations and local modifications it has picked up along the way; hybridity in terms of the Parsi relationship to western cultural values, manifest in anglophilia, and evidenced both in Mistry's education and in the European literary influences scattered across his writing; and a hybridity of possible readings – one can read his works in relation to a canonical western tradition, in the context of a vibrant body of Indian literature both in English and other languages, or in terms of a Persian storytelling tradition and the specifically Zoroastrian coordinates of the moral dilemmas confronting his characters. Accordingly, although Mistry has sometimes been interpreted as a traditional writer, reanimating the nineteenth-century novel and nodding reverently in the direction of its foremost practitioners, it is equally possible – and, I would argue, more rewarding – to think of his texts as subtle enactments of the postcolonial injunction to reiterate and subvert colonial categories, from the inside, as it were, through echoes and mimicry, rather than aggressive opposition. In this way, Mistry's use of the novel form, for example, corresponds to Abdul JanMohamed and David Lloyd's account of how a 'minor literature' can reshape the novel, 'thus transforming what were once efficacious vehicles for the representation of individually, atomistically oriented experiences into collective modes of articulation'.[30] Indeed, Mistry's characters often personify the position of the Parsi community as a whole: they tend to be marginal figures living in ghettoised circumstances, and with an attendant siege mentality; they are frequently conscious of their difference from the surrounding population – something which is occasionally played out in snobbery or prejudice; and they are usually brought to an awareness that they need to take up a moral position, but are also conscious that this may have a limited impact against political and social forces much more powerful than they.

In this respect, then, Mistry's writing can be situated firmly within the postcolonial project of dialogue with, and appropriation of, colonial generic forms. It speaks through existing literary models, while at the same time disrupting what W. H. New has called 'the codes and forms of the dominant language in order to reclaim speech for oneself'.[31] Mistry's adaptation of narrative norms develops from *Tales from Firozsha Baag*, where words in Hindi, Gujarati and the ancient Avestan, Persian and Pahlavi languages describing Zoroastrian ritual and accoutrements, are italicised to stand out from the surrounding English, to a more subtle technique wherein such words are woven into the very fabric of the English narrative, providing sudden little tremors of defamiliarisation for the English-language reader. As Frank Kermode puts it: 'Mistry … occasionally leaves whole sentences in languages few Western readers understand. Others are part Hindi, part Gujarati and part English.'[32] However, while this is a strategy straight out of the manual of postcolonial appropriation, there is a danger in overlooking the cultural specificities of Mistry's narrative materials that inhere in the history and the experience of the Parsis. While Mistry's texts are concerned to examine the complexities of contemporary alienated identities rather than to obsess over the bitterness of the colonial experience, the legacy of empire perforce appears strongly in the self-perception and tastes of the Parsi community he describes.

But what are these cultural specificities when it comes to literary influence? During the colonial era, anglicisation ensured that Parsi literary endeavours were mainly in English (although Parsis have an honourable role in the creation of Gujarati drama too[33]). As Nilufer Bharucha has observed, writers such as Behram Malabari, Cornelia Sorabji and D. F. Karaka jr. formed the vanguard of Parsi writers in the late nineteenth and early twentieth centuries. After a period in the doldrums, Parsi writing reemerged spectacularly in the 1980s with a number of voices – including Mistry, Bapsi Sidhwa, Boman Desai, Farrukh Dhondy, Firdaus Kanga and Ardashir Vakil – articulating the position of the modern diaspora.[34] However, perhaps the key text in the Indian Parsis' consciousness of tradition is the thousand-year-old *Shah-Namah*, or *Book of Kings*. The *Shah-Namah* stands at the beginning of the Indo-Persian literary tradition that flowered for centuries across south and central Asia. The tradition effectively began when Sultan Mahmud of Ghazna introduced Persian to India when conquering the northern parts of the country in the tenth century. It spread with the extension of Muslim rule under the Mughals, enjoying a golden age between the sixteenth and late nineteenth centuries, during which time Persian has been described as 'the literary and cultural language of most of the Islamic countries east of the Tigris and north of the Fertile Crescent'.[35] The influence of Persian literary, and especially poetic, forms was felt in writings in Urdu, Turkish, Pashto and Sindi.

The *Shah-Namah* was composed by the gentleman scholar Abul Kavim-i-Mansur, known as Firdausi (or Fardusi), circa 1000 CE. Writing at the time of Mahmud of Ghazna, Firdausi was both a Muslim and an Iranian, and his work fuses both traditions to create what has been described as the national epic of Iran.[36] The *Shah-Namah* is made up of fifty thousand rhyming couplets which trace the story of the Iranian nation from its first ruler to the defeat of the last Sassanian king by Arab armies in the mid-seventh century. In it, a number of narrative strata are woven together: a Creation myth; local legends such as the cycle involving the hero Rustom; dynastic struggles; romance; and the appearance of Zarathustra and the spread of his religion. As it progresses it 'shifts from myth and legend to historical romance, and then to history',[37] and could thus been seen as a hybrid narrative in its own right. Historically, the *Shah-Namah* marks the point at which the ancient oral storytelling tradition gives way to a literary incarnation, although it retains strong echoes of its oral origins in both form and content. In terms of theme, this epic text can be read as inscribing concerns which resonate down the years, and are picked up once more by Rohinton Mistry writing in the present day. Chief among these are the family feuds and generational conflicts that pepper Firdausi's text. Such interests also form the core of Mistry's examination of how men and women behave in the various affiliative units with which they are involved. Moreover, not only is the *Shah-Namah*, like

Mistry's work, concerned with what the Persian scholar Amin Banani has described as 'the tyranny of Time and the paradox of human existence',[38] it also develops from an initial represen- tation of the struggles of good versus evil as a war of opposites to a more complex understanding of moral ambiguity whereby 'we are led to an increasing awareness of the permeation of good with evil, to a realization of pollution and corruption and, inescapably, death as the final gift of Time'.[39] Likewise, Mistry's texts also explore that sense of loss through time, and the impossibility of moral purity and action without consequences for characters who are, nevertheless, adherents of a belief system founded on the notion of good and evil as absolute antitheses. The achievement of Mistry, and those other recent Parsi writers, is, in part, to have kept alive a critical dialogue between the formative myths of their culture and the require- ments of an on-going history.

Of course, the Persian legacy constitutes only one part of Mistry's multiple literary inheritance. The author has cited among his favourites such luminaries as V. S. Naipaul, Ivan Turgenev, Vladimir Nabokov, Muriel Spark and Albert Camus.[40] To these names we can safely add those masters of the nineteenth-century novel: Balzac, whose attention to the quasi- scientific recording of the effects of environment on character Mistry shares; Dickens, whose power of good storytelling and eye for quirky character traits he replicates; and the Russians, Dostoyevsky, Chekhov and Tolstoy, whose breadth of social vision and expansive sympathies he reproduces in his epics of contemporary Bombay life. There, too, are traces of British literature's canonical modernists, Joyce, Eliot and Yeats, whose sudden epiphanies and quest for order through art prove attractive but somewhat illusory to Mistry's highly literate narrating personae. And finally, the reader can recognise some of the lyrical and meditative qualities of the Bengali Tagore (especially in *Gitanjali*), and echoes of Indian writers whose primary medium has been English: R. K. Narayan, Mulk Raj Anand and Nayantara Sahgal among others. It is not my intention to claim each of these writers as exerting an equal influence on Mistry. Rather, such influences – inasmuch as they *are* influences – emerge as intertexts, as hints and whispers tugging at the reader, setting up reverberations that bring these other writers to mind, and situate Mistry's writing within a global as well as a local tradition.

In recent times this notion of a global tradition has, in some quarters, become synonymous with migrant or diaspora writing. The term 'diaspora' has come to encompass several categories of displaced persons, and numerous ethnic and religious groups. As James Clifford has observed, diaspora discourse 'is loose in the world, for reasons having to do with decolonization, increased immigration, global communication, and transport – a whole range of phenomena that encourage multi-locale attachments, dwelling and traveling within and across nations'.[41] One thing the writers of such diasporas seem to share is the search for some new order, some pattern, to help make sense of their unfamiliar new surroundings. Mistry's writing is full of examples of this search for pattern in the chaos of a dislocated life. The protagonist Kersi gropes for a way of ordering and giving narrative shape and, thus, meaning to his experiences and those of his brother Percy and school-friend Jamshed in 'Lend Me Your Light'; while Nariman Hansotia's stylised and exaggerated telling of the story of Sarosh-Sid in 'Squatter' is a way of metaphorising the experience of cultural dislocation. In this quest, the hybrid heritage of a writer like Mistry is brought fully into play. As Elleke Boehmer says: 'If the postcolonial text generally is … a hybrid object, then the migrant text is that hybridity writ large and in colour. It is a hybridity, too, which is form-giving, lending meaning to the bewildering array of cultural translations which migrants must make.'[42]

When one comes to Indian literature, however, there has been, in recent years, increasing controversy over the perceived privileging of Indian writing in English, and especially of the diaspora, over more 'indigenous' literatures from the subcontinent. The work of writers who have chosen to remain domiciled in India is, it is claimed, overlooked in favour of a fetishised migrant aesthetic, which casts a cold and often critical eye over

India's recent past and contemporary situation. Such arguments depend on a particular, yet fundamentally accurate, understanding of the processes of production and dissemination of South Asian writing in the West. The argument runs that western publishers and critics are guilty of setting an agenda wherein the preoccupations of diaspora writing are inflated to occupy the whole of the available market space of fiction on India. Writers such as Rushdie, Amitav Ghosh, Bharati Mukherjee, V. S. Naipaul and, according to some versions, Rohinton Mistry are the particular *bêtes noires* of such critiques.[43] Leaving aside the rights and wrongs of metropolitan publishing agendas, it is true that Mistry's writing interrogates contemporary definitions of India and Indianness 'from the outside'. However, as both writers and critics have argued, not only is this distance sometimes valuable – creating a penetrating new perspective on long-held commonplaces – the importance accredited to writers of the diaspora in India itself indicates the extent to which their work constitutes what has been described as a 'return of the repressed for the nation-state', or 'a mirror in which modern India seeks to know itself'.[44]

In essence, there is a kind of doubleness at the heart of the immigrant experience, which Mistry's writing, especially in the short story collection, *Tales from Firozsha Baag*, admirably captures. In this volume, the central protagonist replicates Mistry's movement from the tight-knit and reasonably self-sufficient Bombay Parsi community to the unknown and potentially hostile spaces of Canada. Both here, and in the later works, where the thorny relationship between the Parsis and majority social formations becomes the focal point, there is a pervasive sense of an art springing not from one culture alone, but from the tension between overlapping cultures and contexts. As Amin Malak has said:

> The immigrant imagination is dichotomous by nature, locked on the horns of a dilemma, neither affiliated with the old root culture, nor fully fitting with the new adopted one. Accordingly, writers negotiating and articulating such an experience have to inhabit an alternative world, a *third*

world: a world of their imagination, their memory, their nostalgia.[45]

There is often also a contradictory set of impulses at work: both attraction to the new society, and at the same time a fear of such total assimilation that the old coordinates of identity may be lost. This manifests itself, in the later stories in *Tales from Firozsha Baag*, in a tension between the desire to belong in the new host society and the urge to hold onto something of the old one. Sometimes involuntary or even subconscious, such ambivalence appears to be at work in Kersi in 'Lend Me Your Light', whose desire to settle into his new Canadian home is tempered by a need to cross-refer his experiences to the known and familiar structures and relationships of Bombay.

As far as Rohinton Mistry's place in Canadian literature is concerned, his migrant status renders him representative of a host of relatively new literary voices who have changed the way the notional category of a national literature is constructed. Lynette Hunter has described the search for a Canadian identity as one of the most consistent strands in Canadian literary criticism in recent years.[46] For a long time this took the form of an attempt to distinguish Canadian literature from those imposing (and encircling) canonical monoliths, English and American literature. However, with the rise to prominence of an ever-growing number of writers of different ethnicities and cultures, the notion of a single 'Can. Lit.' has had to give way to a recognition of plurality as central to the project of writing in Canada today. Indeed, Canada seems to be a popular destination for writers coming from other parts of the formerly colonised world. Along with Mistry stand the Sri Lankan-born novelist Michael Ondaatje, the Caribbean exiles Neil Bissoondath and Cyril Dabydeen, M. G. Vassanji from Uganda and Suniti Namjoshi, who hails from India (via spells in Britain and the United States), to name only a few. In view of this cultural complexity it is invidious to generalise too much about 'the Canadian experience'. However, as Linda Hutcheon has pointed out, this situation is nothing new. The history of Canada is itself the history of different waves of immigration. Except for native

North Americans, all Canadians are immigrants, or the descendants of immigrants, who came from somewhere else. Over the
last three hundred years, Canada has seen the English and
French settlers joined by loyalist Americans after the United
States' Declaration of Independence in the late eighteenth
century; African blacks, many of whom arrived as slaves
destined for the auctions at Louisbourg and Halifax; Highland
Scots after the Clearances; Irish after the Famine, along with
French Huguenots, Italians, Japanese, and Swiss Germans.[47] The
experiences charted by writers such as Mistry are really only the
latest wave in an on-going historical process.

However, there *is* something different about the way such
immigrants are viewed and talked about. This discrimination
appears based on their skin colour and cultural origin as much as
anything else. Hutcheon identifies and deconstructs such prejudice as it is manifest in the language of official discourses. Of the
word 'ethnic' she says:

> The first strand – the Greek root *ethnos*, meaning 'nation'
> or 'people' – should suggest *all* Canadians are ethnic,
> including French and British; the fact that the word is *not*
> so used points to a hierarchy of social and cultural privilege
> … the word 'ethnic' always has to do with the social
> positioning of the 'other', and is thus never free of rela-
> tions of power and value.[48]

In order to counteract such discrimination 'on the ground', in
the society at large, Canada passed a Multiculturalism Act in
July 1988. Its purpose was to protect and nurture the multicultural heritage of which Canadians had become increasingly
aware. This 'Act for the preservation and enhancement of
multiculturalism in Canada', enshrined in law a recognition of
the positive mingling of cultures. However, as progressive as
such legislation may seem, the initiative was not without its
critics. For one thing, as JanMohamed and Lloyd have pointed
out, 'pluralism' can function as a sop to the white liberal
conscience: 'The semblance of pluralism disguises the perpetu-
ation of exclusion insofar as it is enjoyed only by those who
have already assimilated the values of the dominant culture.'[49]

Mistry is among those who have voiced a degree of ambivalence about the value of state-sanctioned multiculturalism. While accepting that it springs from benevolent instincts, he has expressed the fear that 'Multiculturalism creates Multi-Cul-de-Sacs. Dead Ends from which the ethnic community cannot participate, or be assimilated more fully into Canadian life.'[50] Nariman Hansotia, the storyteller in the tale of emigration and cultural (and physical) discomfort, 'Squatter', is more forthright in his misgivings:

> The Multicultural Department is a Canadian invention. It is supposed to ensure that ethnic cultures are able to flourish, so that Canadian society will consist of a mosaic of cultures – that's their favourite word, mosaic – instead of one uniform mix, like the American melting pot. If you ask me, mosaic and melting pot are both nonsense, and ethnic is a polite way of saying bloody foreigner. (*TFB*, 160)

Mistry's viewpoint from the margins allows him to probe the faultlines and contradictions of such theories when they are put into practice. The same marginal or 'minor' perspective also proves fruitful when applied to the historical and political landscape of post-independence India in his three novels. Like Rushdie and several other authors, Mistry sees India's recent political culture as characterised by deceit, decline and the sacrifice of those ideas of freedom and secularism cherished so devoutly in 1947. This decline is associated most closely with Indira Gandhi's administration, which governed, with only a short hiatus, between 1966 and 1984. Corruption, nepotism and authoritarianism rear their heads in events like the Nagarwala embezzlement scandal, which ran like a jarring antiphon to the hymn of heroic patriotism at the time of the Indo-Pakistan war of 1971, and which provides the main plotline in *Such a Long Journey*; in Indira's promotion of her wayward, ruthless – and unelected – son Sanjay to the upper reaches of the Congress Party hierarchy; and in the antidemocratic brutality of the 1975 State of Emergency, characterised by the suppression of opposition and a programme of civic 'beautification' which quickly degenerated into the nightmare cavalcade of violent slum clearances and enforced sterilisations recorded in *A Fine Balance*. According to Sunil Khilnani, among others, a note of communalist antipathy entered the mainstream of Indian politics with Mrs Gandhi's shameless attempts to play off the anxieties and aspirations of one community against another for electoral purposes.[51] One of the most recent results of this downward spiral has been the rise to power of the regionalist and Hindu nationalist Shiv Sena in Mistry's beloved Bombay, and the creation of a monologic agenda associating Indianness with Hinduism. Mistry's character Dinshawji is an early witness to their burgeoning power and Mrs Gandhi's responsibility for it: 'And today we have that bloody Shiv Sena, wanting to make the rest of us into second class citizens. Don't forget, she started it all by supporting the racist buggers' (*TFB*, 39). Likewise, Shiv Sena activities form a strong undercurrent in *Family Matters* which snatches away one of the central characters and impinges on the lives of the others.

Despite these preoccupations, Mistry has refused to be labelled a political writer, insisting that didacticism is the death of true art, and commenting that 'If politics … come in to my work, they come in a secondary way.'[52] This is of a piece with a more general reticence and unwillingness to pontificate on the subjects often deemed within the remit of today's postcolonial practitioners; he is a reluctant interviewee and, unlike several other authors, has thus far resisted the temptation to commit to paper his reflections on art, society and the role of the writer. Nevertheless, even a cursory examination of his novels will leave readers in no doubt as to his commitment to the principles of personal freedom and human communication, and, while this may not take the form of a recognisably socialistic programme for change, one can certainly see Mistry's interventions – with their outrage against institutional injustices and oppression – as being similar in spirit to Rushdie's observation on fiction as a weapon against exculpatory political revisionism:

> At times when the State takes reality into its own hands,
> and sets about distorting it, altering the past to fit its

present needs, then the making of the alternative realities of art, including the novel of memory, becomes politicized. 'The struggle of man against power,' Milan Kundera has written, 'is the struggle of memory against forgetting.' Writers and politicians are natural rivals. Both groups try to make the world in their own images; they fight for the same territory. And the novel is one way of denying the official, politicians' version of truth.[53]

Mistry's novels can indeed be described as novels of memory, and this memory centres most vividly on the Bombay of his youth. While some critics have found Mistry's version of the city to possess an anachronistic quality, shimmering through a haze of nostalgia as the Bombay of the 1970s, when he left it, rather than as the contemporary metropolis with its contemporary problems,[54] it should be remembered that his Bombay is as much a construct, as much a part of his own 'India of the mind', as the locations created by any other writer. As Amit Chaudhuri has rightly observed, 'The Bombay he writes about he carries inside him, for inside him are streets and institutions and the voices of people – many voices.'[55] Mistry's novels are truly polyphonic affairs. His tone captures both the rhythms, colloquialisms, hesitations and digressions of oral storytelling, and the social sweep and measured ironies of the novel. In this respect, he is one of those writers who complicates the sanctified critical categories which govern our language when we seek to classify literature. Words such as realism, modernism, postmodernism and so on do not adequately describe the 'feel' of a Mistry novel. This generic hybridity can be seen as the direct result of the migrations, both cultural – in the Parsi experience of the last thousand or so years – and personal – in Mistry's own long journey – which have allowed the fermentation of those ingredients outlined above.

The degree to which Mistry's perennial subject is loss, memory and the possibilities for new beginnings, is evidenced in his uncollected story, 'The More Important Things', which appeared in *Canadian Fiction Magazine* in 1989 as a trailer for an as yet unfinished second volume of short stories. It is the tale of a young Bombay boy caught up in a school craze for marbles, and how the transformative work of the imagination charges the loss of his marble collection – they are scattered on the rough pavement below his parents' balcony – with a vividness which passes into memory and ensures a change in the way the developing child views, and describes, the world.[56] 'The More Important Things' is a characteristic Mistry story in several ways. With its young narrator, Tony, it recalls the child's-eye narratives of *Tales from Firozsha Baag*, especially 'The Collectors', and anticipates aspects of *Such a Long Journey*, like family dynamics and generational conflicts, and the Indian tendency to superstition. Once more the body and its functions are in the spotlight, as are the little tyrannies of school life – the viciousness and sadistic frisson of Jesuit corporal punishment – and the quirks, shared anxieties and tenderness of domestic affection. Above all, perhaps, this narrative, like the last few stories in *Tales from Firozsha Baag*, although on a more modest scale, is about finding a voice of one's own. Tony moves from parroting the phrases he hears from parents, teachers and the news media, describing the hardships and paradoxes of adult life and international politics, to being able to find words of his own to describe the magical effect created by the scattered marbles on the moonlit pavement, and to record the sustaining power of shared experiences and stories. This imaginative awakening takes on, in its own way, a greater significance than 'the more important things' drummed into him at home and at school. Similarly, despite the setbacks they suffer, Mistry's adult characters continue to uncover meaning in the minutiae of family life and intimate friendships. They are not always natural optimists, and they are in no way guaranteed a benevolent fate or redemption, yet they carry on with their respective journeys: 'Perpetual spiders in the waterspout', as Stacey Gibson has put it.[57] Their faith may be Zoroastrian, and their intended path that of *Asha*, the Truth that leads to God, or it may be the more general human journey on which we are all embarked. Either way their credo could be said to be encapsulated in the cry of a consumptive character in one of Mistry's touchstone texts,

Dostoyevsky's *The Idiot*: 'It is life, life that matters, life alone –
the continuous and everlasting process of discovering it – and
not the discovery itself.'[58]

'Throbbing between two lives': the structures of migration in *Tales from Firozsha Baag*

the further they go, the more they'll remember, they can
take it from me (*TFB*, 72)

IN 1987, Rohinton Mistry's first volume, a collection of linked short stories, was published in the United States as *Swimming Lessons and Other Stories from Firozsha Baag*, and in Canada and the United Kingdom as *Tales from Firozsha Baag*. It contained the two Hart House Prize-winning stories, 'Auspicious Occasion' and 'One Sunday', but also, in retrospect, can be seen to have introduced themes, symbols and techniques that recur in his later writings. These include topics such as families and their often spiky internal politics: a sense of entrapment and the desire for escape; memory and the pull of the past; the body, its functions and inevitable decay; connections between individuals, and often abortive attempts at communication; the search for balance amidst life's turbulent elements; the use of parallel characters; the slipperiness of language; and the redemptive power of storytelling. Although many of these interests were to receive a more extended treatment in his subsequent novels, they can all be seen at work in the lives of the characters who inhabit the eponymous Bombay apartment block. Indicative of Mistry's style is a subtle, but increasingly sophisticated and insistent, temporal weaving of past and present, enabling an exploration of characters and their motivations, and of the intricate tangle of cause and effect which directs events on both personal and national levels. Likewise, symbols are never static in Mistry's writing. Places, water, music, the weather, cooking, sport, journeys and journeying, and, above all, Bombay itself, enjoy shifting symbolic resonances as they appear and reappear within and across the texts. Their significance changes (and is sometimes even inverted) as the writer – both the real, corporeal personage, Rohinton Mistry, and that author implied by, and occasionally involved in, the text we are reading – seeks to grasp the complexities of experience and turn them into narrative.

Mistry's characteristic tone is even and engaging, detached but sympathetic, finding wry humour in serious situations, even managing to trace the lineaments of the absurd in the tragic, but also drawing profound lessons from apparently trivial incidents and encounters. Yet it is at certain points also marked by almost whimsical flights of exaggeration, satire and meta-fiction which carry the narrative high above the variegated, textured landscape of a prose filled with particulars and quotidian detail: one thinks of Nariman Hansotia's rampant imagination as he spins his yarns in 'Squatter', or the last story, 'Swimming Lessons', where the narrative's 'fourth wall' is broken as the narrator's parents read the stories we too have been reading. Yet such moments are darker and more serious than mere whimsy, and they often act to expose the difficulties and sometimes delusions involved in fiction-making, whether in the seemingly innocent attempt to create order out of chaos in one's personal life, or – in Mistry's later work – as part of a smokescreen of propaganda and disinformation on the governmental level.

As this may suggest, a distinctive feature of Mistry's style is his deployment of irony. The gentle humour he extracts from characters' foibles and the absurdity of the situations in which they frequently find themselves at times recalls that other Indian master storyteller R. K. Narayan. In *Tales from Firozsha Baag* irony takes the form either of a knowing relationship between characters – as when the older boys in the Baag appreciate the serious message of Nariman's stories which goes over the heads of his younger listeners – or a conscious invocation of literary heritage(s) as the narrator distances himself from his characters or from his younger, more naïve, self. Moreover, one can trace a political dynamic in the ironic register. According to

Linda Hutcheon, irony is a particularly appropriate vehicle for writing from the margins of a host society. In the context of so-called 'immigrant' or 'ethnic' writing in Canada, it becomes an expression of the inherent doubleness of identity, a way of establishing one's difference from the dominant discourse, of operating within its parameters while, at the same time, subverting it. She says, 'irony allows "the other" to address the dominant culture from within that culture's own set of values and modes of understanding, without being co-opted by it and without sacrificing the right to dissent, contradict and resist'.[1] So, in the form of the linked story collection, or short story cycle, Mistry appears to have adopted one of the most fruitful and appropriate forms for an exploration of hybrid and fragmented identities.

Forrest L. Ingram, a pioneering critic of the genre, defines the short story cycle as, 'a set of stories linked to each other in such a way as to maintain a balance between the individuality of each of the stories and the necessities of the larger unit. ... [and where] the reader's successive experience of the whole significantly modifies his experience of each of its component parts'.[2] There is no clear consensus as to when the short story cycle form began. Some critics claim the connected stories of Homer's *Odyssey*, Boccaccio's *Decameron*, Chaucer's *Canterbury Tales* and the *Thousand and One Nights*, as precursors. Others locate the genesis of the form very specifically in the nineteenth century, with Dickens's *Sketches by Boz* and Turgenev's *A Sportsman's Sketches*.[3] Such debates over origins are always subjective to an extent, and, in the case of the short story cycle, depend on how one evaluates the internal connections of a given volume. However, there is more general agreement about the concurrence of the genre's popularity with the rise of literary modernism. (Joyce's *Dubliners* is always cited as the definitive example of this confluence and it appears to have influenced some of Mistry's themes and techniques in *Tales from Firozsha Baag*.) The short story cycle's use of fragmentation, foregrounded symbolism and epiphanic revelation, and a differently inflected version of conventional, teleological plotting has proved especially attractive to writers with an oblique relationship to established literary traditions.

The short story cycle contains features such as thematic and symbolic patterns of recurrence and development, and is often structured and given unity by events occurring in a particular locale. Such locales can be so vividly realised, and impact so strongly on the characters who inhabit them as almost to constitute a character in their own right: examples include the American deep south in Faulkner's *Go Down, Moses*, Joyce's Dublin, and, here, Mistry's Firozsha Baag.[4] The sequence of stories also sometimes traces the psychological and intellectual development of a particular character from childhood to maturity. Finally, time is often depicted as cyclical rather than linear, with repetition and variation of situations allowing for a deepening of perspective on key themes: in *Tales from Firozsha Baag*, the stories 'Squatter', 'Lend Me Your Light', 'Exercisers' and 'Swimming Lessons' explore feelings of entrapment by replaying the ambiguous attempts to escape of various characters at different points in time. Eschewing the comforts of linearity and neat resolutions, short story cycles make demands on the reader, requiring that he or she look for unifying elements between stories and across the volume as a whole, elements the writer may have left implicit.

In fact, as Gerald Lynch makes clear, the short story cycle has proved particularly attractive for Canadian writers.[5] Moreover, its formal hybridity – part story collection, part novel – makes it a suitable medium for articulating what Rocio Davis calls the 'between-worlds' position of the 'ethnic' or migrant writer, and indeed of the postcolonial condition in general.[6] This is a quality Mistry takes full advantage of as he crams *Tales from Firozsha Baag* with quotes and paraphrases from, and allusions to, a variety of literary traditions from India, Britain, Ireland, France, Russia and ancient Persia.

The stories in *Tales from Firozsha Baag* describe a sequence of events, mediated through a shuttling temporality, taking place over the space of several years in the 1960s, during which the main recurring protagonist, Kersi Boyce – who also turns out to be the narrator who assembles the stories and effectively 'writes' the book we are reading – grows from youth to maturity. Thus, the stories describe and enact the sometimes uncomfortable journey from innocence to experience, as well as, in the later tales, from Firozsha Baag to Canada. In true short story cycle fashion the volume is constructed in such a way as to show how the lives of the Baag residents are connected beyond the individual narratives in which they may be personally involved. Each tale contains references to other characters and their experiences in other stories in the volume, experiences we have read about previously or will encounter as we read on. This adds resonance and contributes to that sense of a larger, unifying pattern, which the attentive reader will recognise on completing the text. Characters such as Najamai, Rustomji-the-curmudgeon and Jehangir Bulsara seem to stroll through each other's stories as easily as if they were strolling through the apartment block itself. There is a mix of first and third person narration and characters often throw the light of personal reflection over events narrated, sometimes by others in other stories. In effect, what we have is a series of linked stories which, taken together, create a kind of novelistic superstructure, and although individual tales can be, and have been, extracted and anthologised, no individual story is 100 per cent freestanding. One critic has described the shape of *Tales from Firozsha Baag*, which reproduces on the formal level the community that inhabits the compound, as 'the book as an apartment building'.[7] Yet, if the volume replicates a notion of community, it is also able to illuminate some of the darker corners of lives otherwise lived in full view of the neighbourhood: as when we are privy to the tender private memories of Daulat Mirza as she comes to terms with the loss of her husband and the communal pressures to observe the public cycle of the Parsi mourning ritual in 'Condolence Visit'; or to Jehangir's anxious struggles to reconcile his own sexuality with the expectations and stifling attentions of his mother in 'Exercisers'. Nor is community merely celebrated. Mistry parodies the excesses of Parsi exclusivity in stories such as 'Auspicious Occasion', with its sneering protagonist

Rustomji brought down to earth by an encounter with the India from which he has tried to cut himself off, and 'The Paying Guests', where Boman's communal pride prevents him from asking the Baag's sole Muslim tenant to testify against his fellow Parsi 'squatters'.

On the level of the volume as a whole, one can trace a growing sophistication in the narrative style, especially in the use of temporal fluidity – past and present are intermingled in increasingly intricate ways – reflecting the growing personal and literary awareness of the writer-protagonist, Kersi. From Nariman Hansotia's deceptively simple but actually multi-layered stories in 'Squatter', to Kersi's wary consciousness of the easy allure of clichéd fictional resolutions in 'Lend Me Your Light', the art of the storyteller is foregrounded. Indeed, the last few stories, describing what, to borrow and mangle George Lamming's phrase, one might call the pressures of exile, are not merely about the experience of double-edged cultural trans-lation, but also about how one narrates such experiences. In view of the structure and degree of sophistication outlined here, Mistry's chosen epigram from one of Henry David Thoreau's letters, 'Not that the story need be long, but it will take a long while to make it short', seems particularly apt.

Writing of one favoured mode of arrangement for short story cycles, J. Gerald Kennedy notes that, 'Small clusters of three or more stories may give special attention to a particular idea … [while others] may be yoked by formal or thematic features so that they comment explicitly upon each other'.[8] This seems an apposite observation with regard to *Tales from Firozsha Baag*. So, for the convenience of study, it has been chosen to treat the eleven stories in the volume according to the four dominant sets of concerns discernible. It should be noted that such divisions are inevitably arbitrary since themes raised and devices used in the first story recur throughout; they merely force themselves on the attention to differing degrees in differ-ent stories. However, it is possible to break the volume down into the following manageable units: the first three stories, 'Auspicious Occasion', 'One Sunday' and 'The Ghost of Firozsha

Baag' each deal with kinds of isolation from surrounding environments, and are to do with vulnerability and outsider status;
'Condolence Visit', 'The Collectors' and 'Of White Hairs and
Cricket' introduce the inevitability of death and attempts to
come to terms with change and loss; 'The Paying Guests' and
'Squatter' focus on belonging and the spaces protagonists would
call home but, for one reason or another, are unable to; and the
final triptych, comprising 'Lend Me Your Light', 'Exercisers'
and 'Swimming Lessons', interrogate the experiences of migration, exile, return and unsuccessful attempts at escape. (It would
certainly be possible to make a strong case for 'Squatter'
belonging in the last category too, but as there are specific issues
regarding narrativity and cultural influence I wish to address
through this story, it seemed preferable to place it in another
category.)

Outsiders: 'Auspicious Occasion', 'One Sunday' and 'The Ghost of Firozsha Baag'

'Auspicious Occasion' introduces us to the crumbling world of
Firozsha Baag, and to one of its most irascible inhabitants
Rustomji, dubbed 'the curmudgeon' by the local wag Nariman
Hansotia. It also introduces us to the insular, tradition-bound
world of Bombay's Parsi community, as Rustomji and his wife
Mehroo prepare for the important *Behram roje* celebrations.[9]
Rustomji is sixteen years her senior and already wearing
dentures. He pretends indifference to the ceremonies his wife
cherishes, but secretly enjoys the element of display which
festivals such as *Behram roje* allow, as he dons the ceremonial
Parsi dress which marks him out as different from the predominantly Hindu India that surrounds him.

The story begins as the couple prepare for their visit to the
fire temple. The rituals and superstitions surrounding this most
auspicious occasion – the concern that everything be just right
and to avoid unwanted distractions – illustrate the central
conundrum facing the Parsis in the modern world: how to

balance the requirements of tradition with the need for change to keep up with modernity. The retrospective urge, which in the Parsis is often linked to anglophilia and which the story reveals to be central to Parsi identity in postcolonial India, is symbolised by Rustomji's lament that two of Britain's most valuable legacies, Lifebuoy Soap and Johnnie Walker Scotch, are now only available on the black market. If Rustomji is, to a certain extent, living in the past it also seems that the Baag itself has seen better days. The building is decaying badly. Their flat bears the imprint of last year's rains in damp patches on the walls and, much to Rustomji's chagrin, the upstairs toilet is leaking in a steady drip that disturbs his morning motion. As someone who values regularity of all kinds he is discomfited by the drops of water which spatter his head, befouling him on a day which demands from the faithful a particular attention to purity. Dismissing the idea of using his neighbour and arch-enemy Nariman's lavatory – in an image that anticipates the central conundrum of 'Squatter' we learn that, 'his bowels were recalcitrant in strange surroundings' (TFB, 7) – he anticipates constipation 'with perverse satisfaction'.

The Parsi sense of separateness from, and superiority towards, other Indians is represented by Rustomji's nonetheless ambivalent attitude to the Indian servant who comes to clean their flat. He thinks of Gajra as a *gunga*, the generic and somewhat patronising name bestowed by some Parsis on their non-Parsi servants, a racialised slur anticipating his hurling of the pejorative *'ghatis'* at the crowd that surrounds him later. Yet there is desire as well as condescension in his attitude to the voluptuous Gajra, and he engages in covert sexual fantasies as he watches her work, perhaps indicating a latent desire for acceptance by this symbol of unalloyed Indianness. However, the sense of a fundamental separation of the Parsis from their surroundings is most vividly epitomised in the use of the colour white. The couple's special attire – his *dugli* and her sari – is spotlessly white. Whiteness here operates as both a traditional symbol of purity prescribed by religion, but also a visual signifier of the attempt to remain unsoiled by the bustling, chaotic swirl of humanity that is Bombay. Rustomji in particular relishes the elegance of his white *dugli*, his external fastidiousness an indicator of self-worth. We learn that on his way to the fire temple, 'he decided to pass the H route bus stop and walk further, to the A-1 Express, past Tar Gully and its menacing mouth. His starchy whiteness aroused in him feelings of resplendence and invincibility, and he had no objection to the viewing of his progress by the street' (*TFB*, 16). Suitably armoured Rustomji pushes his way to the front of the bus queue. However, his composure is about to be shattered. As he descends from the bus a *paan*-chewing mouth from the upper deck emits a stream of red juice which catches him 'between the shoulder blades: blood red on sparkling white', sending him into a paroxysm of rage, and he starts 'screaming as painfully as though it was a knife in the back' (*TFB*, 17). Rustomji vents his ire on the curious crowd which has gathered around, drawn by his bellowing, berating them as 'sisterfucking *ghatis*'. But the mood of the crowd quickly changes and Rustomji is man-handled, threatened with violence and has his festival finery pulled off in a symbolic disrobing. In immediate danger from the angry mob he hits on the only escape strategy available, one that punctures the assumed stance of superiority he has so carefully been cultivating all morning. As sometimes happens in a school playground, so here the weaker party escapes through comedy and self-mockery. He spits out his dentures: 'The collapsed mouth and flapping lips appeased everyone. A general tittering spread through the assembly. Rustomji the clown was triumphant. He had restored to himself the harmlessness of the original entertaining spectacle' (*TFB*, 18). This moment has been seen as an instance of Mistry consciously reworking the well-known stereotype of the Parsi *bawaji*, beloved of Indian film directors for generations. Tanya Luhrmann describes how this figure is typically 'an old, eccentric man, the kind of elderly man who needs to get off the bus, battling his way to the door, at exactly the wrong moment for everyone', while Nilufer Bharucha reads this incident as symbolising 'the social decline of the "Bawaji", who in the British Raj was a "sahib", but has now become a figure of fun; somebody who can be spat upon with impunity'.[10]

Meanwhile, Mehroo has made her way to the fire temple ahead of her husband, only to find the gates locked and police swarming everywhere. It transpires that the priest, *Dustoor* Dhunjisha, has been murdered, 'stabbed in the back' by an attendant at the fire temple whom he had interrupted in an attempted theft. Of course the phrase 'stabbed in the back' takes on a figurative as well as a literal dimension in this context: the real horror is that *Dustoor* Dhunjisha has been murdered by a fellow Parsi: the ultimate betrayal for a beleaguered minority. Suddenly, a sense of moral and communal decay is added to the personal decay of the aging Rustomji and the structural decay of the Baag buildings. Returning home disconsolately, Mehroo suffers another shock when, on entering, she spies her husband's discarded *paan*-stained *dugli* and mistakes it for the blood-stained vestments of the murdered *dustoor*. In this symbolic misrecognition, Rustomji is momentarily conflated with the dead priest, accentuating the sense of a community under attack from elements in the uncomprehending outside world and, more worryingly, from uncontrollable forces within. 'Auspicious Occasion' strongly conveys the Parsis' internalised sense of siege as a marginal entity in a populous nation. It also prepares us for the later struggles by the next generation to break free from the stifling confines of what the text depicts as an introverted and hidebound, if fiercely loyal, community.

The security derived from repetition and routine is again a feature of the next story, 'One Sunday'. Here the predictable events of an ordinary Sunday, on which the middle-aged widow Najamai goes to visit her sister's family in Bandra, leaving her upstairs flat in the care of her neighbours, are upset by the alleged theft of eighty rupees. The prime suspect is the local odd-job man, Francis, who sleeps under the awning of a nearby shop, waiting to assist any of the Baag residents for the sake of a few *paise*, and whom the Parsis consider 'really no better than a homeless beggar' (*TFB*, 30).

Mistry establishes the interconnectedness of Baag life as he describes the mutual dependence of Najamai and her neighbours. She allows Tehmina from next door and the Boyces from the floor below to use her refrigerator to store their meat and much-needed supplies of ice, while they receive her morning deliveries of bread and milk and let her borrow their newspaper. However, here again, as in 'Auspicious Occasion', the quotidian markers of habit are rent by an unexpected intrusion of terror. Francis is surprised behaving suspiciously by Najamai on her return. She screams in shock and he immediately bolts into the surrounding streets. At the same time, Silloo Boyce's son Kersi – perhaps *the* central figure of the volume as a whole, here introduced for the first time, but at this stage in the third person – is repairing his much-used cricket bat. We learn that he formerly enjoyed playing cricket and marbles and kite-flying with Francis, much to the dismay of his parents, who find it inappropriate for a good Parsi boy to be fraternising with one so much beneath him. Kersi's cricketing ambitions are in the process of yielding to a more adolescent set of concerns and urges, and childish pleasures have given way to teenage ennui. For Kersi, the deadening emptiness of Sunday routine is suddenly interrupted by Najamai's frantic cries for help and, bat in hand, he rushes to her aid, stimulated by heroic fantasies.

The pursuit, also involving Kersi's older brother, Percy, takes them out of the compound gates and into Tar Gully. Tar Gully is in certain respects the antithesis of Firozsha Baag, its dark, disturbing double, a place of poverty, dirt and crime to contrast with the order and regularity of the Parsi enclave. It is a predominantly Hindu space – it even has a resident sacred cow – and its inhabitants spit on those passing through who consider themselves better-heeled than they. In a replay of Rustomji's encounter in the first story, the Gullyites taunt Kersi and Percy as 'Parsi *bawaji*', while they, in turn, determinedly ignore the 'bloody *ghatis*'. Yet, despite their differences, there is a conciliation of sorts which takes us to the heart of this story's concern with outsider status, as both the Tar Gully Hindus and the Firozsha Baag Parsis are united against their Christian prey, Francis, by the accusation of theft and the cry of '*Chor! Chor!*'

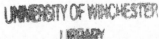

('Thief! Thief!'). Earlier we are told that Kersi's cricket bat is nowadays used to kill rats in the Baag. As well as acting as symbols of that decay we have already encountered, rats are, significantly, vermin who intrude from outside, just as the non-Parsi Francis is felt to have gnawed his way into the trust of the Firozsha Baag tenants. With Kersi brandishing his cricket bat, the pursuit soon turns into a kind of sport, where the spectators eagerly become participants in the hunt. Francis is quickly apprehended, given a beating by the less scrupulous among his pursuers, and brought back into the presence of his accuser. Throughout the story there is a strong sense of Francis as a victim: no evidence is produced to prove the allegation of theft, and Najamai reflects on his ignominious return, 'How silly they looked. Going after poor Francis with their big bats! As if he would ever have hurt them' (*TFB*, 38). Significantly, the Baag's solitary Muslim tenant takes the chance to ingratiate himself with his aloof neighbours by offers of sympathy to the wronged Najamai, while his servant aims a kick at the prone, quaking Francis. The whole incident, and particularly its disturbing denouement, illustrates the potential that exists for communities who themselves feel vulnerable as minorities to vent what little power they have on an individual from another minority. However, with the heat of the chase abating, Kersi finds himself succumbing to feelings of shame about his vainglorious part in hounding the powerless Francis. Back in his room he angrily smashes his cricket bat in disgust at himself. Along with the bat his fantasy of heroism, and the ideals of fair play enshrined in the game of cricket, are shattered too. With insider and outsider roles reversed, 'One Sunday' is a kind of mirror story to 'Auspicious Occasion'. It is still a tale of victimisation of the weaker outsider, but this time by a community one might have expected to know better.

The next tale is told in the first person by the Goanese ayah of a professional Parsi couple who live upstairs in B Block. But as a devout Catholic, as well as a servant, Jacqueline (whose name is corrupted to Jaakaylee by Parsi mispronunciation) is, like Francis, something of an outsider despite her forty-nine years of service. She observes how ayahs live close to the floor, grinding *masala* and chopping vegetables. Significantly, after attending midnight mass, Jaakaylee sleeps outside the flat, by the stairs, so as not to disturb her employers. It is here she witnesses the first manifestation of the ghost of Firozsha Baag.

One of the most striking features of Jakaylee's narration is the vernacular style and her use and mixing of languages. Mistry captures the register of the half-educated, aging Goan servant as she laments in her idiosyncratic English, 'Nowadays my weight is much more than it used to be, and is getting very difficult for me to get up from floor. But I am managing' (*TFB*, 45). Her narrative is marked by untranslated words from Gujarati and Hindi, which puncture the stilted English, not merely adding 'local colour', but signifying 'a certain cultural experience which they cannot hope to reproduce but whose difference is validated by the new situation'.[11] The narrative conducts a low-key but probing interrogation of the issues of language and power – thereby anticipating a central theme of *Such A Long Journey* – as Jaakaylee recalls the process by which she was renamed:

> All the fault is of old *bai* who died ten years ago … Old *bai* took English words and made them Parsi words. Easy chair was *igeechur*, French beans was *ferach beech*, and Jacqueline became Jaakaylee. Later I found that all old Parsis did this, it was like they made their own private language … I don't care about it now. If someone asks my name I say Jaakaylee. And I talk Parsi-Gujarati all the time instead of Konkani, even with other ayahs. Sometimes also little bits of English. (*TFB*, 44)

There is certainly a degree of alienation in this for Jaakaylee – she laments 'Forgetting my name, my language, my songs' (*TFB*, 45) – but her experience can also be seen as part of that cosmopolitan mixing resulting from the influx into Bombay in the 1950s and 1960s, which included 'Tamils and Keralites, with their funny *illay illay poe poe* language' (*TFB*, 46).[12] While there is no suggestion that linguistic dexterity has brought the central protagonist any advantages, Mistry's narration through Jaakay-lee's voice, seems, in its very hybridity, to add an extra dimension to Ashcroft, Griffith and Tiffin's well-known observations about postcolonial challenges to linguistic norms. Speaking of the deployment of the English language, they say, 'the most interesting feature of its use in postcolonial literature may be the way in which it also constructs difference, separation, and absence from the metropolitan norm'.[13] Here this challenge gains an extra dimension as the norms of the colonial language, English, *and* the Gujarati of her employers, are contravened by Jaakaylee's mix-and-match idiom.

At first Jaakaylee's reports of a ghost are dismissed by the Baag residents as the ramblings of an old woman from a backward part of the country where everyone believes in such things. However, interpretation for the reader is guided by the blend of Catholicism, sexuality and repression, woven into her narrative. The ghost first appears early on Christmas morning when Jaakaylee returns from midnight mass. We learn that the other, younger ayahs have gone off somewhere with their boyfriends. Her mistress and master, *bai* and *seth*, react with scepticism when awoken by their unnerved ayah. *Bai* is angry, but *seth* responds with good humour which Jaakaylee is soon able to account for: the audible creaking of their bed carries the sounds of intimacy, as the household settles down again. The next spectral visit occurs at Easter. This time the brazen apparition materialises in Jaakaylee's bed, 'sitting on my chest and bouncing up and down' (*TFB*, 46). Subsequent supernatural pranks include trying 'to put his hand up my gown or down from the neck', and we are told, 'For almost a whole year the ghost slept with me' (*TFB*, 48, 49). The ghost's antics spark a copycat incident in which Dr Mody's wayward son, Pesi, terrorises the nubile sisters Vera and Dolly by probing under their mini-skirts with the light from his clearly phallic torch. They also remind Jaakaylee of a childhood acquaintance called Cajetan – named after a local saint, but rather more of a sinner himself – whose shameless advances to the young Jacqueline had culminated in an incident at the beach. Her account is replete with sexual imagery:

> He rolled up his pants over the knees and I pulled up my
> skirt, and we went in deeper. Then a big wave made
> everything wet. We ran out and sat on the beach for my
> skirt to dry ... Sitting on the sand he made all funny eyes
> at me, like Hindi film hero, and put his hand on my thigh.
> I told him to stop or I would tell my father who would give
> him a solid pasting ... But he didn't stop. Not until the
> fishermen came. Sheeh, what a boy that was. (*TFB*, 49)

The insistence of such circumstances is likely to alert the reader
to the possibility of some form of repression at work. While
there is no countervailing narrative to cast doubt on Jaakaylee's
account, the nature of the ghost's activities is reminiscent of
Henry James's novella, *The Turn of the Screw*, where the
hauntings witnessed by an inexperienced and hysterical young
governess seem just as likely to be the result of psychosexual
repression as posthumous shenanigans.[14] Sure enough, her
confession to the local Catholic priest, Father D'Silva, is immediately effective. Telling the story – and thus, perhaps, working
off the associated feelings which have remained pent up in the
unmarried ayah for all these years – drives the ghost away.

Jaakaylee's relation of the main events of the story is
punctuated at points by italicised passages in which she comments
on the process of making a good curry. As these interruptions
continue, her strictures on how to produce the perfect Goan
masala begin to sound also like a recipe for cooking up a tasty
story: '*secret of good curry is not only what spices to put, but
also what goes in first, what goes in second, and third, and so
on. And never cook curry with lid on pot, always leave it open,
stir it often, stir it to urge the flavour to come out*' (*TFB*, 54).
These judicious instructions, along with the refrain 'believe or
don't believe', accentuate the connection between cooking and
storytelling that, on a second reading, appear to have been
simmering all the way through. *Bai* comes to enjoy her stories
and at the end asks Jaakaylee to sit with her at table and share a
cup of tea, causing the latter to reflect that nowadays, 'She does
not treat me like a servant all the time' (*TFB*, 55). As if to
confirm the connection, *bai* asks for Jaakaylee's help in

performing a magic ritual to determine whether there is a ghost in the Baag, after she has mistaken the ayah, draped in a sheet for warmth one night, for the *bhoot* whose existence she has previously doubted. She now thinks of ghosts as the ayah's 'specialty'. Through her proficiency as a spinner of yarns, Jaakaylee finds herself, at the end, brought 'inside' and she becomes an 'honorary Parsi' as she assists in the séance-like ceremony. The haunted ayah of Firozsha Baag thus becomes the initiator of a long line of storytelling characters in Mistry's work, and offers the first example of Mistry's faith in the redemptive, communicative power of storytelling.

Mortality and memory: 'Condolence Visit', 'The Collectors' and 'Of White Hairs and Cricket'

'Condolence Visit', 'The Collectors' and 'Of White Hairs and Cricket' share a concern with the operation of memory and the potential damage of holding on to that which must be allowed to pass away. In the first tale, we are once more plunged into the world of Parsi ritual. This time we are introduced to the correct sequence to be followed when in mourning. On the tenth day, or *dusmoo*, after the funeral of Minocher Mirza, the appropriate prayers have been said at the fire temple, and now, on the following day, his widow, Daulat, awaits with trepidation the inevitable arrival of visitors, taking advantage of the opportunity afforded them by calendrical convention to offer their condolences. She has thus far been careful to observe the niceties required of her. Yet now she is aware that she will have to recite the story of his last days to the condolence visitors, who will request it 'tenderly but tenaciously, as though it was their rightful entitlement' (*TFB*, 60). Already weary at the thought of reliving the painful recent past, she wishes she had taken advantage of her nephew, Sarosh-Sid's offer of the cassette player he has brought back with him from Canada. Then she could simply tape an account of Minocher's last days and replay it automatically for the sympathisers: 'When they held out their hands in the condolence-handshake position (fingertips of left hand tragically supporting the right elbow, as though the right arm, overcome with grief, could not make it on its own)' (*TFB*, 61). The mechanical quality of these ritual requirements might as well have a mechanism to satisfy curiosity.

Here is a case where the oppressiveness of tradition and ritual weighs heavily. What is more, Daulat is pestered by her well-meaning but interfering neighbour, Najamai – whom we have met before in 'One Sunday', of course – who, on the strength of her own bereavement, has become the self-appointed authority on 'Religious Rituals And The Widowed Woman' (*TFB*, 62). She polices the observance of correct Parsi rituals concerning mourning, importuning Daulat with offers of extra drinks and seats to accommodate the anticipated deluge, and generally embodies culturally sanctioned notions of propriety. For instance, she tells Daulat never to sell the pugree belonging to her deceased husband, and wants her to extinguish the lamp still burning at Minocher's bedside, which has become a source of comfort to the grieving woman. Conventionally, the lamp is there to aid the journey of the soul to the next world, but leaving it to burn beyond the prescribed four days risks confusing the soul by distracting it. Yet, as the story shows, things of ritual can outgrow their conventional meanings. For Daulat, the lamp works as a conduit for memory. As she gazes into the flame, fragments of her life together with Minocher return like the fragments of old tickets and concert programmes she finds among his effects. She recalls her husband's surreptitious deposits of the food he can no longer stomach, in an Ostermilk tin behind the bed, and his more recent craving for oxtail soup: a last little luxury they share together. Thinking of these things, and earlier memories such as their mutual love of music, Daulat is able to begin to come to terms with loss in her own way.

The tension here is between private feelings and the culturally sanctioned public appearance (and consumption) of grief. In this respect, 'Condolence Visit' is reminiscent of Maupassant's short story, 'Family Life', which also examines the rituals attendant on death, the visit of mourners, the obligatory tears and so on. Both stories explore the gap that exists between human emotion in bereavement and the observances sanctioned by society to mark a passing. These include what Maupassant, in a phrase also applicable to Mistry's subject matter here, calls 'the emblems and symbols which it is meet to set out in the presence of Death'.[15] (Of course, Maupassant, with his caustic view of human nature in general and of the French petite bourgeoisie in particular, uses the apparent death of Monsieur Caravan's mother to produce black humour about Madame Caravan's crocodile tears and pre-emptive greed, whereas Mistry's take on death rituals exhibits a more Chekhovian sympathy.)

Floating back from memory to the present, Daulat hears in the hush of the afternoon outside the mourning room a ragman passing by offering new things for old. She then resolves to give away Minocher's wedding pugree to a young man who has advertised for one in the newspaper, and who is due to come and inspect it that afternoon. The young man's plans for a traditional Parsi wedding offer to link the past and present that have been so recently sundered for Daulat, and give Minocher's pugree new life and significance. The act of giving up the pugree is symbolically linked to 'giving up' her dead husband. Daulat here acts spontaneously rather than according to notions of propriety. Now she finds she can also extinguish the bedside lamp and begin the process of healing.

The theme of an imposed duty to remember in a particular way versus a spontaneous response which answers the inevitable need to let go is also present in the equally moving but more complex tale, 'The Collectors'. From the start there is significant temporal fluidity in the narrative: a leakage of the 'present-of-narration' into the 'past-being-narrated' in the story. This shows a greater degree of sophistication on the part of the narrator, whose identity is still hidden from us at this stage. We are made aware of this as a retrospective narrative, partly through the tumbling temporality of the second paragraph, recalling Rushdie's helter-skelter, barely controlled time in *Midnight's Children* and *Shame*. We are told of the things Dr Mody did not know at the time of his arrival in Firozsha Baag:

Dr Mody did not know it then, but he would be seeing a lot of Jehangir, the Bulsara boy; the boy who sat silent and brooding every evening, watching the others at play ... Or that just when he would think he had found someone to share his hobby with, someone to mitigate the perpetual disappointment about his son Pesi, he would lose his precious Spanish dancing-lady stamp and renounce Jehangir's friendship, both in quick succession. And then two years later, he himself would – but that is never knowable. (*TFB*, 79)

This sophisticated opening, blending prolepsis (anticipation) and analepsis (flashback), provides what is virtually a synopsis of the plot, and does so in such a way as to direct our attention in this tale as much to the mode of narration as to what is narrated. Additionally, the story has a sectioned structure, the sections corresponding to the stages of Dr Mody and Jehangir's relationship: I, meeting and mutual interest; II, the beginning of Jehangir's stamp-collecting; III, the growth of his collection, but also his corruption by Eric D'Souza, the disappearance of the Spanish dancing-lady stamp for which he is blamed; and IV, Dr Mody's death, the bequest of his stamps to Jehangir and their destruction.

At first, Jehangir, quiet, contemplative and an avid reader, seems potentially a surrogate child for Dr Mody, to take the place of the perpetual disappointment that is his loutish and high-spirited son, Pesi. The latter's prodigious spitting and emissions of wind are matched only by his casual cruelty to animals: he organises games involving stoning the local cats – a particularly ironic pastime for the son of a vet – and he frequents the backyards that constitute the 'squalid underbelly' of Firozsha Baag. In a memorable deployment of 'Indianised' English we learn that 'Pesi was the worm in Dr Mody's mango' (*TFB*, 81). Little wonder, then, that the doctor attempts to live the fantasy of the life he has projected for his son, with the more temperamentally suited Jehangir. And this includes introducing him to his favourite hobby of stamp-collecting.

The stamps Jehangir admires in his Sunday morning sessions

with Dr Mody come from different parts of the world. They represent the outdoor life and the possibility of travel to foreign places, which it is unlikely he will ever see (this story takes on an additional resonance when we have read the later 'Exercisers', and realise just how complete the domestic stranglehold on this character really is). Dr Mody encourages Jehangir to make new friends and ask them to save stamps for him to help begin his collection. Collecting becomes a means by which to encourage the painfully shy boy to mix, but it also satisfies a mutual need, establishing a bond between these two lonely characters. However, as soon becomes evident, reaching out to others inevitably involves corruption. Jehangir is cultivated by his wayward classmate Eric D'Souza, whose burgeoning homo-sexuality soon involves Jehangir in 'not unpleasant' mutual masturbation sessions, in return for Eric stealing stamps for him from local stallholders. This arrangement is only disrupted by complaints from the traders and the threat of punishment from a prefect, after which Eric's attitude towards Jehangir changes dramatically, and he is forced to return many of the stolen stamps, and his collection shrinks pitifully overnight. Worse follows when, on his next visit to Dr Mody, he learns that the beautiful Spanish dancing-lady stamp, an object of admiration bordering on reverence for Dr Mody, has gone missing. The doctor interprets Jehangir's feeling of culpability about his recent misdemeanours as evidence of his guilt, and their relationship is promptly terminated. The Spanish dancing-lady stamp – with its alluring flamenco dancer – becomes an image, simultaneously, of perfection and the unattainable. Stamps in general, but this one in particular, form a substitute for Dr Mody's unsatisfactory relationship with his hectoring wife, who berates him for spending more time with Jehangir than with his own son, and appears to starve him of affection; it seems no coincidence that the doctor is to die 'of heart failure' on a trip to Ahmedabad. Kept in a special box and inspected with almost furtive excitement, Dr Mody's Spanish dancing-lady can be associated with the covert pleasures offered by Eric D'Souza. Dr Mody says, 'So you like my Spanish dancing-lady. Everyone who sees it likes it. Even my wife who is not interested in stamp collecting thought it was beautiful. When I retire I can spend more time with the Spanish dancing-lady' (*TFB*, 93). As this stamp is so highly prized by both Dr Mody and Jehangir, it becomes that which can be turned against them and used to divide them. (We discover at the end that it is Mrs Mody, in her jealousy, who has removed and destroyed the Spanish dancing-lady.)

The events of 'The Collectors' take place over a more extended period than in previous tales. At the end of two years, the choric voice Mistry occasionally deploys to inform us of the common view of the Baag gossips informs us of Dr Mody's untimely death. Mrs Mody goes to Ahmedabad to escort the body back to Bombay for disposal in the Towers of Silence, but, unfortunately, during the journey the body begins to decompose in the heat. The theme of corruption and corruptibility which has been running through the narrative reaches a climax when Jehangir, who has reluctantly taken charge of what remains of the doctor's stamp collection at the behest of the tearful and contrite Mrs Mody, discovers, some months after storing his hoard in a trunk under the bed, that white ants and cockroaches have reduced the collection to dust. At this, Jehangir feels a 'sense of relief': relief from the burden of being obliged to remember in a particular way by Mrs Mody's bequest.

This ending carries strong echoes of the climax of Alice Munro's tale, 'Heirs of the Living Body', in her short story cycle, *Lives of Girls and Women*. There too the protagonist, Del, has a memento of her deceased Uncle Craig imposed on her by grieving relatives, in the shape of his painstakingly compiled history of Wawanash county. And, as with Jehangir's stamps, Del puts the manuscript in a box under the bed, later transferring it to the cellar where it is subsequently ruined during a flood. Her words on discovering the loss might also stand for Jehangir's sentiments at the end of 'The Collectors': 'I felt remorse, that kind of tender remorse which has on its other side a brutal, unblemished satisfaction.'[16] Both stories reflect on the impossibility of preserving the past, its memories and the personalities associated with it, through artefacts.

'Of White Hairs and Cricket' is more direct in its treatment of the attempt to come to terms with mortality and physical decline, although the retrospective element – the events are being recalled by the older Kersi, as we learn at the end of the book – add an extra poignancy to the sense of loss. The white hairs on Daddy's head which Kersi dutifully attempts to remove with tweezers, are signs of the inevitable process of aging, as is the fact that he can no longer play cricket on Sunday mornings with the Baag youth. These futile attempts to 'uproot the signposts of mortality' (*TFB*, 107) are linked to other images of decay and of efforts to frustrate the passage of time: like the baby on the outdated Murphy Radio Calendar, which partially hides a spreading patch of crumbling plaster on the Boyce's walls, who must now be the same age as Kersi, but who continues to present an 'innocent and joyous' smile to the world, defying all other time-bound entities; *Mamaiji*'s painful weakness of the spine through which she is unable to stand fully erect, and which leads Kersi to contrast the 'big handsome woman' she once was to the frail figure in front of him; the temperamental Criterion and Primus stoves which date from the days of the British, and which seem to threaten the careless user with imminent cremation; and, finally, the father of Kersi's best friend, Viraf, who lies critically ill after a heart attack, and whose fate seems to enucleate all the losses of which life is composed. The story is perhaps a little relentless in its pursuit of instances of human entropy and the various 'enshroudings' that accompany them. The image of spinning things is held out as balm for Kersi: from *Mamaiji*'s dexterous needlework or a favourite record on the turntable, to the exploits of Jasu Patel, the famous Indian spin bowler, who regularly bamboozled international batsmen. (Indeed, cricket in this story comes to symbolise and encapsulate time and loss, contrasting with its use in 'One Sunday' and, as we shall see, 'Squatter'.) The fate of Viraf's father provides a kind of Joycean epiphany about the facts of mortality for Kersi, who ends by lamenting his inability to communicate directly his love and gratitude to his father for all he has given him.

Home from home: 'The Paying Guests' and 'Squatter'

Just as Sarosh-Sid is a 'squatter' during his ill-fated sojourn in Canada, so, in 'The Paying Guests', the eccentric Korshedbai and her long-suffering husband, Ardesar, become squatters in the more intractable sense. Korshedbai, with her faith in the nocturnal revelations of her pet budgerigar Pestonji, long disappeared or dead, appears partly to be a dry run for Miss Kutpitia and her magic spells in *Such a Long Journey*. The story begins towards the end of the events it narrates and loops backwards to fill in the history of the dispute between the young couple, Boman and Kashmira, who need some extra money, and the unstable tenants who take on the partitioned section of their corner apartment. It follows the progress of Korshedbai's 'dirty protest' – littering the shared veranda with banana skins, orange rind, potato peelings, pendulous gobbets of gristle, strips of newspaper and dog faeces – and the disruption of the old, peaceable way of life by the litigation set in train by Boman in his attempt to reclaim the rooms for his growing family. Korshedbai is compulsive and superstitious. She takes Parsi traditions to an extreme, insisting that Kashmira remain in confinement during her menses, and waking up at five a.m. for her morning prayer. The sole record in her possession, a paean to the rising sun, becomes a weapon in the feud and is cranked up at all hours to disturb the neighbouring couple to the maximum. Mistry places much of the emphasis on the psychological effects of the battle on both sides. Boman is rattled but imperious, while his wife fears that the stand-off may never end, and Korshedbai rejoices over her temporary court victory as Ardesar retreats, in his thoughts, to Chaupatty beach where he feeds the pigeons.

Bird imagery is at the forefront of this tale. Korshedbai is determined not to let Boman and Kashmira peck her to pieces; in her philosophy, in order not to be pecked, it is essential to get one's peck in first. Life for her is as brutal and ravenous as for any bird of prey. Meanwhile, the pigeons that offer the therapeutic qualities of their cooing to Ardesar are, significantly, free to fly away, in contrast to the fetishised Pestonji who was caged. Moreover, there is a sense of inexorability about the train of events that culminate in Kashmira's new baby being stolen by Korshedbai and placed in the empty birdcage. Just as Pestonji was both talisman and child substitute for Korshedbai, so the new baby provides a focus for those instincts she has repressed and which have been warped.

In certain respects this is the weakest story in the collection: the ending is uncharacteristically melodramatic and the symbolism of the baby in the birdcage is rather obvious. However, it does serve to introduce the issue of what physical space one can call one's own, which comes to dominate the remaining narratives. And issues of belonging also entail questions of physical migration, as well as communal acceptance or rejection. The international dimension to this is explored in perhaps the most complex and satisfying of all the tales, 'Squatter'.

The play on the word 'squatter', in the story of that title, draws our attention not simply to its use in relation to an unwelcome intruder in a property or, as here, an unassimilated immigrant in a new country, but also to the only position in which the central character, Sarosh-Sid, can effectively evacuate his bowels. And, just as the title has a double meaning, so, too, the story as a whole displays a twofold concern. It is not merely about the disorientating experience of emigration, but also the power of language to encode these experiences in different story-types – heroic, epic, tragicomic and so on – and the role of listeners and readers in creating meaning. (As such, it takes us to the core concern of the volume, and Mistry's oeuvre, as a whole.)

Nariman Hansotia, the communal storyteller who beguiles the boys of Firozsha Baag with his tales, is especially adept at encoding experience in narrative form. After a ritual which involves tooting his car horn and polishing the Mercedes star on the bonnet to alert the boys, he launches into one of his amazing stories. His most sensitive listener Jehangir, also known as Bulsara Bookworm, admires the style and structure of Nariman's stories. In certain respects he may be seen as a kind of ideal reader/listener every writer/storyteller has in mind. He describes Nariman's technique in terms that might also be applicable to Mistry:

> Unpredictability was the brush he used to paint his tales with, and ambiguity the palette he mixed his colours in ... Nariman sometimes told a funny incident in a very serious way, or expressed a significant matter in a light and playful manner. And these were only two rough divisions, in between were lots of subtle gradations of tone and texture. Which, then, was the funny story and which the serious? Their opinions were divided, but ultimately, said Jehangir, it was up to the listener to decide. (*TFB*, 147–8)

This active engagement with interpretation is just one feature of the traditions of oral narrative invoked here. Listeners have an active role to play in the storytelling circuit. As an oral narrator, Nariman relies on a close relationship with his listeners. They, in turn, participate to the full, prompting, enquiring, egging him on, interjecting exclamations at appropriate moments. The boys who surround Nariman and clamour for a story join in the ritualised dialogue which critics have seen as central to the oral tradition. In an essay on Mistry's use of storytelling devices, Amin Malak has described what he sees as the distinctive features of oral storytelling transcribed in the novel *Such a Long Journey*, but which, in many respects, are more evident in 'Squatter'. Malak writes of 'A Sense of Audience': certainly present here as the boys give up their games of cricket and rough-and-tumble to come and hear Nariman's latest tale; 'A Sense of Heritage and Shared Values', which the community certainly has as Parsis; 'The Reliable Reporting of Private and Collective Memory', something Nariman demonstrates by claiming to recall personally the events he is describing – including his presence at Sarosh-Sid's 'welcome home' party – and the collective memory he evokes in the older boys of the voluptuous sisters Vera and Dolly; and 'The Blending of Modes and Moods', as when the listeners have the vague feeling that there is a serious message behind the humorous scatological story of Sarosh-Sid and his bowel problems.[17]

One of the most significant features of 'Squatter', and one which has not always received the critical attention it warrants, is the fact that what seems to be the main story, that of Sarosh-Sid and his difficulties in Canada, forms only the last part of the tale, the first half being taken up with the amazing feats of the incredible Savukshaw, Parsi cricketer, cyclist, pole-vaulter and hunter extraordinaire. Moreover, both stories are held in the frame narrative about Nariman Hansotia and his spellbinding storytelling skills. (As we shall see, this structure is actually even more complex than it first appears.)

As a cricketer and all-round sportsman, Savukshaw is a latter-day embodiment of those characteristics of manliness and physical vigour which Luhrmann sees the Parsis as having internalised from British public school models. She says, 'Of all gentlemanly athletic pastimes, cricket was the most esteemed. It was fitting to the ethos and aspirations of the community that Parsis played cricket sooner and better than any other community.'[18] Yet, with his incredible skills and prodigious strength, Savukshaw also recalls the heroes from another of Mistry's perennial sources, the *Shah-Namah*. In the great Persian epic, figures such as Sikandar, Afraisab, Asfandyar and, above all, Rustom, traverse the generalised landscape of ancient Iran, fighting battles, killing dragons, slaying demons and generally performing amazing deeds. There is more than a hint of such mythical heroic qualities in Savukshaw, and the tall tales told about him.

Interpretation is problematised here via the response of the listeners. There seems to be a moral message lurking somewhere behind the veneer of success, but different listeners construe this message in different ways. On one level the story of Savukshaw is used to emphasise the dictum that practice makes perfect for aspiring cricketers. Yet Jehangir, also correctly, interprets Savukshaw's restless activity as showing that 'success does not always bring happiness' (*TFB*, 153). Moreover, I would argue that this doubleness also plays a structural role for the narrative. Savukshaw is a fantastical Parsi hero for these young members of a marginal community to look up to and identify

with. Yet his story is also being used by Nariman as a balance for
the subsequent story of Sarosh-Sid's experience of isolation and
failure. The implied message on one level for the young listeners
is that you can achieve anything you aspire to if you try: after
all, Vera and Dolly have emigrated successfully to Canada and
are happily married, so the experience need not necessarily be
completely traumatic. This then sweetens the medicine of the
more salutary story of Sarosh-Sid, told for the benefit of the
older listeners who might be thinking of emigrating themselves
one day.

Sarosh-Sid has emigrated to Canada, but promises to return
to India if, after exactly ten years, he has not become completely
Canadian. Ten years later he feels entirely westernised, except
that he is unable to use western toilets and must still squat,
Indian-style, perched on the toilet rim, to achieve relief. With
the distress this causes him, it could be said that, in terms of
morale, he suffers the same fate as the cricket ball Savukshaw
smashes for four runs. He finds himself, '*Past the boundary line
… lying near the fence. Rent asunder. Into two perfect leather
hemispheres. All the stitches had ripped and some of the insides
had spilled out*' (*TFB*, 149) [emphasis added]. The fact that
Sarosh-Sid's toilet technique is different from that preferred in
his new host country is explicitly linked to xenophobia and
racism:

> The world of washrooms is private and at the same time
> very public. The absence of feet below the stall door, the
> smell of faeces, the rustle of paper, glimpses caught
> through the narrow crack between stall door and jamb – all
> these added up to only one thing: a foreign presence in the
> stall, not doing things in the conventional way. And if one
> outside could receive the fetor of Sarosh's business wafting
> through the door, poor unhappy Sarosh could detect some-
> thing malodorous in the air: the presence of xenophobia
> and hostility. (*TFB*, 156)

The use of defecation difficulties as a metaphor for the
failure of cultural assimilation is typical of Mistry's writing,
where the body often becomes a site for the exploration of social

issues and anxieties. The problems attendant on migration are
narrated by Nariman in a semi-fantastical and satirical way. In
an attempt to cure himself of the cultural constipation which has
cost him his job, Sarosh-Sid visits a pair of advisers specialising
in treating a range of digestive problems among immigrant
communities, all of which correspond allegorically to the very
real obstacles newcomers to the West might face: one man has
not been able to stomach Wonder Bread, but has recently
successfully eaten his first slice, although 'the ultimate goal',
which is 'pure white Wonder Bread', still seems a long way off.
Indeed, in the unlikely stories told by the immigrant specialists
he meets, Dr No-Ilaaz and Mrs Maha-Lepate – the latter's name
roughly translates as Big Yarn Spinner – the overall narrative
spirals further and further away from a grounding in reality.
Essentially, their stories of immigrant problems are framed
inside Sid's story of his experiences as supposedly told to
Nariman, which is, in turn, *inside* Nariman's recounting of the
affair to his young audience, *inside* the collection of tales which
– we discover at the end of 'Swimming Lessons' – is being read
by the author, Kersi's parents, which is, finally, *inside* the
volume we are reading, entitled *Tales from Firozsha Baag*. This
mise en abîme structure is reminiscent of the Persian *dastan*
storytelling tradition. Although the word has now come to
mean a short story in general, it was originally applied to the
narratives forming independent story-units within a larger
narrative whole; the stories of the heroes in the *Shah-Namah*
constitute one example. The *dastan* is a feature of Persian,
Arabic and South Asian literary traditions. Perhaps the most
famous example of the *dastan* form is the *Book of a Thousand
and One Nights*.[19] Of course, Nariman's cautionary tale is not
meant to be taken literally, but these stories-within-stories take
us back through so many layers of 'reality', each more far-
fetched than the last, that we begin to question the veracity of
anything in the tale. Just as Derrida, writing of the *mise en
abîme* structure included in Plato's *Timaeus*, where the story of
the origin of Athens is repeated and passed from one teller to the
next, asks whether we can work back through the layers of

speech to arrive at any base in the 'real', so, too, we may question whether we, as readers, ever pass from simulation to a source reality in Nariman Hansotia's imaginative allegories of migration. (After all, we have heard hints about the 'true' story of Sarosh-Sid in 'Condolence Visit', which is a more prosaic one involving marriage, divorce and repatriation.) Derrida says, 'In truth, each narrative content – fabulous, fictive, legendary or mythic … – becomes in its turn the content of a different tale. Each tale is thus a *receptacle* of another. There is nothing but receptacles of narrative receptacles, or narrative receptacles of receptacles.'[20] In 'Squatter', then, it is not simply a case of a frame narrative as some critics have claimed, but of narrative frames.

Sarosh-Sid finally achieves his desired evacuation, ironically when he himself is about to 'evacuate' from Canada. He manages to use the toilet in the plane that is about to take off bringing him back to India. It is significant that this character, whose very name – hyphenated and culturally ambivalent – indicates his status as, in Homi Bhabha's words 'not quite/not white',[21] can only succeed in the in-between space of the plane. And he returns to a Bombay that is altered and unfamiliar, even down to the labels on coke bottles. There is no way to recover the old life now. The text says, 'The old pattern was never found by Sarosh; he searched in vain. Patterns of life are selfish and unforgiving' (*TFB*, 167). The storyteller is, of course, interested in just such patterns. The warning moral of this story is supposedly offered by Sarosh himself. He chooses to paraphrase *Othello*, another black outsider undone by an alien host culture, in a move which reconciles oral and written traditions:

> When you shall these unlucky deeds relate, speak of me as I am; nothing extenuate, nor set down aught in malice: tell them that in Toronto once there lived a Parsi boy as best he could. Set you down this, and say, besides, that for some it was good, and for some it was bad, but for me life in the land of milk and honey was just a pain in the posterior. (*TFB*, 168)

'Squatter' is inherently a dialogic story in Bakhtin's terms. It burlesques the monologic tone of the epic in the Savukshaw story. Yet it also maintains a dialogic engagement with its target audience. As a 'master of voices' and a good storyteller, Nariman is always aware of the response his utterances seek, and of the different levels on which his crazy stories may be received: the older boys will recognise the 'hidden' message, the literary allusions, and possibly the parody of the *Shah-Namah* heroes, while the younger ones will enjoy Savukshaw's feats of derring-do, or the scatological humour of Sarosh-Sid's toils on the toilet. His story also mixes 'high' and 'low' language forms in the citation of *Othello*. He reveals himself to be a sophisticated weaver of subtle speech acts. Words are never single or free-standing for him. They are always part of an intersubjective process of communication. He gives what Bakhtin calls a 'socially significant verbal performance [which] has the ability … to infect with its own intention certain aspects of language … imposing on them specific semantic nuances and specific axiological overtones'.[22] For Mistry the writer, as for Nariman the speaker, 'The comic style demands of the author a lively to-and-fro movement in his relation to language, it demands a continual shifting of distance between author and language, so that first some, then other aspects of language are thrown into relief.'[23] Nariman, and perhaps Mistry, can be read as a modern incarnation of the professional minstrel or *gosan*, of ancient Iran who, according to Boyce, quoted by Yarshater, was 'present at the graveside and at the feast, eulogist, satirist, storyteller, musician, recorder of the past achievements and commentator of his own times'.[24]

Exile and Escape: 'Lend Me Your Light', 'Exercisers' and 'Swimming Lessons'

For all its playfulness, Squatter's account of the psychological (and physical) effects of migrancy makes a salutary introduction to the final triptych of stories with their themes of attempted escape and the persistence of old ties. The first of these, 'Lend Me Your Light', in a sense offers a 'real-life' equivalent for those allegorised experiences of Sarosh-Sid. Once again, themes of connection and disconnection between past and present, and past and present selves, along with storytelling and types of journey, are explored. The more sophisticated narrative voice of the first person narrator, Kersi – older and more conscious of the pitfalls of literary convention – takes us back over the events of his adolescence and migration to Canada. As narrator, Kersi shares Nariman's love of words and consciousness of their power: he looks back in shame on his complacent boyhood use of the term *'ghati'* for Indian menials, and the arrogance it expressed. This sense of superiority is taken to extremes by Jamshed, a friend of his brother Percy, whom Kersi initially admires. Jamshed's family live in a luxury tenth-floor apartment block with a lift. His lunch is brought to school in a 'chauffeur-driven', 'air-conditioned', 'leather-upholstered' car, and he devours it in what Kersi describes as 'this collection of hyphenated lavishness' (*TFB*, 174). However, as a young Parsi susceptible to the lure of the West and destined to emigrate a year after his privileged compatriot, Kersi, too, might be said to be one of those 'hyphenated subjectivities' of the new 'border' Indian diasporas, described by Vijay Mishra, who keep in touch with the old country through family ties, and make occasional return visits.[25]

Jamshed cannot wait to leave India, a country he views disdainfully as mired in dirt, poverty and corruption and, thus, a lost cause. Later, when they are both ensconced in North America, Jamshed sends Kersi a letter describing the incommodious horrors of a recent two-week visit he has made to Bombay. Kersi, whose attitude to his homeland is altogether more ambivalent, struggles to understand Jamshed's hostility, wondering whether his old friend is seeking to evade something in himself through his disproportionate response. Yet he finds himself in a sense responding in kind, as he attempts to lay claim to a continuity of identity by accentuating his 'Indianness'. In his reply he pretends that he frequents Toronto's 'Little India', although he has been there only once, and mentions his membership of the Zoroastrian Society of Ontario and appearance at

Parsi New Year celebrations, attended by a certain class of ex-patriots who swap stories of Indian incompetence and display exaggerated attitudes and prejudices tantamount to a performance:

> As the evening progressed it took on, at an alarming rate, the semblance of a wedding party at Bombay's Cama Garden ... [but] It was Cama Garden refurbished and modernized, Cama Garden without the cluster of beggars waiting by the entrance gate for the feast to end so they could come in and claim the dustbins. (*TFB*, 182)

They patronise these sanitised simulacra of the India they have left, 'equipped with a supply of ohs and aahs for ejaculation at suitable moments, pretending to discover what they had always lived with' (*TFB*, 182). These exiles play a part. They take on a set of attitudes to the old land that, it is suggested, is an inevitable part of the psychology of migration. Despite the geographical distance, which the younger Kersi hopes will vouchsafe him greater clarity of vision, he too finds himself preparing for a visit home by choosing as presents luxury items unavailable in India; the older narrating Kersi wonders what he was hoping to barter them for: 'Attention? Gratitude?' (*TFB*, 186). (Kersi's position is similar to that of Dr Manny Patel in Bharati Mukherjee's short story, 'Nostalgia', who, despite a successful medical career in New York surrounded by the paraphernalia of western commodity fetishism, 'knew he would forever shuttle between the old world and the new',[26] and who becomes involved in a disastrous one-night stand with a woman who comes to symbolise the Indian life choices he has tried to repress.)

Meanwhile, Percy has decided to remain in India and set up a charitable body to help rural communities escape the grip of usurers. He now runs this with a friend, Navjeet, and expresses his contempt for Jamshed's ostentation and crass materialism. While, to use the central image borrowed from Tagore's 'song offerings', *Gitanjali*, Kersi is hiding his light amidst the dazzling glare of metropolitan brightness, and the 'light' of Jamshed's human sympathy appears to have been extinguished altogether,

Percy seems to be obeying the Zoroastrian call to charitable works, thereby exemplifying the faith's conjunction of light with the Good.[27] To Kersi, Percy's seems the engaged, 'authentic' life choice. He is doing 'real work', while Kersi watches sitcoms on a rented television. However, his visit home coincides with Percy's return from the village in which he has been working, with the shocking news that Navjeet has been murdered by hostile moneylenders. Jamshed's cynicism appears momentarily vindicated: is Percy's idealism any less delusory in a context where violence and brutality are endemic in the feudal power structures of rural India? (In this plotline, 'Lend Me Your Light' comes closer to one of the main themes of *A Fine Balance* than any of the other tales.) Kersi asks, 'In all of this, was there a lesson for me? To trim my expectations and reactions to things, trim them down to the proper proportions?' (*TFB*, 187). Kersi recognises that he is only another tourist in India now, purchasing the specially produced merchandise of the 'Cottage Industries store' to take home: an inauthentic, simulated version of rural culture, to contrast with the brutal reality his brother has experienced at first hand.

The self-consciousness in this retrospective narrative is indicated by its rejection of modernist narrative's quasi-resolutions. At the end, Kersi finds his questions are still unanswered and recognises that the old narrative consolations are illusory too: 'The epiphany would have to wait for another time, another trip' (*TFB*, 192). This issue, of vision and/as revelation, is buttressed by the use of motifs from, and refer-ences to, T. S. Eliot's poem of modernist fragmentation, *The Waste Land*. Kersi observes the 'parched land' of India from the plane on his return: walking disconsolately around his old stamping grounds he is caught up in 'the crowds which were now flowing down Flora Fountain' (*TFB*, 189) – recalling Eliot's crowd which flowed over London Bridge, undone by the metaphorical death of repetition in the 'Burial of the Dead' – and which include 'typists and clerks', like the pair who endure a loveless coupling in 'The Fire Sermon'; while his unexpected meeting with Jamshed, who has turned up in Bombay again, despite his expressions of loathing for it, echoes the poet persona's encounter with the corpse-planting and apparently immortal Stetson from the ships at Mylae.[28] The multiple resonances set forth by these resemblances reach a peak when Kersi, on the eve of his departure, develops conjunctivitis and compares himself to the unifying presence in *The Waste Land*: 'guilty of the sin of hubris for attempting emigration out of the land of my birth and paying the price in burnt-out eyes. I, Tiresias, blind and throbbing between two lives, the one in Bombay and the one to come in Toronto ...' (*TFB*, 180)

Echoes of 'The Waste Land' are also to be found in 'Exercisers', which, moreover, features a deliberate 'false epiphany' constructed by the artful narrative lacunae. In this story, Jehangir Bulsara is now nineteen and at university. The tale is an account of his first relationship with a woman, and the frustrations caused by the interference of his disapproving and over-protective mother. It is structured around two key incidents both of which remain only partially narrated and open to interpretation: the message of Bhagwan Baba, a guru in whom his parents habitually place their trust for healing, benediction and advice; and the moment when the opportunity for Jehangir to consummate his relationship with Behroze arises. Other incidents fan out from these two key moments, in the customary weave of the present time and memory.

In an attempt to persuade Jehangir of the error of his infatuation, his father and mother take him to see the oracular Bhagwan. Lamenting the scepticism which appears to have descended on Jehangir along with his new inamorata, they urge him to 'believe again as you once believed when you were younger' (*TFB*, 208). Indeed, this story charts the shift in the old relationships that often takes place in adolescence. The past is always a more comfortable place, and Jehangir feels himself torn between the pull of the old certainties and the excitement of new love. Yet, this battle is not merely between past and present, or girlfriend and mother. In Jehangir's unconscious and almost obsessive return to the children's playground in Hanging Gardens, where he watches the late-night exercisers working out, the homoeroticism that was a feature of this character's ambivalent nascent sexuality in 'The Collectors' is once more foregrounded. Although he likes to think of this watching as a transient phase that is now over, he automatically returns to it at times of crisis, finding comfort in the precise drill of well-toned male bodies, and indulging his fantasy of joining them in back-slapping camaraderie and exertion which always culminates in the sexually loaded image of sharing a kebab and juice. Such fantasies are, of course, covert. Yet, it seems that sexuality in general is subject to a more widespread interdiction: just as the heterosexual courting couples who come to the Gardens after dark are disturbed by boisterous voyeurs and a night-watchman, the privacy required for sexual experimentation of any kind seems unavailable in this populous yet carefully regulated world. In this context, exercising comes to take on an additional resonance, as Jehangir struggles to 'exercise' control over his own destiny.

The fulcrum of this repressive attention is Mrs Bulsara, who decides that her son is old enough to go out alone in the evenings providing he returns by eight o'clock, and who embarrasses him by wearing the traditional *mathoobanoo* head scarf when she is first introduced to Behroze. Her objection to the girl is ostensibly based on her greater wealth – in a foreshadow of *Family Matters*, the straitened Bulsaras keep envelopes of carefully saved money for essential items – but this is, in fact, just one of a series of reasons she rehearses for refusing to relinquish her hold over her son. As Behroze observes, the apron string by which Jehangir is tied is far more visible than the *kusti* cord he wears as a mark of his Zoroastrianism. Their relationship is an extreme example of what Luhrmann calls the 'double-bind' of the Parsi mother-son relationship, where the mother's attentions are perceived as powerful and stultifying: 'The explicit verbal statement to the son … is "succeed". But … the underlying message is "don't succeed, you can't".'[29]

This is part of the narrative's concern with traps and entrapment. Bhagwan Baba speaks of life being full of traps, and Jehangir wonders how to interpret this typically enigmatic piece of intelligence. Is Behroze trying to trap him? Or is he subject to the altogether more refractory operations of Fate, or *Karma*? Yet, the one interpretation Jehangir does not venture is that the trap is always already sprung, that it exists in the maternal over-protection which has become part of his very psyche: why else does he desert Behroze at their most intimate moment to obey the arbitrary curfew his mother has imposed? The theme of entrapment is most memorably captured in the image of the hedges cut into the shapes of animals and birds in Kamala Nehru Park, which Jehangir sees at twilight. They are beautiful but, significantly, petrified – 'possessing neither the randomness of nature nor the manicured discipline imposed by man' (*TFB*, 216) – and all frozen at points of movement, points of becoming: 'the birds on the verge of flight, the camel and elephant and giraffe about to lumber off into the darkness. But all of them ultimately frozen. Trapped, like Bhagwan Baba said' (*TFB*, 220).

Meteorological phenomena quite literally add atmosphere to the tale. Events take place in the oppressive heat that pre-figures the monsoon season. The visit to the guru is conducted under a 'sombre, rainless cloud cover' (*TFB*, 211) recalling the aridity and anticipation of the 'What the Thunder Said' section of *The Waste Land*, and is followed by a gust of wind which bears the unfulfilled promise of rain to relieve the drought. On the night when Jehangir makes his fateful tryst with Behroze at her empty home, a storm brews, promising freshness and relief. As readers, we are left anticipating a consummation of their relationship when the couple draw closer, only to be tantalised by a fresh ellipsis, after which we see Jehangir racing homeward through the streets in the rain. The conventions of countless romantic novels and movies suggest that the storm in such circumstances will symbolise the release of sexual climax, and that Jehangir is swept along by the exuberance of an experience that will break his mother's spell once and for all. Instead, it soon becomes clear that he is racing home because he has missed his eight o'clock deadline and has left the shocked Behroze in mid-kiss. He arrives home, breathless and soaking, only to find the door to the flat – the only entry he truly desires – locked against him. The false epiphany here traced is of a piece with the knowing rejection of literary resolutions shown by the narrator Kersi in 'Lend Me Your Light'. Thus, while, on the level of content, this story allows us to catch up with a character whom we have met earlier in the volume – and who is, in many respects, a parallel figure for Kersi – formally, it adds further impetus to those considerations of the craft of storytelling which have been growing throughout the volume, and which reach their culmination in the final story, 'Swimming Lessons'.

In 'Swimming Lessons', we find that Kersi has moved to Canada. The story develops through the use of what one might describe as binocular focalisation. In addition to Kersi's reflections, we are introduced, in italicised sections, to his parents' literary musings as they read the volume of short stories their son has sent them: the volume we too have been reading. Through the use of this metafictional framework,[30] as well as in the incidents narrated, 'Swimming Lessons' reprises and draws together several key themes visited previously, such as story-making and memory, physicality, detritus and decay, problems of clarity of vision, exile and how to turn this, and other experiences, into narrative.

In Ontario, Kersi occupies an apartment block which has certain similarities with the Firozsha Baag he has left behind, parallels which appeal to his eye for shape and order. This building too has its characters (in both senses of the word): like the Portuguese Woman, who keeps an eye on events and offers snippets of the day's stories to Kersi on his return at night; the Yugoslavian Berthe, with her uncoordinated slabs of English hurled like weapons at her feckless husband; or the wheelchair-bound old man, who reminds Kersi of his own stricken grandfather, and whose concern that Kersi guess his age is both a ritual to mark off time and a challenge thrown down to the fledgling writer. This is the apartment block as exile community, and the haphazard encounters which paper over the monadic isolation of its inhabitants can be likened to those of the international community of down-at-heel migrants who populate the boarding-house in Kensington at the beginning of Naipaul's classic novel of exile, *The Mimic Men*.[31] In a sense, the immobilised old man, who seems to guard the entrance hall, becomes the Tiresias figure in this story as he observes the comings and goings of the apartment, but, as his illness takes hold, his all-seeing gaze gradually moves from the world outside to the blank wall of the lobby 'As though he is not interested in the outside world any more, having finished with all that, and now it's time to see inside' (*TFB*, 247).

An interest in narrative and symbolism is integral to this tale's wider concerns. Although Kersi's parents complain about the curt missives he sends home – they lament that 'everything about his life is locked in silence and secrecy' (*TFB*, 232) – they eventually discover that imaginative narrative can break this silence, sometimes offering 'truths' more replete and vivid than mere facts. Moreover, Kersi muses on the prevalence of water imagery in his life, as he makes his abortive first attempts to learn to swim. He remarks that, 'The universal symbol of life and regeneration did nothing but frustrate me' (*TFB*, 234) and, using hyphenated adjectives which recall Joyce, observes: 'symbols ... should be still and gentle as dewdrops, tiny, yet shining with a world of meaning. But what happens when, on the page of life itself, one encounters the ever-moving, all-engirdling sprawl of the filthy sea' (*TFB*, 234). Just as, in India, the sea is the site of the consolatory but polluting rituals of religion, symbols may make a little order in the chaos, but they are themselves intrinsically linked to the life that produces such effluvia. Kersi's reluctance to immerse himself in the swimming pool can be read as representative of his resistance to that cultural assimilation by Canada which, on another level, he desires. Experiencing casual racism in the swimming pool changing area, he goes home to reflect on his failed 'watery rebirth' (*TFB*, 240). According to Smaro Kamboureli, invoking Homi Bhabha:

> The biologism of the image of being born as ethnic in the host country ... is conditioned by the essentialist and appropriating strategies practised by the host country ... The hiatus between *being* (what the ethnic subject was, and what it thinks it still is) and *becoming* (what becomes

of that subject in the host country, how it is perceived) is what structures "the spectacle of otherness".³²

Such considerations should alert us to the problematic status of language for the émigré, and the importance of perspectives, of ways of seeing. In a symbol of the first mental step necessary for a degree of assimilation, Kersi, having previously only been able to recognise the emblematic maple tree among the flora surrounding him in Canada, ends by resolving to buy a book on trees so that he can put a name to more of them. Humans are less biddable, however. Despite writing of the old man, Kersi never discovers his name. He thinks to check the designation on the mailbox only after the old man has died, and finds all identifying traces erased, there is nothing to signify his ever having existed there. He, along with the trees, remains somehow outside the realm of language, beyond the narrator's ability to speak for him: one more example of what Beckett might have called the 'nameless things' and 'thingless names' which confront the writer in a new environment. There is, in such incidents, a paradigm of the condition of the exile groping his way to a new relationship with language, new words for a New World. More particularly, Kersi's need to reshape in words the alien circumstances confronting him, recalls the problems of naming, of making one's language adequate to one's surroundings, which also confronted early European settlers to Canada.³³

A sense of perspective is also essential. Kersi is disappointed to discover that the bikini-clad sunbathing women on the lawn, about whom he has been fantasising, are actually older and less attractive than they appear from a distance. However, it is suggested that this kind of remove might be valuable for a writer, when Kersi's father, reading his son's first volume in Bombay, predicts future success for him if he continues to write about his immigrant experiences in Canada, while preserving 'the important distance' (*TFB*, 248). And, finally, when Kersi plunges his head beneath the surface of his bathwater, the different perspective on things he discovers when he opens his eyes is symbolic of both the personal and cultural immersion he must undergo, and of what Linda Hutcheon has called 'the doubleness or bifocality of the ethnic vision':[34]

> The drain plug looks different, slightly distorted; there is a hair trapped between the hole and the plug, it waves and dances with the movement of the water. I come up, refresh my lungs, examine quickly the overwater world of the washroom, and go in again. I do it several times, over and over. The world outside the water I have seen a lot of, it is now time to see what is inside. (*TFB*, 249)

Anticipating *Family Matters*, issues of cause and effect are interrogated in 'Swimming Lessons'. When the building's heating breaks down, Kersi wonders: 'It's the hot water that goes through the rads and heats them. Or is it the other way round? Is there no hot water because the rads have stopped circulating it?' (*TFB*, 244). And remarking on the high incidence of divorce in the Parsi community, Kersi comments on its degree of westernisation, speculating as to whether the former is a result of the latter, or vice versa. However, whether it is possible to resolve such questions when posed in these terms, is less clear. During one of their discussions on what has motivated their son to write, Kersi's mother wonders whether he '*is remembering because he is a writer, or whether he started to write because he is unhappy and thinks of his past, and wants to save it all by making stories of it*' (*TFB*, 243). Yet neither possibility seems to offer an adequate account of the flexible and complex interaction of character, past and present as we have witnessed it in this volume.

Nevertheless, such reflections exemplify the way in which Kersi's father and mother are used as vehicles for a discussion of writing and inspiration in this story. His father explains a theory of literary creation he has come across which suggests that it takes a writer around ten years to absorb and understand experiences before he can attain the 'artistic distance' necessary to turn them into stories. His mother, however, has little time for such critical niceties, preferring to allow interpretation to emerge from the stories themselves. Ultimately, as Jehangir Bulsara might have observed, it is up to the individual reader to discover connections and form interpretations.

It is, in fact, possible to object to the violation involved in these intrusive parental meditations, in having Kersi's parents disgorge chunks of semi-digested literary theory. The two figures reading these stories at home in Bombay appear to bear little relation to the carefully drawn characters in 'Of White Hairs and Cricket', for example. The voices in the last story do not 'feel' as if they belong to the same people. A certain amount of arbitrary grafting seems to have been involved to get the discussion underway. However, the tone makes sense if one reads their sections as taking place *within* the reflexive framework: in other words, they are also fictional constructs consciously produced by the narrator for this purpose. A kind of metafictional loop is at work in this story. The parents read Kersi's stories about his youth and the move to Canada. But when they read the last story, do they read themselves? And who is writing them reading this? The fact that they are being written and read too is as important as what they themselves read. The metafictional element ensures that these figures never break free of the diegetic gravitational pull, to exist 'outside' the writing. As well as explaining the technique here, such an understanding also makes it difficult to sustain the neat distinctions between fact and fiction, memory and creation, and writing and reading posited by the father at one point. While the writer does not elbow his way into his own text in 'Swimming Lessons', we *are* witnessing a kind of metafictional commentary couched in the third person and propounded via specific characters.

Craig Tapping has offered an excellent synopsis of *Tales from Firozsha Baag*'s aims and themes. He says that it is,

> an exemplary postmodern, postcolonial literary collection. It stages the translation of oral cultures into literature with a commentary on the traditional society from which such practices derive; it reflects on textuality and on the growing consciousness and literary abilities of its protagonist-author, it mocks well-meaning Anglo-Saxon liberalism through satire; and it appropriates the inherited narratives of the imperial canon in parody which opens our understanding of such figural systems.[35]

One might add that, in its rigorous structural integrity, which yet allows for a fluid investigation of universally recognisable but specifically grounded experiences, it can also be seen as an apprenticeship for the ambitious novels that were to follow.

Mistry's Hollow Men: language, lies and the crisis of representation in *Such a Long Journey*

Truly there are two primal Spirits, twins renowned to be
in conflict. In thought and word, in act they are two: the
better and the bad. And those who act well have chosen
rightly between these two, not so the evildoers.
(*The Gathas*, Yasna 30, v. 3)

We are the hollow men
We are the stuffed men
Leaning together
Headpiece filled with straw. Alas!
Our dried voices, when
We whisper together
Are quiet and meaningless
As wind in dry grass
Or rats' feet over broken glass
In our dry cellar
(T. S. Eliot, *The Hollow Men*, lines 1–10)

COMMENTING on the possibilities for narrating the colour-
ful story of India's historical experiences, Rukmini Nair writes:

It sometimes seems apt to imagine the history of this
subcontinent as a palimpsest of literary forms. First a
substantial layer of myth and epic, then a burning layer of
tragedy, then farce and so forth. Lately, the furious
discovery of political scandals we've witnessed might
suggest that it is now an action thriller, Hindi-film style,
which is currently being written out in subcontinental
space.[1]

Rohinton Mistry's first two novels, *Such a Long Journey* and *A Fine Balance*, appear to bear out this suggestion. Both have something of the political thriller about them, although, as always in Mistry's writing, the operations of history are linked to, and impinge on, humdrum, quotidian life. In the earlier novel, published in 1991, political events put pressure on a family already under strain.[2] Gustad Noble becomes alienated from his disobedient elder son, his precious daughter falls mysteriously ill, and he struggles with memories of a financially secure and emotionally stable past that only serve to highlight his family's current plight at a time of shortages and rationing. Additionally, the outside world with its political intrigues and threat of war seeps into their flat in the Khodadad Building, a Parsi housing development similar to Firozsha Baag. As a Parsi loyal to Indira Ghandi's government, Gustad finds himself, along with his friend Major Jimmy Bilimoria, used and duped as part of an apparent plot hatched by the Prime Minister to embezzle money. The Bilimoria sub-plot is based on a true-life financial scandal that engulfed Indira Gandhi's government at the beginning of the 1970s, and offers a point of entry to one of the texts central concerns, the manipulation and misuse of language. The theme of language versus reality is played out in the propaganda and doublespeak of the government: the Prime Minister's vocal denial of involvement in a conspiracy bearing the hallmark of her arbitrary power; the renaming of Bombay streets by the Shiv Sena which leads to acute existential anxieties in Gustad's dying friend, Dinshawji; and a 'hollowness' at the heart of communication more generally in this tale of misunderstanding and the limitations of verbal communication. This, in turn, is linked to a wider Platonic investigation into the relationship between shadow and reality operating on a number of levels, and which can also be connected to the Zoroastrian struggle to reconcile the spiritual (*menog*) and material (*getig*) realms. The echoes of T. S. Eliot, begun in *Tales from Firozsha Baag*, redouble in significance and are extended to include 'The Love Song of J. Alfred Prufrock', 'The Journey of the Magi' and 'The Hollow Men', as well as 'The Waste Land'. Many situations and characters are multi-layered or enigmatic, and there always appears to be a gap between events and the power of language to describe them and encompass their various resonances; there is always a disjuncture between appearance and actuality, intention and outcome, utterance and reception, object and surrogate. One is constantly aware that, on the personal as on the political level, nothing is quite what it seems. Once again the role of stories and storytelling is considered – as with all Mistry's works the text features emblematic storytelling figures – but this time it is given a dark, political edge too. Gustad's initial desire to hold the outside world at a safe distance, symbolised by the blackout paper he keeps over his windows even in peace time, is part of the related theme of activity versus withdrawal, again traceable to the Zoroastrian demand that the true devotee be actively engaged in the fight against evil. *Such a Long Journey* is in part the story of Gustad's battle to confront and overcome the urge to withdraw. After all, it is only through the activity of the righteous that evil may be defeated and good advanced. As always, in this novel about contending evils of various kinds, Mistry gives the Zoroastrian ethical imperative a political dimension. Many paths to truth are charted, some of them spiritual or supernatural, and some of them mundane and material. Yet the important thing is never to be merely passive, always to go on with the journey.

The novel is set in 1971, the turbulent year of the struggle between what were then East and West Pakistan, which eventually drew in India and culminated in a brief, two week war and the creation of Bangladesh. However, it also harks back to the political history of India in the 1960s, the decade that saw the death of Jawaharlal Nehru, who had led India to independence from Britain and become its first Prime Minister, and the accession of his daughter Indira Gandhi. Events in the 1960s – including the Indo-Chinese War, the sudden death of Nehru's successor Lal Bahadur Shastri, superpower meddling, and the rise of Indira and her tearaway son Sanjay – are all mentioned in the text and seem to be characteristic of a political landscape of decline, deceit and corruption.

However, the most important background feature of all, described in the latter part of the novel, is the Indo-Pakistan War of December 1971. This was triggered by a divided election result in the two 'wings' of Pakistan left, predominantly Muslim but geographically and racially separate, after Partition in 1947. The larger force in West Pakistan, led by Zulfikar Ali Bhutto and General Yahya Khan, refused to accept the election result in the East which had gone against them, ordered the arrest of the East's victorious candidate and embarked on the suppression of opposition in the territory in an unprecedented clampdown. Brutal repression led to an enormous refugee crisis with, eventually, approximately ten million people fleeing across the border into Indian-controlled Bengal.[3] Of course, such an influx was inevitably a severe strain on India's resources; one result was the Refugee Tax which pushed up prices, and which characters complain about in the novel. There was also a groundswell of popular opinion supporting the deployment of Indian troops in defence of the Bengalis. Not wanting to appear the aggressor, Indira Gandhi initially rejected such a move, preferring instead to train and equip guerrilla bands based in India but operating across the border. And this is, of course, the point of overlap with the political sub-plot of *Such a Long Journey*.

Major Jimmy Bilimoria, Gustad's close friend from the Khodadad Building, suddenly disappears, leaving no other explanation than that he has embarked on a covert mission in the interests of national security. Eventually we discover that he is involved in the activities of RAW – the Research and Analysis Wing of India's secret service. It seems that he is engaged in providing funds for the cross-border guerrilla groups. However, it is soon apparent that Jimmy has become deeply embroiled in an altogether more murky set of events involving the embezzlement of large sums of money. The outline of his story is based on that of a parallel historical figure – also a Parsi and, by all accounts, an agent of RAW – Captain Sohrab Rustom Nagarwala. On 24 May 1971, the chief cashier of the State Bank of India received a telephone call, apparently from the Prime Minister, instructing him to withdraw six million rupees and hand them over to a person whom he would find waiting on a road, and who would identify himself simply as 'a man from Bangladesh'. The cashier obeyed these instructions and then went to the Prime Minister's residence to ask for a receipt. To his surprise, he was told by the Prime Minister's private secretary that she had made no such telephone call, and advised to contact the police. He did so, and Captain Nagarwala, who had taken delivery of the money, was swiftly arrested. He seemed to have left an easy trail for the police to follow, and confessed that he had impersonated Indira Gandhi's voice to obtain money to support guerrilla activities in Bangladesh. However, what began to raise suspicions at the time, and what was never adequately explained, was the hasty and highly unorthodox manner in which Captain Nagarwala's trial was conducted. Three different judges presided over the case in just three days, at the end of which he was sentenced to four years imprisonment. The police failed to produce in court the tape they claimed to have of Nagarwala's remarkable impersonation of Mrs Gandhi, and contradictions between his story and that of the State Cashier were never investigated. Moreover, after his arrest, Nagarwala appears to have had a change of heart. From prison he appealed for a retrial and tried unsuccessfully to gain an interview with a journalist and fellow Parsi from a Bombay weekly newspaper. A few months later, Nagarwala was removed to hospital, allegedly complaining of chest pains, where he died in March 1972.[4]

So, was Nagarwala a scapegoat, a 'patsy', taking the blame for corruption at the highest level? And did the Prime Minister's private secretary, unaware of the unorthodox financial arrangement, unwittingly expose it by sending the cashier to the police? Just how was it possible for the Prime Minister simply to telephone the State Bank and demand money from it anyway? And what was the money really intended for? (A further twist to the tale was added when the police officer in charge of investigating the case also died under suspicious circumstances soon afterwards.)[5] In Mistry's fictionalised version of these events, the Nagarwala substitute, Jimmy Bilimoria, tells Gustad that he has been made a stooge in the interests of Mrs Gandhi and her family who act extra-constitutionally and for their own ends: 'it is beyond the common man's imagination, the things being done by those in power' (*SLJ*, 280). Mistry partly undercuts these shocking allegations by having Jimmy utter them on what turns out to be his deathbed, in disjointed fashion, and in a drug-addled daze. Yet they do appear to represent more insistent, gnawing malefactions in the body politic as a whole.

Against this, the Parsi world of the Khodadad Building seems something of a haven: the novel commences with Gustad's morning orisons to Ahura Mazda, while ritually tying and untying his *kusti* cord, and later he reflects fondly on his elder son's *navjote* ceremony, initiating him into Zoroastrianism. As in *Tales from Firozsha Baag*, ritual is linked to the security of the known and familiar. Such moments are often retrospective, and the narrative works through a shuttling temporal schema that is the formal corollary of the thematic concern with memory and identity. Of course, the locus for the most powerful memories is to be found in the tender minutiae of family life. Gustad's image of lost perfection arises in the ghostly shape of his mother, seen through a mosquito net on a family holiday before her untimely death, 'saying goodnight-Godblessyou, smiling, soft and evanescent, floating before my sleepy eyes, floating for ever with her eyes so gentle and kind' (*SLJ*, 242). Since then the Noble family – like the noble community they appear to represent – have fallen on hard times. Gustad recalls the halcyon days when the family had servants, but now they cannot even afford to buy milk from the Parsi dairy. He therefore invests his hopes for the future in his elder son, Sohrab. However, rather than appreciate the sacrifices his parents have made to facilitate his education, Sohrab refuses to accept entry into the prestigious Indian Institute of Technology, preferring – much to his father's outrage – to pursue an arts degree elsewhere. The generational split which results, culminates in a series of bitter arguments, after the last of which Gustad disowns Sohrab declaring, 'he is not my son. My son is dead' (*SLJ*, 52): thereby metaphorically recalling the slaying of Sohrab by his father, Rustom, on the battlefield in *The Shah-Namah*.[6] In fact, by attempting to impose his personal ambitions on his son, Gustad is at once hoping to reclaim vicariously his own lost opportunities, clinging to the remnants of the old father-child relationship and attempting to perpetuate his role as protector: a role which once saw him seriously injured in a traffic accident while thrusting the young Sohrab to safety. This inability to come to terms with time, change and endings – fundamental to human life – characterises Gustad's dealings with those around him. He aims to keep everything, family, friendships, his environment, pristine and inviolate. Ironically, he attempts this by surrounding himself with the detritus of the past: old furniture, books and other possessions saved from the bailiffs who ransacked his childhood home after a profligate uncle had run up enormous debts. Beyond this habitat he is much less confident, and recalls Eliot's Prufrock, diffident, paralysed by doubt and confronted by seemingly hostile forces in the outside world; during one misunderstanding with his wife, Dilnavaz, he even laments, 'That is not what I meant at all' (*SLJ*, 292).

An early collision between the private man and the exuberantly public spaces of Bombay comes when he reluctantly visits Crawford Market to buy a chicken. 'Dirty, smelly, overcrowded,' Crawford Market represents the chaotic, threatening, and sometimes bloody world, with its 'wicked-looking meat hooks' and 'sight and smell of blood … and bone' (*SLJ*, 21). The cavernous 'hall of meat' proves especially traumatic, and draws our attention to the novel's preoccupation with bodies. From the flakes of skin which fall from the milk-selling *bhaiya*, Dilnavaz's repulsion from Tehmul's begrimed toenails, the body parts sold as tokens of healing at Mount Mary, or the stomach cancer – and its attendant halitosis – that eats away at Dinshawji, bodies are maps of corruption, pain and decay. (This is a theme which will be explored to its agonising limits in *A Fine Balance*.) Additionally, while at Crawford Market Gustad remembers that he once stopped buying meat when militant Hindu *sadhus* began protesting against cow slaughter; 'offences of the flesh' also have a communal dimension for minorities in India.

Most redolent of the minority mindset is the physical space of the Khodadad Building itself. It is a Parsi enclave in the heart of Bombay, almost a ghetto, with all the attendant paranoia such an environment suggests. At one point, the complex is likened to a museum, and it is no coincidence that many domestic items in Gustad's apartment seem to be in a state of atrophy and decay too. In this atmosphere, municipal proposals to demolish the wall surrounding the compound as part of a road-widening programme take on the qualities of a threatened invasion, further underlining the community's sense of being at siege. The wall keeps the hectic, disordered world out. Yet even this space cannot be maintained in its purity: it is used as a public latrine by passers-by, like dogs marking their territory, and as events unfold, Gustad's worries start 'walling him in, threatening to crush him' (*SLJ*, 177). In *Gitanjali*, one of the intertexts that provide epigraph quotations at the start of the novel, Tagore describes a devotional crisis which, nevertheless, mirrors Gustad's own self-inflicted isolation: 'I am ever busy building this wall all around; and as this wall goes up into the sky day by day I lose sight of my true being in its dark shadow.'[7] The dark shadow cast by the wall becomes Stygian gloom within the apartment on account of the blackout paper Gustad has put up at the time of the Indo-Chinese War, and which he has refused to remove ever since. We are told that the paper restricts 'the ingress of all forms of light, earthly and celestial', and despite Gustad's regular dawn prayers, Dilnavaz remarks, 'In this house, the morning never seems to come' (*SLJ*, 11). The blackout answers a psychological need in Gustad in that it keeps out the frightening historical events he reads about in the newspaper every day, as the nation prepares for war and its propaganda machine grinds into action. Moreover, as he has discovered in his dealings with Sohrab – and with his neighbour Jimmy Bilimoria, whose disappearance leaves him baffled and angry – to reach out to others, even members of one's own family, is to risk betrayal. He increasingly retreats into dreams of the past, and soon stops taking newspapers altogether.

Gustad's is the predicament of all those characters who

attempt to preserve the things of the past as a bulwark against inevitable mutability. Like Sohrab's childhood butterfly collection whose contents nevertheless continue to decay, change and development cannot be artificially arrested. One of the most memorable personifications of this attempt to hold on to what must be allowed to pass is the eccentric spinster Miss Kutpitia. A Parsi Miss Havisham, she preserves in a locked room the belongings of her beloved nephew, Farad, killed in a car accident thirty-five years previously, and carries on conversations with the shadows in her dusty flat. Yet, in a lesson Gustad would do well to learn, an accidental fire acts as an emotional purgative, freeing her from the grip of the past by destroying these old things, and allowing her to move on. Such rare moments of cathartic release paradoxically serve to highlight the themes of imprisonment and freedom, every bit as insistent in this text as in Dickens's *Great Expectations* or *Little Dorrit*. There are real prisons, such as that which contains the disgraced Jimmy near the end, and the self-imposed variety, of which Gustad is the most notable inmate, confirming Eliot's tautological dictum, 'We think of the key, each in his prison / Thinking of the key, each confirms a prison.'[8]

Ironically, it is Major Jimmy Bilimoria, Gustad's best friend and, in many respects, a surrogate brother for him, who is the 'agent' that brings the outside world in and destroys Gustad's insulated existence. He does so by embroiling his friend and a work colleague, Dinshawji, in the embezzlement scam, sending bulky packages of crisp new banknotes along with a prevaricating letter requiring them to make regular bank deposits on his behalf. As an undercover operative, Jimmy has certain affinities with Verloc in Joseph Conrad's novel of intrigue and evasion, *The Secret Agent*. Both novels explore the theme of loyalty, and the respective protagonists keep secrets even from those nearest to them. Secrecy and agency are themes in a more general sense too, as characters are empowered or disempowered to varying degrees according to the amount of knowledge they possess. And, crucially, both texts are concerned with the way language can be used to obscure and disinform as much as to enlighten.[9]

Indeed, *Such a Long Journey* demonstrates an insistent concern with the slippery, manipulable nature of language, and how reality can often be very different from appearance. This is nowhere more evident than in the nature of names and naming. Characters adopt and discard names, give and take nicknames, and find that certain names stick, while others are forgotten: the bank manager, Mr Madon, has a secret first name that no one knows; old Mr Cavasji did have a nickname, 'the watermelon', but shed it along with the pounds as he aged; Ghulam Mohammed knows Jimmy as 'Bili-boy', while the latter uses the anagram Mira Obili when communicating with Gustad incognito; and Dr Paymaster, who treats Roshan's unnameable illness, is completely in thrall to nomenclature when he finds that his patients will not allow him to replace the name of the previous doctor on the sign outside his surgery with his own.

As this last example indicates, to name is to exert power. In an interesting essay on the novel, David Williams invokes Jacques Derrida on the appropriative nature of naming: '"The Battle of Proper Names" in *Of Grammatology* concludes that what's in a name is nothing less than the whole coercive network of relations bounding the subject.'[10] Nowhere is this more evident than in the ailing Dinshawji's lament over the Shiv Sena's campaign of street renaming in Bombay, designed to expunge signs of the British presence and reassert majority Marathi identity:

> Names are so important. I grew up on Lamington Road. But it has disappeared, in its place is Dadasaheb Bhadkamkar Marg. My school was on Carnac Road. Now suddenly it's on Lokmanya Tilak Marg. I live at Sleator Road. Soon that will also disappear. My whole life I have come to work at Flora Fountain. And one fine day the name changes. So what happens to the life I have lived? Was I living the wrong life, with all the wrong names? Will I get a second chance to live it all again, with these new names? Tell me what happens to my life. Rubbed out, just like that? (*SLJ*, 74)[11]

As Williams observes, 'What Dinshawji laments in the loss of the old names is the loss of the old logocentric security, that metaphysical reassurance via language "of the meaning of being in general as presence" ... Ultimately, he experiences the rewriting of the map of his neighbourhood as an interruption in his self-presence.'[12]

Unfortunately, Dinshawji fails to take on board the lesson about names and power inherent in his disorientation. His own behaviour when flirting with the alluring new secretary at the bank, Laurie Coutino, is an example of the potential sexual violence involved in language and naming. He tells Laurie that he would like to introduce her to his own 'little Lorri', neglecting to mention that *lorri* is the Parsi slang word for penis. When she finds out, Laurie feels demeaned and insulted, telling Gustad, '"If someone speaks my name now ... I feel bad. It reminds me of the dirty meaning. Mr Dinshawji has ruined my own name for me"' (*SLJ*, 176). Although Dinshawji means no offence, the misalliance between intention and effect here offers a prime example of how, in Eliot's words, 'Between the idea / And the reality / Between the motion / And the act / ... Between the emotion / And the response / Falls the Shadow.'[13] As if to compound both the indignity and the linguistic vacillation, Laurie's complaints about the harassment take place in one of the 'private' upstairs rooms at a local restaurant, where illicit sexual encounters take place, and which contains a sign proclaiming, 'Please Ring Bell For Waiter Under The Table': '"Now why would they put a waiter under the table?" said Gustad' (*SLJ*, 174).

From Dinshawji's crude double entendres, to the damaged Tehmul with his rapid-fire speech, words have a habit of sliding around, of changing meaning between sender and recipient. Throughout the book attempts at communication tend to obscure as much as they reveal. Gustad and Dilnavaz use a special *'asmai-kasmai'* code when they want to communicate without the children understanding, and a Gujarati child's rhyme is cryptically deployed as a veiled threat to Gustad as he wavers over the bank deposits. When Jimmy realises that he has been framed he sends an apologetic letter to Gustad, imploring him to undertake a visit to the jail in which he now languishes, as, '"you will not believe words on paper, because *I sent you words on paper before and could not keep them from turning false* ... I want you to know and understand, *hear from your own lips that you forgive me*"' (*SLJ*, 216) [emphasis added]. Yet, despite Jimmy's faith in the power of direct verbal communication, he is here succumbing to what Derrida would describe as the logo-centrism characteristic of western thinking, wherein language itself is seen as a guarantee of presence, and spoken language in particular is viewed as a more authentic mode of communication, giving immediate access to the speaker's thoughts and intention, whereas writing is a bastardised form, forever divorced from the originating utterance and at best a 'warmed up' re-presentation, at worst downright falsehood.[14] However, the deceptive charac-teristics of writing also turn out to hold true for the spoken word. On Gustad's arrival, Jimmy's jailor asserts that his charge is suffering from 'jungle sickness', despite the clear textual indication that paralysing drugs are being administered. The story of the set-up emerges little by little, stifled and blurred by the injections: Jimmy's words require patient listening and disentanglement, emerging slowly, 'As though each one was being sculpted painstakingly, out of stubborn granite' (*SLJ*, 272). And during his account he recalls an observation by that 'Very clever woman', Indira Gandhi, at a personal briefing: '"under the proper conditions, people will believe anything"' (*SLJ*, 277). During a lull in the interview when Jimmy lapses into catalepsy, Gustad emerges, exhausted, to seek refreshment: 'The policeman said there was tea and snacks in the canteen downstairs. He pronounced it snakes' (*SLJ*, 272).

The Janus-faced nature of language is also illustrated by the discrepancy between the propaganda offered by the newspapers at time of war – about evil, baby-bayoneting Pakistani troops confronted by their impossibly heroic and virtuous Indian counterparts – and the reality which seems to involve shady dealings at the highest level. In time of war, when demon-strations of loyalty are *de rigueur*, no one is immune from the effects of the political uses and abuses of language. Ultimately, some things, such as hope, can be expressed extra-linguistically, as Gustad discovers when a chance meeting with an old friend, Malcolm Saldanha, heralds memories of the well-being and transcendence their mutual love of music used to provide, arming him for the traumatic yet therapeutic experience of Dinshawji's funeral. Music here – whether Cesar Franck's Sonata for violin and piano, or Nat King Cole singing 'You Will Never Grow Old' – seems a purer, less equivocal mode of communication. And in a reference to the song from the film *Mary Poppins*, 'supercalifragilisticexpialidocious', that fantastical, arbitrary word signifying nothing (and everything you want it to), becomes the last word Gustad murmurs into Dinshawji's ear as he awaits the hearse. Under the circumstances, it seems as good as any sacrament.

As suggested above, Gustad offers the main example of how misrecognition and the fundamental gap between appearance and reality are key themes in *Such a Long Journey*. Initially, this relates to his bewildered and resentful dealings with Jimmy which draw him further into the world of double-dealing and intrigue he seeks to avoid. Baffled by his neighbour's unexplained disappearance, Gustad no longer knows what to believe about him. His absence allows Gustad to project all manner of sinister motivations onto him and his actions, viewing him as a traitor to the close friendship they have shared. In the first half of the book the Major operates almost as an absurdist 'absent presence', an off-stage orchestrator of events, *à la* Beckett's Godot or Pinter's menacing dumb waiter. In this respect, Jimmy is one of several characters who invite their interlocutors – and the reader – to project interpretations onto them. For instance, Dinshawji plays the role of 'the Casanova of Flora Fountain', and maintains a façade of good humour and ribaldry despite the fact that he is actually dying. As a result of this discrepancy between appearance and reality, Gustad is shocked by the speed of his decline when, in the interests of discretion, the joking is silenced:

> When Gustad came across him later in the day, he was surprised at how authentically Dinshawji projected his new image. Till he remembered that it seemed authentic because Dinshawji was no longer playing a role; reality, at

last, had caught up with him; and Gustad felt awful for confiscating his mask. (*SLJ*, 181)

Another character onto whom it is even easier to project interpretation is Tehmul-Lungraa. With his swaying gait and impaired mental faculties, Tehmul lurches around chasing butterflies, running simple errands and disconcerting residents by his tendency to follow them around; he becomes particularly attached to Gustad with a childlike loyalty and faith. In the novel as a whole, Tehmul functions as a kind of divine idiot or fool figure. Like Dostoyevsky's eponymous character, Prince Myshkin, in *The Idiot*, Tehmul appears too good, too innocent for the duplicitous society in which he is placed. His tumbling, repetitious utterances can be compared to Myshkin's relapse into idiocy at the end of Dostyevsky's novel, symbolising a rejection of that language which has been used throughout for deception and dissembling. Likewise, both Tehmul and the Prince have no knowledge of women, although Tehmul's beatific innocence is alloyed with a disturbingly adult sexuality: his drooling and crotch-rubbing antics alarm Dilnavaz, particularly when he appears to set his sites on the attractive pink plaster doll Roshan has won in a school raffle.[15]

Both Gustad and Dilnavaz in their different ways take advantage of Tehmul and project their anxieties onto him: Gustad, by frightening him with the threat of violence when he finds out about the hoard of money; Dilnavaz by conspiring with Miss Kutpitia to displace onto him the 'evil spirits' afflicting little Roshan and making her ill. Indeed, the text appears to maintain the possibility that Tehmul has been gifted some extraordinary qualities and powers to compensate for his other disabilities. We are told that he has the 'ability to ferret out information ahead of others with whole minds and bodies' (*SLJ*, 112), and there is enough evidence to support a reading of his urgent desire to 'touch' Roshan's doll as more than simply an urge to sexual self-gratification. Is it some kind of proxy healing gesture, a laying on of hands, to draw the malevolent forces from her and, thus, effect a cure? Like Joseph Conrad's half-witted Stevie in *The Secret Agent*, Tehmul is an incoherent victim of the machinations and intrigues of those around him. However, unlike the hapless Stevie, Tehmul becomes a redemptive figure: he is the receptacle into which the bad spirits plaguing Roshan will be poured, and his death at the end of the novel effects a reunion between the estranged Gustad and Sohrab over his corpse. He is, on one level, a kind of sacrificial lamb – just as, one might say, Major Jimmy Bilimoria is made a sacrificial lamb on the national level (although, in the latter case any redemption is rather more ambiguous and short-lived, as Mistry will show in *A Fine Balance*).

Tehmul, like Jimmy, is one of Mistry's 'hollow men' in *Such a Long Journey*, embodying the text's insistent concern with shadows and doubles, surrogates and simulacra. For example, at one point Jimmy poses alongside a projection of the crime-fighting superhero the Shadow to entertain Gustad's children, but is later described on his deathbed as 'nothing more than a shadow. The shadow of the powerfully-built army man who once lived in Khodadad Building' (*SLJ*, 267). Similarly, in a last trip to the Noble home before the hospitalisation from which he will not emerge, Dinshawji is little more than a shadow of the ebullient joker Dilnavaz remembers from a previous visit: 'The man who had laughed and sung that night, drunk beer and recited rhymes … was not the man who stood before her,' (*SLJ*, 187) shrunken and visibly sick. Meanwhile, Roshan's doll operates as her double – when he hears of his daughter's raffle success Gustad exclaims, 'my doll has won a doll' (*SLJ*, 84) – but it also serves as a surrogate sexual partner for Tehmul, who has been denied the physical comforts of the 'painted dolls' working in the local brothel, the 'House of Cages'. The image of synthetic supplements for organic entities, begun with the doll, reaches a semi-surrealistic pitch in the plethora of surrogate body parts – torsos, limbs, digits, heads – sold to supplicants at the Church of Mount Mary, hoping for miraculous cures to a variety of ailments; just as the statue of the Virgin, supposedly found under supernatural circumstances, like all icons acts as a receptacle for the hopes and dreams of the faithful.

The line between what one might call the deep structures of these psychic correspondences, and 'mere' simulation, is never entirely clear. Dinshawji simulates vitality and cheerfulness for as long as he can; Tehmul simulates sex with Roshan's doll; Ghulam Mohammed – the contact through whom Jimmy communicates with Gustad – alters his appearance to play the roles of taxi-driver or bookseller as the exigencies of espionage require; and the Government of India simulates openness and accountability while actually being mired in corruption and ruthlessness. Ghulam Mohammad makes a comment about Jimmy's predicament that might almost stand as a refrain, or a surrogate title for the novel as a whole: 'things are not what they seem' (*SLJ*, 215).

At one point, when Gustad goes to Chor Bazaar for a rendezvous with Ghulam Mohammad, he purchases a copy of Plato's *Dialogues* at a bookstall. Probably the most famous of these dialogues is *The Republic* in which Plato advances his Theory of Ideas or Forms. Here, Plato explains that most people live as if in a darkened cave. We are chained, facing a blank wall, and behind us is a fire. Between the fire and our backs, others move carrying all manner of vessels, statues and figurines of various shapes and materials. All we can see are the flickering shadows of these objects playing on the screen offered by the wall in front of us. It is only by learning to break our shackles and turn away from the wall and its shadows, that we can hope to escape into the true light of day, and view those archetypal Forms – the ideal paradigms, of which all earthly entities are merely imperfect copies.[16] Although Plato is talking about a general philosophical conundrum, it is tempting to apply his ideas to Gustad in *Such a Long Journey*: trapped in his own dim cave, the earthly and celestial light kept out by the blackout paper and his own fear of change, chasing the shadows that have become threatening only because he cannot face them fully. Throughout the book, the lure of the illusion, of what one wishes to believe, is stronger than that of reality. Examples of the attraction of appearance, or reflection, over reality range from Gustad's unwillingness to entertain Sohrab's insights into the misdemeanours of Indira Gandhi's government – preferring to keep his patriotic worldview intact – to the mosquitoes which plague him, drawn by the stench of urine emanating from the wall, but which, themselves, can be diverted towards the reflection of an electric light in a bowl of water: 'abandoning the real bulb, they played, unswervingly suicidal in their attempts to reach the aqueous, insubstantial light' (*SLJ*, 123).

These Platonic interests and echoes work not merely to lend intellectual *kudos* to Gustad's personal tribulations, but to point up the thematic continuity between Plato and the cosmological and theological preoccupations of Zoroastrianism. Correspondences between Platonism and Zoroastrianism include the tendency both systems have to privilege the verbal over the written. In poststructuralism, Derrida's critique of logocentrism questions that elevation, traceable to Plato, of the spoken over the written in human communication. The comparatively late transcription of the Gathic texts of Zoroastrianism likewise ensured the pre-eminence of oral performance in ritual observance: 'The sound of the words themselves were thought to convey power and instil religious experience, a power and experience which could not be captured by the written word.'[17] Susan Stiles Maneck has recounted how the twelfth-century Sufi mystic, Suhrawadi, developed his *Ishraqi* philosophy by integrating Platonic and Zoroastrian elements.[18] Similarly, Platonism, like the revealed religions, of which Zoroastrianism is one, interprets truth as an absolute hidden from humankind, but which can yet be attained by those following the path of light.

Indeed, it is in their mutual recourse to images of light that Platonism and Zoroastrianism seem most apposite as compatible modes of approach to *Such a Long Journey*. In the parable of the cave, light becomes, for Plato, a symbol of the ultimate Good: the nearest we can approach to the Divine Form itself; 'the good may be said to be not only the author of knowledge to all things known, but of their being and essence'.[19] He continues:

> my opinion is that in the world of knowledge the idea of good appears last of all, and is seen only with an effort; and, when seen, is also inferred to be the universal author

of all things beautiful and right, *parent of light and lord of light* in this visible world.[20] [emphasis added]

In Zoroastrianism, the *Yasna* ceremony, the highest of the liturgies, may only be performed at sunrise, 'since this is said to represent the fire of *asha* scattering light and heat over creation'.[21] And in the ninth century *Pahlavi* text, the *Bundahishen*, *Ohrmazd*, otherwise known as *Ahura Mazda*, dwells outside time, 'in a realm of pure light', while the evil spirit, *Ahriman*, exists, 'in a realm of utter darkness'.[22] *Asha*, associated with truth, is represented in Zoroastrian ceremonial by fire. It is the opposite of evil or the lie, *drug*, and represents that ideal form by which the cosmos should be regulated. Considering the battle between truth and lies that is conducted on all levels in *Such a Long Journey*, Mistry's novel appears to raise once again one of the central questions from the *Yasna* hymns: 'This I ask you, O Ahura, tell me truly: How can I deliver deceit into the hands of truth?'[23]

It has also been suggested that the two planes of existence recognised in Zoroastrianism – the *menog*, or spiritual, and the *getig*, material – correspond to Plato's notions of physical and Ideal realms. The *getig* plane serves as the battlefield between the forces of good and evil, while the *menog* has been read as a prototypical stratum, inhabited by the spirits. According to Clark:

> Both Plato and Zarathushtra advocated a dualistic view of the universe, though their respective forms of dualism are only superficially related … In Zoroastrianism, unlike Platonism, there is an ethical struggle to make the *menog* accessible through the *getig* on the basis that the more good there is in a spatially and temporally finite world the less evil can reside there, whereas the Platonic view tends towards the eventual rejection of the *entirety* of the mundane, allowing the 'ideal' world of forms to be realised and experienced in its totality.[24]

In view of this, Zoroastrianism requires of its devotee a conscious choice to participate in the battle against evil. As a result, asceticism is discouraged as it constitutes a retreat from that worldly engagement on behalf of truth. (This desire to engage is what Gustad lacks at the beginning of the novel and needs to develop. His horror of contamination and urge to withdraw can be seen as an indulging of an ascetic instinct.) Whether or not final victory is achievable in this world is a moot point. What is important is to be always endeavouring to move, to journey, towards perfection.

Thus, Gustad's long journey is to a kind of enlightenment on two levels: that of political reality and that of personal affections and mortality. The central image of the journey recalls that paradigmatic journey of the Parsis in their flight from Iran to India in the eighth century, alluded to in the novel and recorded in the talismanic seventeenth-century chronicle known as the *Kisseh-i Sanjan*.[25] Yet it also encompasses a range of experience, resonating outwards to affect all the characters and situations in the novel. As Anjana Desai says, 'The journey is the journey of a nation, of a city, of an ethnic minority, and of an individual man of this community – and the question it raises is the same one that baffles Eliot's magi – was it for a birth or a death that they travelled?'[26] Meditations on this theme are memorably focalised through the figure of the pavement artist, who is persuaded to turn the stinking compound wall into a canvas on which are depicted the sacred personalities and sites of a variety of religions. The peripatetic pavement artist lives and deals in the mutable and transient. In art as in life, permanence is an illusion, a false consolation: the pavement artist works in coloured chalks and crayon that can be rubbed out or washed away. For him existence, the stuff of art, is 'a cycle of arrival, creation and obliteration … The journey – chanced, unplanned, solitary – was the thing to relish' (*SLJ*, 184). However, at one point his prime location beside the Khodadad Building begins to awaken his old desire for 'permanence', 'roots', 'something immutable'. He becomes protective of his work, wants to build a shelter for himself and plans to start working in oils because they are indelible. This spell is only broken after the climactic riot, during which demolition work on the wall begins. The artist must resume his journey now. By contrast Gustad's own fear is of the end of journeys: a paralysing horror of change, termination and death, which does not allow him to yield to the pavement artist's maxim and start enjoying the journey for its own sake. The acts of betrayal and deception of which he feels himself a victim are experienced as mini-deaths, confirming him in his isolationist outlook. It is only with the actual deaths of his friends Dinshawji and Jimmy – and his decision to undertake the long journey to the latter's bedside – that, through the soothing balm of the funeral rites he participates in, Gustad is able to come to terms with those losses which constitute human experience through time.

Despite the conceptual common ground of Zoroastrianism and Platonism, *Such a Long Journey* is not simply an illustrative Platonic tract. Instead, Mistry appears to be offering what one might describe as a Zoroastrian revision of Plato. To begin with, Gustad is not one of the initiates, the philosopher-kings or guardians of his society. Indeed, the novel as a whole shows a nation state whose governance appears predicated on mendacity, and teeters on the brink of a tyranny that will become overt in the 1975 State of Emergency. Likewise, the existence or otherwise of a spiritual realm of ideal forms is not really the issue. Rather, Mistry appears to understand the necessity of some form of idealism to the whole concept of life's journey: whether it be an ideal of family life, of which the Noble unit inevitably falls short, or the belief that politics ought to be motivated by a sense of social responsibility and altruism instead of self-interest and corruption.

Typical of Mistry's attitude to human belief systems – that they are a bulwark against contingency and chaos – is the text's treatment of religion and superstition. For example, Dilnavaz, with her reflex gestures to ward off evil if someone mentions unpleasant possibilities, is a prime candidate for belief in Miss Kutpitia's magic, which offers the chance, 'to understand the hidden meaning of mundane events and chance occurrences' (*SLJ*, 4). In Miss Kutpitia's cosmology endowments such as health, strength or the ability to see things more clearly are stolen from one person by another. Such a simple explanatory system attracts Dilnavaz at her lowest ebb – when Roshan is ill and Sohrab has left home – even though it also requires her to concoct a sort of noxious witch's brew to shift the eviscerating forces. Arun Mukherjee has objected to the portrayal of the female characters as indulging in superstition and black magic, while 'the men make money, tell tall stories, do adventurous things'.[27] However, this is to overlook the constant juxtaposition of superstition with culturally sanctioned religious ritual and belief throughout the novel. Miss Kutpitia's belief system is not ridiculed or simply dismissed any more than are the pilgrims to Mount Mary who seek miraculous intercession in their daily affairs. Rather, when first mentioned in the novel's opening pages, it is surreptitiously bracketed by the introduction of Gustad, engaging in the altogether more 'respectable' activity of morning prayers. Similarly, his religious instincts are aroused by the fates that have overtaken Dinshawji and Jimmy, and Roshan's worrying illness. Where is the line between cultural custom and superstition where religion is concerned? As explanatory metanarratives both aetiologies offer an apparent pattern in the chaos of existence. Moreover, while the material and metaphysical may be opposed as ways of seeing, both medical science and supernatural intervention are maintained as possible explanations for Roshan's swift recovery. (In this, *Such a Long Journey* is reminiscent of Amitav Ghosh's fantastical, 'subaltern' account of the discovery of the means of transmission of malaria, *The Calcutta Chromosome*, where scientific rationalism and indigenous arcana are held together as possible explanatory narratives.)[28] Once more, Mistry's apparently valorised spokesperson, the pavement artist, takes a pragmatic view of people's belief in miracle and magic, consonant with the power of the imagination his pictures embrace: not examining phenomena too closely, but accepting the story 'if it helps'.

Indeed, the proliferation of storytelling, and the power of art more generally, is again celebrated in *Such a Long Journey*, making a final, decisive distinction from Plato who famously wished to banish artists and storytellers from his republic. For him, not only did the 'trickery' involved in art have the potential to call reality into question, and its examples of flawed personalities and behaviour risked influencing its viewers in negative ways, in imitating the earthly copy of the ideal paradigm, art is a derivative exercise three-times removed from its original. Plato uses the example of a bed. There are, essentially, three beds: 'one existing in nature, which is made by God … another which is the work of the carpenter … And the work of the painter is a third'.[29] As such, the imitation inherent in representative art is, for Plato, the mark of a third-rate activity. Likewise, citing the impracticality of art, Plato uses a horse's saddle as illustration to distinguish between the art which uses (that of the horseman); the art which makes (that of the leatherworker); and the art which imitates them (that of the painter who depicts it).[30] These, possibly rather reductive, conclusions have of course been reinterpreted and challenged over the centuries, not least by Plato's own disciple, Aristotle. Certainly, the author of that exuberant celebration of story-telling, *Tales from Firozsha Baag*, might not be expected to agree with such an uncharitable view of his trade. And, indeed, it seems as if Mistry may be taking a subtle sideswipe at Plato's bed/art parable in the occupations of the Noble patriarchs: Gustad's grandfather was a furniture maker, some of whose tools have been passed down to Gustad and become sources of comfort and continuity; while his father was a bookseller – a purveyor, no doubt, of just those scurrilous imaginings the ideal republic would do without.

Likewise, this novel is replete with storytellers too. Jimmy is a great storyteller, regaling the children with heroic tales of India's previous post-partition clashes with Pakistan: Dinshawji is an accomplished story and joke teller; and Dr Paymaster meta-phorises the political situation between Pakistan and Bangladesh as a 'diarrhoea of death', municipal corruption as gangrene, and, along with his faithful compounder, is likened to Don Quixote with Sancho Panza as he joins the *morcha* to tilt at the local government's incompetence and sloth. The doctor's surgery is near both the cinema, where the unending appetite for stories is temporarily sated, and the House of Cages, where the gaudily arrayed prostitutes, like fantastically plumed birds, draw punters into a fantasy environment. The latter is presided over by the local *paan* salesman and raconteur, Peerbhoy Paanwalla, whose racy stories inspire and elevate the sordid and carnal, encouraging clients to think of their sexual prowess and encounters as something grander than they really are. With his centrally placed stall, Peerbhoy is this text's Tiresias figure, all-seeing with 'wrinkled, old-woman dugs ... [and] ageless navel that watched the street tirelessly, an unblinking, all-seeing third eye' (*SLJ*, 158). His repertoire also includes an erotic satire, attributing the Pakistani leader's fascination with military hardware to the recent failure to function of his own sexual hardware. Peerbhoy's stories are multifaceted and difficult to categorise. In another passage, recalling the description of Nariman Hansotia's storytelling technique in 'Squatter', and which might also be said to be applicable to the complex inter-weavings of Mistry's narrative voice, we learn that:

> Peerbhoy Paanwalla had mobilised his talents for the common good, using his skills to weave a tale that defied genre or description. It was not tragedy, comedy or history; not pastoral, tragical-comical, historical-pastoral or tragical-historical. Nor was it epic or mock-heroic. It was not a ballad or an ode, masque or anti-masque, fable or elegy, parody or threnody. Although a careful analysis may have revealed that it possessed a smattering of all these characteristics. But since things such as literary criticism mattered not one jot to the listeners, they were responding to Peerbhoy's narrative in the only way that made sense: with every fibre of their beings. (*SLJ*, 306)

Yet, the stories in *Such a Long Journey* syncretise experience in non-linguistic forms too. For instance, the pavement artist's polytheistic mural turns the Khodadad building's perimeter wall from a latrine into a sacred site, enshrining India's portable notions of the sacred in a synthesis, albeit temporary, of religious iconography. It reconciles the different religious stories so fundamental to the nation's sense of itself. In figuring the saints and sages, mosques, churches and temples, on the blank canvas offered by the wall, the artist's work foregrounds the role of representation in the perception of 'truths', whether inter-personal, national or metaphysical. On inspecting the rapidly expanding mural, Gustad notices on one of the panels 'a painting of the wall featuring a painting of the wall, featuring a ...' (*SLJ*, 288). The pavement artist explains this by pointing out that the wall itself is now a sacred place, drawing its own share of pilgrims and worshippers. This draws attention once more to the inherently reproductive nature of attempts to give access to 'the real', especially in art and literature, in terms that recall the various other simulations which, as we have seen, epitomise this novel. This, in turn, might act as a metaphor for the issue, amplified throughout, of how versions of reality are created through, and dependent on the vagaries of representation, thereby having implications for an understanding of Mistry's narrative technique which will be examined later. As Michael Ryan has written:

> what we take to be real does not exist prior to simulation; rather it is simulated into being and lent ontological reality by virtue of acts of *representation, masquerade*, and *posturing* that are themselves more prior, funda-mental, generative (of the real). Reality is the successful repression of these processes.[31] [emphasis added]

Upon the wall's destruction, the pavement artist is undeterred. He resumes his travels, responding to Gustad's enquiry as to where he will go: 'In a world where roadside latrines becomes temples and shrines, and temples and shrines become dust and ruin, does it matter where?' (*SLJ*, 338). The stuff of art can be found everywhere, and the spirit of the artist – like the spirit of God or the gods – is omnipresent and immanent.

Such a Long Journey has been described as 'both history and fabulation',[32] and there are certainly elements of the text's treatment of documented national events which appear to propel it towards the category of 'historiographic metafiction' described by Linda Hutcheon, where history and fiction are intertwined, and the boundaries between them blurred to allow a new perspective to emerge.[33] For instance, gossip opens up the interpretative possibilities of the whole of post-independence Indian history, anonymously advancing the suggestion that the causes of the unexpected deaths of Lal Bahadur Shastri and Indira's Parsi husband, Feroze Gandhi may not have been natural. Similarly, at their last meeting, Ghulam Mohammad tells Gustad that he is content to wait for revenge on those in power whom he considers responsible for the death of his friend Jimmy, remarking of Indira: '"I am a patient man. Her life is as easy to snuff out as Bili Boy's, let me tell you. Like that," and he snapped his fingers under Gustad's nose,' (*SLJ*, 323). Reading with a hindsight that encompasses the deaths of both Indira Gandhi – assassinated by a Sikh personal bodyguard in 1984 – and her son, Sanjay, 'the car manufacturer' – killed in a plane crash four years earlier – Ghulam's tirade metafictionally anticipates (perhaps even proleptically participates in) these later reckonings.

In a sense, Rohinton Mistry's first two novels can be read as a diptych, diagnosing the ills of a nation in the early 1970s. The powerful blend of political chicanery and casual brutality which descends on the fiercely guarded private world of sensitive individuals, intrinsic to *Such a Long Journey*, also provides the lineaments of Mistry's novelistic analysis of an even greater constitutional outrage, the 1975 State of Emergency, in his next novel. *A Fine Balance* pursues further the themes of political decline and personal moral responsibility raised in *Such a Long Journey*, but it does so on an epic scale, testing out the fabric of the nation through a swatch of characters, both employer and employee, middle-class and peasant, high-caste and untouchable, caught up in the dangerous delirium of a paranoid political regime.

4

Thread and circuses: performing in
the spaces of city and nation in
A Fine Balance

> you only have power over people as long as you don't
> take *everything* away from them. But when you've
> robbed a man of *everything* he's no longer in your
> power – he's free again. (Alexander Solzhenitsyn,
> *The First Circle*, p. 107)

> you cannot draw lines and compartments, and refuse to
> budge beyond them ... You have to maintain a fine
> balance between hope and despair ... In the end, it's all a
> question of balance. (*A Fine Balance*, p. 231)

MISTRY'S interest in the impact of the historical waves that
wash over the lives of ordinary people, begun in *Such a Long
Journey*, is continued in *A Fine Balance*, published in 1996.[1]
Indeed, the tribulations of the Parsi community, along with its
distinctive cultural orientations and ethical dilemmas, give his
writing some of the qualities of a 'minor literature' as diagnosed
by Deleuze and Guattari. Describing minor literatures as those
'which a minority constructs in a major language' – thereby
allowing for the inclusion of both the Indian novel in English
and the Parsi contribution to it – Deleuze and Guattari identify
two key features: 'everything in them is political', and 'everything takes on a collective value.'[2] In the 'cramped spaces' of the
'minor' novel individual intrigues connect directly to politics:
'The individual concern thus becomes all the more necessary,
indispensable, magnified, because a whole other story is vibrating
within it. In this way, the family triangle connects to other
triangles – commercial, economic, bureaucratic juridical – that

determine its values.'[3] Certainly true of *Such a Long Journey*, the same can be said of Mistry's second novel, where a family of a quite unorthodox kind develops out of an initial atmosphere of squabbling and mutual mistrust, before being torn apart by the blind exercise of a capricious brutality.

Yet, *A Fine Balance* also reveals Mistry's expanding field of vision, now moving beyond Parsi life to embrace the fate of the wider Indian community at the time of Indira Gandhi's infamous State of Emergency (1975–77). As John Ball has put it: 'in its careful exploration of diverse gender, class and religious subject positions, it is a much more inclusive work than its predecessor.' It offers:

> a superabundant social spectrum of Muslim rent-collectors and tailors, Sikh cabbies, wily beggars, disillusioned lawyers, murderous strongmen, corrupt slumlords, profit-eering police, radical students, and – in a cameo no less unflattering than her appearances in *Midnight's Children* and *Such a Long Journey* – Indira Gandhi herself.[4]

Acknowledging that in his first two books he had focused in detail only on the Parsi community, Mistry commented in interview: 'I made a conscious decision in this book to include more than this, mainly because in India seventy five per cent of Indians live in villages and I wanted to embrace more of the social reality of India.'[5] This, in turn, leads to more profound reflections on questions of belonging in relation to the body politic, a point reinforced by the novel's focus on lower caste Hindus, 'Untouchables', Muslims and, of course, Parsis: what one might call a cast list of the marginalized and dispossessed who find themselves at the mercy of the Brahminical and pseudo-secular elites shaping India in the 1970s. Such questions arise with particular poignancy in relation to the role of caste, and are explored through the experiences of two of the central characters, the tanners-turned-tailors Ishvar and Omprakash Darji. They have felt the full force of upper caste disapproval, vented on their family for violating time-honoured stasis by daring to alter their occupation and, hence, their position in the hierarchical social chain. The brutal murder of Ishvar and Om's relatives sends them scurrying to the city, where they meet a fellow migrant, Maneck Kohlah, who has arrived to complete his education at a technical college, and a lonely Parsi widow, Dina Dalal, in whose flat they find employment and a temporary home.

Mistry's broader canvas allows for a rhythmical depiction of rural communities, their comforts and their injustices, as well as the more 'rough and ready' community of the city, which includes slum dwellers and mutilated beggars, among whom the fleeing Ishvar and Omprakash find themselves. On trial too is the neo-colonial economic system which embroils even well-meaning characters, such as the tailors' host and employer Dina, in a network of exploitation and debt stretching from the highest offices of government to the lowest reaches of the dispossessed. The forced evictions and sterilisations that take place as the Emergency swings into action are merely the most extreme manifestation of a mania for social control infecting Indira Gandhi, and articulated by numerous corresponding figures who resort to excessive measures in the face of national and personal instability. By a series of tragic twists of fate, Ishvar and Omprakash eventually find themselves at the mercy of one particularly vicious personification of the conjunction of rural and urban, feudal and capitalist modes of oppression.

Yet Mistry is also concerned to show how real communication can develop through physical intimacy. Ishvar, Omprakash and Dina are thrown together somewhat unwillingly in the latter's flat, along with Dina's paying guest, Maneck. They achieve fruitful interaction leading to genuine affection by co-operation and the sharing of stories emblematised by the never-ending patchwork quilt Dina makes from the tailors' surplus material. From Dina's decaying rented apartment, the novel opens out, creating a whole world – or rather a series of inter-connected worlds – for the reader to inhabit: ranging from Maneck's Himalayan childhood home; the tailors' village and the slum colony in which they find temporary domicile when they start their employment; Ashraf Chacha's workshop where they learn their trade; the Au Revoir export company, making a tidy profit from their relentless labours, and presided over by the viperish Mrs Gupta with her austere, sculpted hairstyles; to the Vishram Vegetarian Hotel, where the tailors fill their well-earned breaks with steaming cups of tea and regale the staff with tales of their adventures. The differing domains of the novel underline its concern with space. At the same time, characters take on roles in relation to one another in these spaces according to the operation of stark inequalities of power: they must perform in the expected and 'appropriate' way, or face verbal denunciation, unemployment, imprisonment, physical violence or even death. For the newcomer to the city such codes have to be internalised and the 'script' learned, and all at a time when the recognisable lineaments of democracy and accountability have been erased: something which makes the lessons of urban living, of staying one step ahead of the now fitful and despotic mechanisms of the law, every bit as haphazard and mysterious as they are for Kafka's Joseph K in *The Trial*.[6] Equally, people are defined in relation to their work. Indeed, it is possible to argue that the spatial economy of Bombay's 'toilers', as described by Sandeep Pendse, is reflected in the movements of Mistry's tailors with their unique and vulnerable relationship to the metropolis. The precariousness of their social position, indeed of their entire existence, is related to the eponymous theme of balance, an imperative articulated by the seemingly allegorical figure of Vasantrao Valmik BA LLB, the Yeats-quoting proof-reader, who surfaces periodically and appears at first glance to be the novel's valorised voice.

A Fine Balance also has a more varied pace and tone than Mistry's other novels, skipping over swathes of the characters' early years and slowing to meditate on defining incidents and unfolding relationships, such as the death of Dina's beloved husband and her battles with her dictatorial brother, Nusswan. Along with the vivid and evocative descriptions of daily life, especially that of the tailors, the text contains elements of the picaresque, as their escapades take them on train journeys, into police vans, and onto buses commandeered by the government to ferry a 'made-to-measure' audience to a prime-ministerial rally. The novel is tragic, certainly, but it also has moments of broad farce, often used to illustrate the absurdity of power and the Emergency's random and sometimes contradictory injunctions. Indeed, the surface of the novel, characterised by the fine detail that brings the text to life, is everywhere marked by eruptions of the symbolic, the satirical, the allegorical and the carnivalesque: thereby indicating that Mistry is here developing a more stylised and syncretic way of representing the world than the conventional critical view, which sees him simply as a realist writer, would allow. Moreover, *A Fine Balance* is the richest of Mistry's texts in terms of intertextual allusions, at times echoing Indian writers such as R. K. Narayan, Mulk Raj Anand and Nayantara Sahgal, and with more nods in the direction of Mistry's European influences such as W. B. Yeats. Likewise, it can be argued that the novel has a similar scope and ambition to those sweeping chronicles of nineteenth- and twentieth-century Russian society – by Dostoyevsky, Tolstoy, Turgenev or Solzhenitsyn – with their relentless attention to power, injustice and enforced social orthodoxies, as it narrates the tailors' encounters with the arbitrary power unleashed in the Emergency.

A full examination of the range of forces which brought Indira Gandhi from the pinnacle of national admiration as victor of the 1971 war with Pakistan, to an isolated and paranoid despotism in three and half short years, are beyond the scope of the present study. However, a broad account of the events shaking India, and Indira – the two became synonymous in the infamous slogan 'Indira is India and India is Indira' dreamed up by Congress party sycophants during the Emergency – can be given. Perhaps most important were a series of economic crises in the early 1970s. The rains failed in 1972–3, resulting in disaster for the harvest, and this was immediately followed by the OPEC oil crisis, which affected both economically developed and developing nations. In India's case the result was rampant inflation, which was running at about thirty per cent by the middle of 1974. At about the same time there was an increased radicalisation of certain sections of the population. The Naxalite peasant insurgency, which had begun in a small village in Bihar, spread to other parts of the country, while the ranks of the disaffected were swelled by the large numbers of unemployed from the educated, professional classes. Forms of direct action included a series of strikes, the most famous of which, the All-India Rail Strike of 1974, Indira saw as a direct, almost personal challenge, and which she crushed in determined manner.[7] As David Selbourne has noted, 'the conjunction of suffering, inflation and recession, and the cyclical collision of mounting opposition from right, left and centre to the misgovernment of India and the draconian intolerance of such opposition began to deepen and quicken'.[8] The same period saw Indira Gandhi, isolated, uncertain of whom she could trust and coming to rely on an ever-smaller band of close confidantes, centralising more and more power in her own hands. The atmosphere of embattled authoritarianism was ripe for abuses, and the early 1970s were also marked by a rise in instances of peremptory arrests, the fettering of prisoners, torture and 'disappearances',[9] experiences mirrored by those of the student politico, Avinash, in *A Fine Balance* who briefly befriends Maneck in his college hall of residence before being swallowed up by dark inquisitorial forces.

The immediate constitutional precursor to the Emergency was a decision of the Allahabad High Court, early in June 1975, that Indira Gandhi had been guilty of electoral malpractices in relation to the 1971 General Election. Although the offences were relatively trivial, the court decreed that the Prime Minister should be debarred from holding public office for six years. Rather than submit to the judgement, and citing the growing tide of 'internal disturbances' threatening India, Mrs Gandhi instructed the President of India to announce a State of Emergency just before midnight on 25 June. Opposition leaders, and even suspect members of Mrs Gandhi's own Congress Party, were taken from their beds and interned: the right to trial was effectively suspended; public meetings were banned; newspapers were subject to strict controls; and even the writings on freedom of Indira's father, Jawaharlal Nehru, and Mahatma Gandhi were censored.[10] Indira even demonstrated her mastery over time itself, by introducing constitutional amendments conferring on herself retrospective immunity from prosecution in respect of past or future criminal offences.[11] In Mistry's novel, Vasantrao Valmik remarks ironically on this development: 'We poor mortals have to accept that bygone events are beyond our clutch, while the Prime Minister performs juggling acts with time past' (AFB, 563).

However, perhaps the most sinister elements of the Emergency were initiated by Indira's son and heir apparent, Sanjay, who, despite having no electoral mandate, used his power base in Youth Congress to add some ideas of his own to his mother's 'Twenty Point Programme' for national rejuvenation. In the guise of 'beautification' a process of slum clearance and family planning was instituted. In practice, the former often meant clearing the poor away from areas they had improved and made habitable themselves, so that these juicy slices of real estate could be utilised by Sanjay's friends, the property developers; while the latter turned into what has been described as 'a grotesque carnival of abduction, mutilation and disease',[12] as people were forced and tricked into allowing themselves to be sterilised, in order that 'motivators', conscripted to impose the unpopular measure, could meet the targets imposed on them by employers empowered to bestow or withhold financial rewards.[13] Sanjay Gandhi came to exert an enormous amount of power during the Emergency as Indira, seeing him as one of the few people she could trust, and unwilling or unable to restrain him and his acolytes, gave free rein to his schemes and turned a blind eye to their consequences.

Ishvar and Omprakash have what is perhaps their first experience of the unrestrained severity of the new order at the beginning of the novel, when their train journey to the city is interrupted by the discovery of a dead body on the line ahead. Disturbing but seemingly innocuous at this stage – the passengers merely lament this passing inconvenience: 'Why does everyone always choose the railway tracks only for dying … No consideration for people like us …What is wrong with poison or tall buildings or knives?' (*AFB*, 5–6) – the discovery can only be set in context later in the book, when we learn that bodies are now appearing on railway lines with alarming regularity, and when it is revealed that one such body belongs to the troublesome Avinash. Likewise, it is only after Maneck's suicide under an oncoming train at the end of the book, that the faint echoes of Tolstoy's *Anna Karenina*, that other tale of a family torn apart, which also begins and ends with deaths under trains, can be fully appreciated. Rather, at this early stage, the focus is on Ishvar, Om and Maneck who are meeting for the first time in the train carriage, recalling the initial encounter of three of the central characters in another of Mistry's Russian textual influences, *The Idiot*. Here, the way the trio are described, with our attention drawn to Ishvar's disfigured left cheek, and Om's frail spine as he is bumped and jostled by fellow passengers, indicates that the body and its fragility is again to be at the centre of what follows.

In his *oeuvre* as a whole, Mistry's focus on the body, the messiness of its functions and its inevitable corruption, emerges from, but offers a striking contrast to, the traditional Zoroastrian obsession with corporeal purity which is at the heart of several of his characters' aversions to the outside world. His protagonists learn that the Zoroastrian injunction to engage with the world must take precedence over such doctrinal niceties. In *A Fine Balance* it is Dina Dalal who must overcome the urge to withdraw and scrape away the suspicion with which her life has become encrusted since the death of her husband. This is not just a suspicion of the other, but specifically of the other body. She is initially discomforted by the physical presence of the tailors when they come to perform their piecemeal work in her home, recoiling at the alien smell of their urine in her toilet, and segregating the mugs in which she serves their break-time tea. But Dina herself has been a victim of bodily discrimination, most noticeably as a teenager when she is physically chastised by her brother and guardian, Nusswan, for ignoring his injunction not to follow fashion and cut her hair, in a disturbing scene where her burgeoning sexual maturity is exposed to his ambiguous gaze (*AFB*, 23–4). Such moments prefigure the later forms of national authoritarianism and the abuse of bodies in the Emergency. In this book, violence against the body takes its most drastic form in the enforced sterilisations. The concern with the fragility of bodies, which encompasses the handless and legless beggar, Shankar, and his disfigured mother, known only as 'Nosey' because of her empty nasal cavity, reaches its culmination when Ishvar and Om are captured and sterilised by the henchmen of the landowner also responsible for the torture and murder of their family. Om is castrated on a whim of the *Thakur*, while Ishvar suffers the fate of many victims of the *nasabandi* process: the paucity of aftercare means that his wounds turn septic, then gangrenous and eventually his legs have to be amputated.

The bodily distress of the characters appears also that of the city they inhabit – and, perhaps, of the body politic more generally – as the tailors realise when, travelling back after a spell in a forced labour camp, they spy one of the remaining slum settlements, with its 'sordid quiltings of plastic and card-board and paper and sackcloth, like scabs and blisters creeping in a dermatological nightmare across the rotting body of the metropolis' (*AFB*, 379). Mutilation metaphors abound. There is a sense in which the tribulations of this society are historically predicated on physical brutality, its wounds self-inflicted. The novel sweeps backwards in time to fill in the earlier lives of its protagonists and their ancestors, forever mutated by the gory 'parturition' of Partition, when markings on the body, speci-fically those of circumcision, take on a literal life or death significance. Partition has robbed Maneck's father of his ancestral lands and threatened the peaceful coexistence of Hindu and Muslim in the community from which the tailors will come.

In this way, the line drawn at Partition, portioning out territory between India and Pakistan, is only the most obvious boundary in a text with an obsessive concern for the ways in which individuals and communities seek to demarcate space and seal themselves off from others. Commenting on Dina's initial attempts to follow the advice of her supplier, Mrs Gupta, and maintain a line between herself and her new employees, Mistry observes the paradox at the heart of the desire for delineation and order: 'all such lines are artificial and there are stronger forces at work and if such a line is made to persist it will lead to chaos or lead to even more problems. Partition was just such a line and history has amply shown this.'[14] To be sure, there are instances where characters reach out across 'the line': Ishvar and his brother, Narayan, the father of Omprakash, protect the Muslim tailor to whom they are apprenticed and whom they look on as their uncle, when a Hindu mob descends on his workshop at the time of Partition. And, indeed, Dina eventually learns that the barriers she is seeking to maintain between herself and the tailors are unsustainable. She initially banishes her unauthorised employees and their sewing machines to the back room, out of sight of the prying eyes of the rent collector, and when she delivers the fruits of their labours to Au Revoir exports she locks them in to avoid any possibility that they may follow her, learn her supplier and cut her out of the transaction. However, while she is away, Ishvar and Om take pleasure in transgressing into Dina's comparatively comfortable living space, lounging in her cushioned chairs and luxuriating in wreaths of cigarette smoke. Eventually, however, with the familiarity borne of intimacy when the tailors become permanent residents and an ad hoc family develops in the cramped apartment, her line begins to waver, and even their scent becomes 'unobtrusive now because it was the same for everyone. They were all eating the same food, drinking the same water. Sailing under one flag' (*AFB*, 399).

In fact, if endeavouring to maintain 'the line' in the interest of some notion of self-preservation is damaging, attempting to re-impose it after it has been dismantled is potentially disastrous. At the end of his course, Maneck leaves Dina's flat for a job in Dubai, working in refrigeration. He returns eight years later to the maelstrom of anti-Sikh violence which has followed the assassination of Indira Gandhi by a Sikh bodyguard, and to the horrific discovery that his erstwhile flatmates, Ishvar and Om, have been mutilated and reduced to beggary. Unable to cope with changes that aggravate his already depressive disposition, he cannot bring himself to speak to the tailors and pretends not to recognise them. The novel emphasises the need to cut through the formalities and imposed proprieties that keep people apart, even though the connections thereby established can only ever be transitory and preserved in the memory. (Indeed, there is also a danger in trying to hold onto the past, as Dina discovers – like other Mistry characters before her – when she clutches at her late husband through the possessions he has left behind. Mistry comments: 'there is a great difference between remembering the past which is creative and life enhancing and trying to preserve it which is detrimental and debilitating'.)[15] Maneck forgets Vasantrao Valmik's wise counsel: 'the secret of survival is to embrace change, and to adapt' (*AFB*, 230), and allows himself to become disconnected from his past and all the support networks that have sustained him. Disconnection leads to death – for Maneck – or death-like experiences. Ironically, not long before his suicide, Maneck has rediscovered an old friend of the tailors in unexpected surroundings. Rajaram, the hair collector, first appears as a fellow slum dweller when the tailors arrive in the city. He helps them to settle in, teaches them the tricks of a scavenger's life, and displays his community-mindedness by sharing food with them. When the slum is broken up he disappears, only to resurface soon after as a family planning motivator, trying to cajole all and sundry to surrender their reproductive futures – a job at which this benevolent figure proves spectacularly incompetent. However, some kind of moral corruption attendant on working for the government seems to have entered his soul, and his reversion to hair collecting culminates in the murder of two beggars with particularly luxurious, and therefore valuable locks. Rajaram confesses his crime in his last meeting with the tailors, and states his intention to do penance by renouncing the world and becoming a wandering mendicant. Eight years later, Maneck finds him back in the city, transmogrified into Bal Baba, a miracle-working *sanyasi*, with a neat line in what Om would describe as 'fakeology', and bolstered by an entourage of devotees and a range of holy merchandise. Maneck tries to make Rajaram confront his past but is rebuffed: '"Rajaram the hair-collector renounced his life, his joys and sorrows, his vices and virtues. Why? So that Bal Baba could be incarnated and could use his humble gift to assist humanity along the pathway to moksha ... That was another life, another person. That's all finished, don't you understand"' (*AFB*, 602–3). Given his guilty past, it seems possible that Rajaram/Bal Baba's may be an exculpatory fantasy rather than true renunciation, and that he is merely peddling consoling fictions. However, as Maneck leaves Bal Baba's marquee, the crowds are still queuing for an audience and a benediction, and the life-cycle transformations sanctioned by the Hindu *Ashramas* maintain the possibility that – like a more sinister version of Raju in R. K. Narayan's novel of dubious saintliness, *The Guide* – he may yet achieve redemption in his new incarnation.[16]

Instead of dividing lines between self and other or past and present lives, the novel endorses balance and pattern. Existence is inherently unsteady, as Ishvar and Om discover when their first tailoring job in the city requires them to perch precariously in a temporary loft made of planks supported by bamboo poles. The theme of balance is articulated most effectively by Vasantrao Valmik in a discussion with Maneck during a train journey. He advises: 'You cannot draw lines and compartments, and refuse to budge beyond them. Sometimes you have to use your failures as stepping-stones to success. You have to maintain a fine balance between hope and despair' (*AFB*, 231). Valmik reveals himself as, in a sense, the moral conscience of a nation that has now 'gone off the rails', so to speak. He seems to take upon himself the sins of the national elite to which he has been a witness during his post as a proof-reader for *The Times of India*. After an abortive career in law – beginning in the year of India's independence but symbolically fizzling out soon afterwards – Valmik has spent twenty-four years reading 'court proceedings, legal texts, stockmarket figures. Politician's speeches too' (*AFB*, 228), as well as 'stories of misery, caste violence, government callousness, official arrogance, police brutality' (*AFB*, 229), until his tear ducts rebel and he becomes virulently allergic to printing ink. He seems to embody the ills currently besetting India. His latest 'incarnation' at this stage is as a *morcha* man, hiring himself out to different parties and producing slogans to be shouted at political rallies. When Maneck meets him he is hoarse: his throat having been unable to stand the strain of such raucous employment after the hushed pursuits of proof-reading. His enforced silence amid the clamour of the Emergency also seems symbolic. He recognises that in selling out to those forces responsible for the present turmoil: 'You could say that I have cut my own throat' (*AFB*, 233). After a brief return to the law – during which he counsels Dina at her lowest ebb: 'Loss is essential. Loss is part and parcel of that necessary calamity called life' (*AFB*, 565) – Valmik ends up in charge of Bal Baba's mail-order business, answering the religious enquiries of a different kind of plaintiff, and 'creating fiction after fiction, which will become more real in the recipients' lives than all their sad realities' (*AFB*, 604); something of an ambivalent fate for a character whose stoicism has earlier made him appear a kind of authorial spokesman. In fact, images of balance are themselves ambiguous in the text. As John Ball has noted, balance 'becomes something of a mantra in the novel and takes on ever deeper shades of meaning and association.' While Valmik advocates his 'fine balance between hope and despair':

> 'Balance' is not always so benignly commonsensical … For a village thug enforcing caste discipline, an Untouchable's transgression of his prescribed profession 'distorts society's timeless balance' and must be punished by a hideous death … The street performer Monkey-man [who balances small children on the top of a pole] … enacts a different kind of balance in his retributive tit-for-tat killings. At times, the invocations of balance here are as gruesomely ironic as in Shakespeare's *Measure for Measure*.[17]

The search for pattern in chaos is also preferable to line drawing. By definition, the tailors' business is the creation of shape and order by following a pattern. Dina takes this a stage further by utilising the scraps of material left over after the day's work to make a quilt. The many different colours and textures of the quilt come to represent the experiences which the little 'family' in her flat share during their time together, and quilting spirals away to take on a series of metaphorical, and metaphysical, associations: Om wistfully pictures time as a bolt of cloth, and wishes he could stitch together the good parts and take out the bad; while Maneck imagines that God is a giant quilt maker whose handiwork has grown so expansive that the pattern is impossible to see. Sewing and quilting are connected to other kinds of creative act by which the randomness of life can be redeemed, such as the sharing of memories and stories. As Dina gets to know her boarders they slowly unburden themselves of their harrowing life story: 'she added the pieces to what Maneck had already revealed about their life in the village. Like her quilt the tailors' chronicle was gradually gathering shape' (*AFB*, 385). Just as memory allows one to connect with one's own past, so too it allows one to reach out and connect with others. The Forsterian valorisation of connection in this text is emphasised by Ishvar, who encourages his fractious nephew to 'keep connecting', when confronted with a particularly intricate pattern to follow.

This quest for pattern is likewise written into the book's very structure. Its shuttling temporality, employing both prolepsis and analepsis, allows us to understand character and motivation as well as filling in the political and historical background. As I have claimed elsewhere, these echoes and prefigurements are 'a formal corollary of the thematic concern for pattern'.[18] Mention has been made of the mangled bodies that appear from time to time on the railway tracks. Another reverberation begins when Dina's doomed husband, Rustom, wobbles through the city traffic on his bicycle before a collision claims him: later Omprakash will rent a bicycle and be involved in a less serious accident while trying to follow Dina to her supplier. Likewise, on page 68, Dina puts her foot through a rotten plank of wood while scouring the neighbourhood for available tailors: an incident echoed when (on page 153) we learn that Om has earlier done the same thing on the same spot. The looping narrative ensures that, in 'real time', Om has stumbled over the plank first, but that Dina's experience is narrated first. The reader is thus equipped to register the textual obsession with pattern, and patterns within patterns. Moreover, for characters too the past is constantly intruding on the present: as it does when memories of her departed husband prevent Dina from enjoying intimate relations with a potential suitor. Thus, memory invests everything with significance for both readers and characters. The cyclical structure of the novel is confirmed when, after their encounter with the steriliser, Ishvar and Om come to replace the now-dead beggar, Shankar, in a chapter significantly entitled 'The Circle is Completed'. The involutions of India's political life also appear cyclical in the Epilogue: on his return to India, Maneck finds that Rajiv Gandhi has been sworn in as Prime Minister after his mother's assassination; while hindsight for the reader includes the 'foreknowledge' of Rajiv's own assassination, seven years after the novel's action ends.

In terms of symbolism, Mistry's technique is reminiscent of that 'repetition plus variation' recommended by E. M. Forster in his chapter on 'Pattern and Rhythm' in *Aspects of the Novel*.[19] Symbols do not atrophy by being made to stand for a single set of correspondences. They shift, evolve, find new combinations, achieve new resonances, sometimes even have their meanings inverted. Just as balance throws up a multivalent set of symbols, so too hair and animals are freighted with different symbolic connotations at different times. Hair is a banner of individuality for the defiant young Dina in her battles with her brother, while Rajaram can initially read the 'whole life' of the person whose hair he has collected through their follicular peculiarities. Later, however, when he returns to hair collecting, he develops an unbalanced obsession for his quarry, which leads him eventually to murder. We are also reminded of the well-known divisive incident of the hair of the Prophet's beard, which led to riots and communal tensions in Kashmir in the 1960s. Similarly, something of Dina's initial insularity and gradual opening-up is symbolised through the kittens abandoned by their mother in her kitchen. She is initially perturbed by this insalubrious invasion, but she eventually yields to her new guests, as she does to the tailors. Likewise, the kittens are at first dependent additions to the developing 'family': then, as they grow bolder, plucky embodiments of the scavenging principle also necessary in human society as depicted here; and finally – when, to mix a metaphor, they 'fly the nest' altogether – anticipatory symbols of the inevitable emptying of Dina's flat and the scattering of her makeshift brood.

The echoes of Forster and the concern for order through narrative, symbol and repetition gives a modernist flavour to *A Fine Balance*. The text appears to be saying that the chaos of human life can yield to pattern through the intervention of the creative faculties, whereas the rigidity represented by lines that divide is purely destructive. The modernist inheritance would seem to be underlined by the quotations from Yeats, Valmik's favourite poet and one with much to say about the kind of 'blood-dimmed tide' loosed by the Emergency. Certainly, all the lives on display here appear to be tossed from order to chaos and back again by the myriad upheavals of fate. Yet, in fact, the use of this motif is part of a more complex dialectic played out in the text. Mistry cites the upper caste response to a higher birth rate of male children among its low caste neighbours as an example. To the Brahmins: 'This is the result of chaos in the universe brought on by some transgression in this world of the natural social order. They then talk of increased vigilance and a more rigorous adherence to the caste system which obviously means more floggings and beatings, which is the real chaos.'[20] Mistry explores the paradoxes of the terms 'order' and 'chaos' in this context, transvaluing them in a manner reminiscent of Chinua Achebe's celebrated inversion of colonial discourse's claim of bringing order into the chaos of nineteenth-century Nigeria in *Things Fall Apart*.[21] There may be a different kind of authoritarian impulse at work in 1970s India, but it is an oppressive, all-pervading one nonetheless. The multivalent use of the idea of chaos in *A Fine Balance* inverts the discourse of power to show that, although Mrs Gandhi's Emergency claims to be bringing order out of chaos, it does in fact introduce chaos (and fear) into a situation which – while previously characterised by a degree of social disorder – does have a pattern discernible to the attentive eye: that of the heterogeneity of lived experience. Therefore, order and chaos are not simply inverted, but consciously played off against each other in the shifting symbolic economy of the novel, in search of that elusive balance of the title.

But above all, *A Fine Balance* is a book about space. At first sight the novel's different locales appear neatly divided. The middle-class characters such as Dina, the doctor's daughter, and the proud shopkeeper Mr Kohlah enjoy the comparative luxury of independent living spaces, however tarnished they have become, whereas the early life of the tanners-turned-tailors, marked by poverty and discrimination, is nevertheless communal, with burdens and tasks being shared and local news discussed throughout their village. This would seem to be of a piece with the theme of rootedness versus uprootedness, and the deeply-felt danger of forgetting who you are if you leave your own earth, which plays most insistently on the conscience of Maneck. However, these spaces are not discreet, distinct from each other, or immune to the intrusion of other ways of life. Such lines are crossed too: Dukhi and Narayan break the bonds of caste by changing their occupation; Dina's flat is 'invaded' by 'foreign bodies'; and Mr Kohlah's visceral identification with the mountains in which he has always lived and worked is eroded by the incursion of developers and 'nation-builders' (*AFB*, 215), whose vision of bigger and better roads carries the seeds of destruction for both Mr Kohlah's home-brewed carbonated drink – squeezed out of business by a multinational latecomer – and for his whole way of life.

Indeed, capitalist and pre-capitalist (or feudal) forces are compared and contrasted too. Capitalism is embodied by Mrs Gupta, doyenne of Au Revoir Exports. Her control-freak tendencies are evinced by regular trips to the hairdresser to tame her unruly locks, and, with her slogan-pocked speech, she is a vocal supporter of the Emergency. Indira's motto, 'The Need of the Hour is Discipline' (*AFB*, 74), holds good for her too. She recommends that Dina preserve the distance between herself and her tailors, and rejoices that Emergency legislation has meant a curb on the trade unions. (One of Indira's trusted advisers, P. N. Dhar, has noted how the middle classes 'were impressed by the immediate gains of the Emergency: no strikes ... industrial peace, quiet on the campuses ... stable prices, spurt in economic activity.')[22] As an exploitative personification of the entrepreneurial spirit allowed free rein under the Emergency, Mrs Gupta recalls the callous and arrogant 'New Entrepreneurs' Wives' group in Nayantara Sahgal's novelistic indictment of the Emergency, *Rich Like Us*.[23]

The tailors' village is a site where a feudal economy of power remains in place. It is a space of continuity and community in adversity, at least among the lower castes. But it is certainly not an idealised locale: superstition and violence are rampant, and gender inequalities are shown in the fact that sweetmeats are circulated when a male child is born, but no such celebration attends the birth of a girl. Moreover, it is also a site of the repetitions of caste-based brutality. The lower castes are beaten, tortured and killed for a number of trivial offences. The proximity of a summary 'justice' and barbarity feeds into Mistry's exploration of the ambiguous coordinates of order and chaos. Most outrageous of all in this rigidly hierarchical society is the transgression signified by Dukhi's decision to better his family's prospects by turning from tanning to tailoring. Partha Chatterjee's comments on caste may suggest what is at stake in Dukhi's refusal to endure hereditary and perpetual servitude: 'The essence of caste, we may say, requires that the labouring bodies of the impure castes be reproduced in order that they can be subordinated to the need to maintain the bodies of the pure castes in their state of purity. All injunctions of dharma must work to this end.'[24] The unfulfilled promise of uplift offered by the nationalist campaigners early in the book appears as illusory for Mistry's characters, in the face of ingrained prejudice, as it does for the eponymous hero of Mulk Raj Anand's pre-independence classic, *Untouchable*, whose experiences are replayed in intensified form.[25]

A Fine Balance is a novel exploring what Rukmini Bhaya Nair calls 'the complex ecology of exploitation. All the Dinas and the Ishvars and the Manecks and Beggarmasters ... and Mrs Guptas form a complex chain of survival in which both mutual need and mutual suspicion exist intertwined.'[26] Indeed, it is strongly suggested that everyone, regardless of good intentions, is in some way implicated in, or profiting from, exploitation. Even Dina is part of the exploiting capitalist network. She is economically dependent on her brother and seeks a way out of his clutches by surreptitiously employing her piece-working, non-unionised labour to provide cheap textiles which Mrs Gupta then exports at a profit. The full complexity of inter-dependence is made explicit when the sinister Beggarmaster – a character who, in contrast to others individualised in minute detail, is never physically described, and who has previously protected street beggars like Shankar, making 'professional modifications' where necessary – becomes protector of Dina's vulnerable household against a thuggish landlord keen to evict her. The text asks whether it is possible to behave morally in a world turned upside down. Perhaps there is even a perverse benevolence in Beggarmaster's horrific activities. He mutilates his charges because he knows that those with the worst disfigurements earn the highest profits in the warped economy of beggary. Yet, as well as being 'a thoroughly modern businessman' (*AFB*, 446), he does demonstrate a concern for his beggars, albeit out of self-interest: so much so that one is led to wonder what use freedom will be to them after his violent death. In this respect, with its attention to the mutual exploitation sanctioned by the Emergency, and examples of human tragedy underpinned by dogged endurance, the 'City by the Sea' in *A Fine Balance* recalls Balzac's Paris in *Père Goriot*, where the protagonist Rastignac reaches a conclusion equally applicable to Mistry's hunted characters: 'he must, as on the battlefield, kill or be killed, deceive or be deceived; ... he must give up conscience and heart at the entrance, put on a mask, mercilessly exploit others and ... seize his fortune without being seen in order to earn his laurels.'[27] Equally, a culture of parasitism is also being fostered, symbolised in the extensive worm imagery. The Emergency breeds enforcers, like the slum landlord who accepts a job at the head of a government slum clearance programme and bulldozes the ramshackle dwellings of his own tenants; 'motivators' who prod, pester and push people into waiting sterilisation vans; 'facilitators' who offer to forge ration cards and sterilisation certificates; protection racketeers thriving in the atmosphere of paranoia and banditry; and those using the invasive new laws to settle old scores.

Inevitably, such activities are concentrated in the city. Yet the city still operates as a magnet to Ishvar and Om when they seek a new start after the massacre of their family. It may be a stage on which the starkest social disparities are played out, but the city still fires the imagination of all sections of the populace,[28] and the tailors come to it with naïve optimism and dreams of a better life. Moreover, after their experience of the murderous re-imposition of 'the line' in their village, the tailors' first experience of the city is of the bustle of its railway station, 'a roiling swirl of humanity' (AFB, 153), which does not so much allow mixing as enforce it. The unfamiliarity of their surroundings is emphasised during their first night, spent under an awning, when their sleep is disturbed by a woman being beaten, a drunkard shouting abuse and a pavement-dweller shrieking as he is attacked for stealing someone else's spot. The city is initially depicted as corrupt and corrupting in the eyes of the newcomers. It contains the same 'thieving-shops, the stews and the rookeries, the fetid cellars and the dangerous tenements', which Raymond Williams finds in eighteenth-century literary evocations of London.[29]

In fact, the position of Ishvar and Om in relation to their new environment calls to mind Sandeep Pendse's definition of the 'toilers' of contemporary Bombay who perform menial tasks in unstable occupations within the city, 'are sellers of labour power' – sometimes in covert and unofficial ways – and who lack control over most aspects of their lives. Toilers thus 'acquire a sense of impermanence, instability, and insecurity':[30] a far cry from Valmik's vaunted balance. Ishvar and Om's new habitat is one of ad hoc dwellings: street corners, shop doorways, railway stations and temporary shacks on waste ground. Pendse argues that the cityscape impacts on three aspects of the toilers' lives: space, time and the rhythms of existence. For example, they are often relegated to peripheral parts of the city, both figuratively and literally, and form a large proportion of those slum dwellers who haunt the least desirable and developed patches of urban land. Ishvar and Om come to inhabit one such slum, beside the railway line, where a volatile but supportive community develops to complicate the picture of the city as a place of alienation and isolation. Equally, for new arrivals from the country, the city forms a daunting, unknowable space, very different from the manageable dimensions of the rural village:

> The occupied space does not form a gentle and negotiable territory under leisurely control of its inhabitants. It cannot be easily traversed. It is, as a whole, beyond the intimate knowledge and comprehension of any of its inhabitants … [while] Movement in the city … similarly involves an effort [and] the use of specialised modes of transport.[31]

Ishvar and Om experience this when they squeeze onto overcrowded trains, and are corralled into a variety of vehicles by the authorities as their fortunes ebb and flow. Likewise, informal conceptions of time, dependent on natural phenomena like sunrise, sunset or the cycle of the seasons, are superseded in the city by a more disciplined temporal regime organised around carefully controlled schedules and shifts, which also serve to determine the overall rhythm of life.[32] (Once again, the novel illustrates this facet of urban experience in the tailors' constant anxieties about being late for work: something that also emphasises their precarious status as casual labourers.) But above all, the most striking impression of city life for the new arrival is one of sensory overload. As well as the sounds that interrupt their sleep, Ishvar and Om have their noses assaulted by smells such as that which hovers over the railside latrine the slum dwellers use, and their sense of direction is confused at the intersections of streets that all look the same.

Disorientating as all this may be, city space does allow for the possibility of the kinds of creativity elsewhere valorised. As

Michel de Certeau has suggested, stories – such as those the tailors share at their favourite café, the Vishram Vegetarian Hotel – 'traverse and organise places; they select and link them together; they make sentences and itineraries out of them. They are spatial trajectories.'[33] By narrativising their experiences in the spaces of the text – village, town, city, slum, shop doorway, Dina's flat – they not only contribute patches to the symbolic quilt, they also show how narrative structures 'regulate changes in space (or moves from one place to another) made by stories in the form of places put in linear or interlaced series,'[34] thereby also offering an object lesson in how narrative stitches together different locales to create an image of the nation at this crucial time in its history.

I will have more to say about this imagining of the nation later. The key point here is that, for Michel de Certeau, 'space is a practiced place'.[35] In other words, he distinguishes between mere location, made static by cartography, and the movements between points which are also potential narratives. Even as 'ordinary practitioners of the city', who normally fall well below the administrative gaze of those who think they control such space – and who, indeed, strive to eliminate such 'waste products' as slums and beggars in the name of 'beautification' – Ishvar and Om are part of a host of bodies whose sheer number allows them sometimes to evade the panoptic gaze. This does not mean they escape altogether, as their tragic fate reveals. For them, urban life is often 'an immense social experience of lacking a place – an experience that is ... broken up into countless tiny deportations':[36] quite literally, as they are rounded up and shunted off along with others to (variously) a political rally, a forced labour project, and a sterilisation camp. Yet, in their very travels they probe the points of differentiation, the frontiers – between castes, communities and classes – which have been erected and preserved in fiat and in practice, thus fulfilling what de Certeau sees as the role of stories: 'to *authorize* the establishment, displacement or transcendence of limits'.[37] *A Fine Balance* sets up such limits, such dividing lines, only to have characters transgress them.

This is not to say that the various spaces of the novel – the 'City by the Sea', the 'Village by a River' and the 'Mountains' – are not circumscribed and defined by relationships of power. In the village these include the religious nationalism that infects previously placid human beings at partition, as well as the blatant atrocities of caste power. In Maneck's beloved mountain home, the neo-colonial strength of the multinational cola company prevails over the indigenous product. And, of course, in the city numerous arbitrary impositions have been generated by the Emergency, and are gleefully pursued by those with an eye to the main chance. As Dina has always known since her youthful confrontations with Nusswan, those on the disadvantageous end of such power imbalances must perform the roles expected of them by their tormentors. These roles include obedience, gratitude, deference, hard work and patriotism – the latter being orthographically subverted when Shiv Sena activists besiege a cinema audience, forcing them to stay for the national anthem, while brandishing placards declaring 'PATRIOTISM IS A SCARED DUTY' (*AFB*, 281).

Indeed, the text is full of performers and performances: Monkey-man is an entertainer whose skills include juggling, gymnastics and tightrope walking, but who specialises in acts involving monkeys balancing on the back of a dog and small children perched atop a long pole; street performers are coerced into amusing tired workers in the forced labour camp; Shankar has a repertoire of whimpers and wriggles on his wheeled platform, approximating to Beggarmaster's ideal 'dramaturgy of begging' (*AFB*, 445); and even the *morchas* that Valmik co-ordinates are essentially orchestrated performances for political effect. Yet, less sportive characters too are caught up in the logic of performance in their daily dealings with others: the rent collector, Ibrahim is required to look menacing – a task made difficult by his rebellious smiling muscles; and Maneck's parents feign disappointment at their son's mediocre college marks. However, there are dangers in fostering relations based on imposed obligations and the denial of basic freedoms. This is symbolically illustrated when Monkey-man's dog turns on the monkeys with whom he has been made to caper: the implication being that if you force relationships into unnatural and abusive channels, sooner or later there will be a price to pay.

Mistry does not show the political opposition with which the Emergency was met. Instead, he exposes the pomposity and absurdity of the governing regime in set piece scenes of exuberant satire. Foremost among these is the scene in which Ishvar, Om and Rajaram are dragooned into attending a rally to be addressed by the Prime Minister, in a chapter tellingly entitled 'Day at the Circus, Night in the Slum'. The motif of performance shifts up a gear as we are introduced to the extended metaphor of the circus that accompanies the antics of Indira's placemen and lackeys as they arrive in the slum to round up an audience. Party officials pick their way gingerly across the waterlogged terrain: 'Their performance on the tightrope of mud soon collected a crowd. A puff of wind caught the umbrellas; the men wobbled. A stronger gust pulled them off balance.' (*AFB*, 258) A 'drumroll' of water in an empty bucket under a tap accompanies the spokesman's invitation to the rally, giving him the air of a barker touting at a side-show, and, when the punters prove unwilling, Sergeant Kesar waddles across the mud to direct operations, his flat feet and megaphone held like a trumpet, giving him the demeanour of a clown (*AFB*, 259). Ironically, Monkey-man is prohibited from bringing his monkeys in case their presence gives the Prime Minister's address the appearance of a circus. However, the apparatchiks prove more than capable of doing this themselves, as they compete in fawning self-abasement, prostrating themselves like tumblers at the feet of their leader. The stage on which the rally is to take place is bedecked with flowers and illuminated by coloured lights, and there is even an eighty-foot cardboard-and-plywood cutout of the Prime Minister, with arms outstretched, an outline map of India forming a battered halo behind the head. Dwarfed by this paraphernalia, Indira herself, and her speech, are rather less impressive. Her gesture of flinging the garlands with which she has been overwhelmed into the crowd is not well received:

'Her father also used to do that when he was Prime Minister,' said Ishvar.

'Yes,' said Rajaram. 'I saw it once. But when he did it, he looked humble.'

'She looks like she is throwing rubbish at us,' said Om.

Rajaram laughed. 'Isn't that the politician's speciality?'

(*AFB*, 263)

But the rally takes on a farcical air – and the parody is cranked up further – when a helicopter takes to the sky scattering packets of rose petals, one of which fails to open concussing an onlooker, and the event is blessed by a quasi-divine visitation from Sanjay Gandhi, hovering above the field in a hot-air balloon and strewing the fidgety audience with leaflets outlining the Twenty-Point Programme. The master of ceremonies surpasses himself in sycophancy: '"Behold! Yonder in the clouds! Oh, we are truly blessed! ... Mother India sits on stage with us, and the Son of India shines from the sky upon us! What a blessed nation we are!"' (*AFB*, 266).[38] The farce reaches a peak when the giant cutout, disturbed by the wind whipped up by the helicopter's blades, topples onto the crowd below:

> The crowd shouted in alarm. The figure with outstretched arms groaned, and the ropes strained at their moorings. Security men waved frantically at the helicopter while struggling to hold onto the ropes and braces. But the whirl-wind was much too strong to withstand. The cutout started to topple slowly, face forward. Those in the vicinity of the cardboard-and-plywood giant ran for their lives. (*AFB*, 267)

The rally disintegrates as ambulances arrive 'to collect the casualties of the eighty-foot Prime Minister's collapse'. This *tour de force* scene, reminiscent at times of the uproarious debunking ironies of J. G. Farrell's *The Siege of Krishnapur*,[39] can be said to be an example of how 'national politics as symbolic display ... must be fought on the symbolic level'.[40] Thus, while Mistry's text may not show many instances of direct opposition to the Emergency, it nevertheless participates in an essentially postcolonial subversion of power by pinpointing its excesses and absurdities.

I would argue that this subversion continues on the level of form, and can be seen in the very fabric of the narration. Although he may carefully ground his inventions and surround them with the meticulous detail characteristic of social realism, Mistry's tone in *A Fine Balance* blends comedy with pathos, rumbustious farce with tragedy, and journalistic matter-of-factness with domestic sentimentality. In fact, his novel could be said to exemplify 'the deliberate multi-styled and hetero-voiced nature' Bakhtin cites as characteristic of 'carnivalised literature'.[41] The world of the Emergency is depicted as a carnivalesque environment where distinctions between performers and spectators have been obliterated and all participate in the carnivalistic life ... 'life turned inside out'.[42] While it may be too much to claim that the Emergency heralds an interruption in the hierarchies normally regulating society – it is, of course, meant to have just the opposite effect – it *is* the case that all manner of eccentric and bizarre behaviour has been unleashed as opportunists scramble for advantage, while inappropriate speeches and performances abound as 'the laws, prohibitions, and restrictions that determine the structure of ordinary ... life are suspended'.[43]

However, there is one particular scene in which the egalitarian potential of carnival appears temporarily to be realised. This occurs when the local beggars join Shankar's funeral procession after he has been run over on his wheeled platform and crushed. In the Indian context, Sandeep Pendse has claimed that 'Occupation of public space, at least periodically [via religious festivals, processions or demonstrations] ... acts as a mechanism of assertion and cathartic release.'[44] Likewise, carnival allows for the reclamation of the street from the oppressors. Shankar's funeral procession joins the protest march of disaffected citizens in *Such a Long Journey* as a mode of popular expression and an inversion of established precedence. The assembly of crippled and mutilated individuals is compared to a circus and a freak show, while the novelty of the occasion for its participants gives it the air of a festival rather than a funeral. Moving along at a snail's pace to allow those with the worst deformities to keep up, the ramshackle procession brings traffic to a standstill. At one point, the line of mourners is charged by a phalanx of riot police and in the mayhem Shankar's decapitated remains tumble from the bier. Beggarmaster's influential presence soon convinces the apologetic commanding officer of his mistake:

> a report had been received on the wireless that a mock funeral was underway, intended to make some kind of political statement ... Suspicion had been aroused, in particular, by the assembly of so many beggars, he explained. 'They were mistaken for political activists in fancy dress – troublemakers indulging in street theatre, portraying government figures as crooks and criminals embarked on beggaring the nation. You know the sort of thing.' (*AFB*, 506)

The police then provide an official entourage for the remainder of the journey. Shankar's funeral procession even offers a moment of that ritualised decrowning that Bakhtin identifies as part of carnivalised life and literature, when figures of authority are stripped of their power and ridiculed.[45] Dina's tyrannical brother Nusswan rolls up in his car and is shocked to find his sister participating in a beggar's funeral. He demands that she get into the car at once, but Dina refuses:

> Beggarmaster and the commanding officer approached them. 'Is this man bothering you?'
> 'Not at all,' said Dina. 'He's my brother. He is just offering condolences for Shankar's death.'
> 'Thank you,' said Beggarmaster. 'May I invite you to join us?'
> Nusswan faltered. 'Uh ... I'm very busy. Sorry, another time.' He slipped inside the car, hurriedly pulling the door shut. (*AFB*, 507–8)

Ultimately, the more power warps relationships the more bizarre behaviour becomes in *A Fine Balance*. In the Dina–tailors relationship, it is only as the co-ordinates of power begin to blur that real communication can take place and connections start to grow. In the flat that becomes home for the main characters this thaw occurs as they traverse the increasingly porous boundaries between one another's spaces. Tabish Khair has objected that caste and class differences mean that 'Mistry's main protagonists in the novel would not even be able to hold an extended, "intellectual" conversation with each other in real life – thanks to the widely separate linguistic-discursive and socio-economic spaces that they occupy.'[46] However, as I have indicated above, the text as a whole is concerned with probing and crossing divides such as that which Dina at first seeks to maintain. Objections such as Khair's are, of course, predicated on a reading of the novel as simply a realist text, something that I have argued is hard to sustain given its multiform texture. The realist hand is shown again when he complains that whereas 'Dina's past is realistic in every classic sense of the term, the stories of … Ishvar and Omprakash borrow heavily from different genres: the fantastic, the fairy tale, newspaper reportage, etc.'[47] – an objection which answers itself if one accepts the idea of the novel as a generic patchwork, the literary equivalent of Dina's quilt. *A Fine Balance* is made up of a bricollage of narrative styles at once creating and transcending verisimilitude, as well as describing transgressions across the material dividing lines of caste and class, country and city.

Two final examples should illustrate this point. In an unexpected plot twist, the lowly Shankar and the all-powerful Beggarmaster are discovered to be half brothers. The father who bore Beggarmaster also sired Shankar during a drunken encounter with the beggar's mother, Nosey. Beggarmaster is thereafter wracked with anxiety about how to ease Shankar's life and whether to tell him about their kinship. This unlikely turn of events spirals away from all pretence of realism and into the realm of pure symbolism. Even the names of this trio – Shankar is also known as 'Worm' – call forth the heightened archetypes of a morality play. If the author had wished to make his point about the moral dilemmas raised by the inevitable interconnectedness of oppressors and oppressed in a realist way he could easily have avoided such contrivances, which suggest another set of narrative priorities at work. Moreover, Mistry has decided in this text not to specify his locations. Although the City by the Sea has the topography and many of the characteristics of Bombay, it is also allowed to resonate with the unexpected dangers of a Kafkaesque cityscape, and contains obfuscating legal labyrinths reminiscent of Dickens's Inns of Court. More pertinently for the India of Mrs Gandhi's time, it allows the author to bring together on one stage, so to speak, regional patterns of oppression – sterilisations and slum clearance were given special emphasis in Delhi, Haryana and U.P. The generalised locations mean that *A Fine Balance* takes place in a palimpsest-like 'everyspace', and the City by the Sea is Bombay and not-Bombay at the same time. Thus, it might be argued that the novel is consciously symbolic rather than historical. Taken together, the City by the Sea, the Village by a River and the Mountains, constitute an unmarked literary map of the nation as it undergoes its terrible beautification.

The practice of reading postcolonial fictions, especially those of India, as national allegories in which texts provide a focus for the exploration of national experience and characters take on a representative quality is widespread in western academia.[48] Amit Chaudhuri, among others, has criticised this preoccupation which is accompanied by 'the tautological idea that since India is a huge baggy monster, the novels that accommodate it have to be baggy monsters as well', and which inscribe 'a mimesis of form, where the largeness of the book allegorizes the largeness of the country it represents.'[49] Despite a length that would appear to lend itself to such a construction, *A Fine Balance* is more fruitfully read as one of those texts about, in Chaudhuri's words, 'cultures and localities that are both situated in, and disperse the idea of, the nation'.[50] I would suggest that, pre-eminently among Mistry's works, *A Fine Balance* is a narrative about the persistence, against the odds, of that form of collective life – incorporating but transcending the nation – that Michael Sprinker has identified as offering a more profitable way of conceiving the panoramic tendencies of some postcolonial fictions.[51] Moreover, as I have argued in *Fictions of India*, Mistry's position as a member of the Parsi minority within India means that his 'writing is able to stand as an oblique commentary on the processes of identity formation the Indian nation has undergone pre- and post-1947, based, of course, on selective inclusions and exclusions.'[52] As Homi Bhabha has taught us, the nation – any nation – is 'internally marked by the discourses of minorities, the heterogeneous histories of contending peoples, antagonistic authorities and tense locations of cultural difference', which challenge the crafting of legitimised, 'authentic' or official versions of national identity.[53] It can be claimed that *A Fine Balance* at once allegorises national experience – in Valmik the proof-reader with his ailments figuratively linked to national decline, and in the toppling cardboard personification of India at the political rally – *and* reaches beyond these configurations to the daily life in which human beings live, breathe and form new combinations. Ultimately, a statement by Paul Ricoeur might serve best to illustrate the way in which narrative is always and inherently an intersubjective, communicative act:

> Storytelling displays its imaginative skill at the level of a human experience which is already 'communalised'. Plots, characters, thematic elements, etc. are forms of a life which is really a common life. In this respect, auto-biographies, memoirs, … confessions [and novels] are only subsections of a narrative arc which as a whole describes and redescribes human actions in terms of interactions.[54]

On his return to India in the Epilogue to *A Fine Balance*, Maneck finds himself in a city now torn apart by the sectarian violence that is both a consequence of Indira Gandhi's ill-fated introduction of a communal note into Indian politics, and a foretaste of the even more cataclysmic Bombay riots of 1992. After the Emergency, Indian politics fragmented, with parties such as the *Bahujan Samaj* emerging to articulate the claims of those, like the lower castes, previously excluded from the political scene.[55] Some of these developments may be welcomed as having brought democracy within the reach of those effectively disenfranchised before. However, it also opened what

Rushdie has called the 'Pandora's Box'[56] of corruption and religious majoritarianism that provides the background to Mistry's next novel, *Family Matters*.

Running repairs: corruption, community and duty in *Family Matters*

it is their characters, indeed, that make people what they
are, but it is by reason of their actions that they are
happy or the reverse. (Aristotle, *Poetics*, Book 6)

The world as evil let us not resign,
But be good whilst to good we still incline.
Nor good nor bad forever will remain;
Let us in memory the good retain.
(*The Shah-Namah of Fardusi*,
trans. Alexander Rogers, p. 60)

ON 6 December 1992, the Babri Mosque at Ayodhya was
destroyed by a large crowd of Hindu militants, claiming the site
on which it stood as the birthplace of the god Ram and therefore
sacred to their religion. In its place they proposed the construction of a Ram temple. Within hours of the news reaching
Bombay, angry Muslims had taken to the street in protest. But
they soon found themselves confronted by highly organised
groups of Hindu activists celebrating the 'victory' at Ayodhya.
The horrific violence that ensued continued sporadically throughout December and January. By the time it came to an end almost
eight hundred people were dead and many more had been made
homeless. In a few short weeks Bombay's reputation as a haven
of tolerance and communal eclecticism lay in tatters.[1]

The Maharashtrian state elections of 1995 took place against
a background of anti-Muslim sentiment consequent on the civil
unrest which had followed the destruction of the Babri Mosque
two and a half years earlier. At the polls the Shiv Sena (Army of

Shiva), depicting itself as the 'defender of Hindus', won enough support to form a coalition government with the BJP (Bharatiya Janata Party). This success represented the culmination of thirty years of activism by the Shiv Sena in Bombay, fuelled by its charismatic and ruthless leader, the *Senapati*, Bal Thackeray, which had seen the organisation develop from a cadre concerned with employment opportunities for Maharashtrian speakers to a major player in the Hindu nationalist movement on the metropolitan, and hence national, stage.[2] Drawing on its appeal to a broad spectrum of the Bombay population, and raising the banner of Hindu majoritarianism, or *Hindutva*, the Shiv Sena exploited the inevitable consequences, in terms of inequality, fostered by capitalist development in the city. It employed flexible tactics and a posse of young, vigorous activists trained to see political work as part of a larger struggle sometimes requiring unscrupulous methods and direct physical violence, and was involved in such nefarious activities as protection rackets, illegal land deals, and drugs and contraband smuggling. The movement of the Shiv Sena from fringe player to main actor in the unfolding drama of Bombay politics both indicates, and is a symptom of, what Novy Kapadia has described as the 'criminalisation of politics and the politicisation of crime, so rampant in India in the last decade of the twentieth century'.[3]

It is against this backdrop of communalist politics and corruption that the action of Rohinton Mistry's third novel, *Family Matters*, takes place.[4] Ostensibly the story of the pressures faced by one down-at-heel Parsi family in their attempts to care for an aged and infirm patriarch, the novel, like its predecessors, also offers a consideration of how, despite all efforts to keep them separate, the public world impinges on the private space, and how the taint of corruption can mark even the most insular and apparently upright of communities. Characters are caught in a complex web of actions and reactions in their dealings with each other and with the wider world they inhabit. Physical corruption and the inevitable change and loss accompanying mortality are linked with the social and political corruption characteristic of modern Bombay, and with the moral corruption of characters who, often for laudable reasons, perpetrate deceits and engage in subterfuge. For example, Yezad Chenoy uses his family's precious housekeeping money to gamble on the illegal lottery, the *Matka*, making losses they can ill afford. Yet he does so in the hope of meeting the increased expense caused by the arrival of his Parkinson-raddled father-in-law who, in turn, has been ousted from his home by the devious machinations of an embittered stepdaughter at her wit's end. Similarly, in a move connected to the endemic municipal and national corruption that sees politicians and criminals in league, his son, Jehangir, is tempted to betray his role as school homework monitor and take money for overlooking his class-mates' mistakes. In particular, Yezad's attempts to influence his ecumenical employer to stand for election on an anti-communalist, anti-corruption ticket – prompted less by concern for Bombay than for the promotion he anticipates for himself as a result – backfire in tragic fashion. The cost of such actions is investigated as part of the novel's interest in moral ambiguity and causality, means and ends, which often centres on the distinction between duty and free will. In this it recalls the strictures of Kantian ethical philosophy, and, emphasising the text's hybridity, the Zoroastrian injunction to 'good thoughts, good words, good deeds'. The question of how to identify the good course of action in a world seemingly devoid of moral absolutes casts a shadow over the best intentions. Mistry explores the inevitable fragmentation of such ideals in practice and the overlapping, and sometimes contradictory, compulsions of duty to family, to community, to the Zoroastrian faith and civic duty. What is revealed is a Parsi community whose response to its glorious past and attenuated status in postcolonial India is fundamentally split between an urge for physical and imaginative escape and a hidebound orthodoxy that, ironically, echoes the purist agendas of the very Hindu nationalism that threatens it.

Although set in the mid-1990s, the novel again blends past and present as Nariman Vakeel, progressively immobilised by Parkinson's disease, reflects, in italicised passages, on the

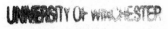

incidents leading to the joint deaths of his wife and former lover, a cataclysm to which the family's subsequent fractures and barely suppressed hostilities can be traced. Nariman is the narrative's initial controlling consciousness, but he is gradually reduced to silence and ultimately death, and the voices of his stepson, Yezad, and nine year old grandson, Jehangir, take over as the novel progresses. In a final Epilogue, 'five years later', Jehangir takes over completely. More mature and reflective now, he is able to piece together more of the jigsaw of adult motivation and cunning his grandfather's tangled love life has so painfully scrambled.

As the double play of the title suggests, family is important both as the site of primary loyalties – 'filiation', as Edward Said might say[5] – and the locus of tangled and often unresolved issues. Family in the novel comes to have both positive and negative connotations. The Chenoy–Vakeel–Contractor family unit is already fractured by loss: Coomy and Jal Contractor's own father dies young and they are unwillingly swept into a new domestic arrangement when their mother seeks the security of a marriage to Nariman Vakeel, who, in turn, carries with him the whiff of scandal and divided loyalties owing to his liaison with a non-Parsi, Lucy Braganza. When his father refuses to countenance his exogamous intentions, Nariman reluctantly yields to the marriage with Yasmin Contractor. Nariman soon adds a daughter of his own, Roxana, to his newly acquired stepchildren, leading to longstanding jealousies and resentment about favouritism.

As these almost ad hoc arrangements indicate, families develop, change and some branches die out while others are propagated and flourish. Beyond this, as in *A Fine Balance*, there are affiliations independent of blood ties that come to take on the supportive qualities of the family ideal: the letter-writer and bookstore owner Vilas Rane seems part of a multitude of 'ready-made families' as he preserves the link between illiterate workers forced to leave their birthplaces and come to the city for work and those they have left behind; 'writing and reading the ongoing drama of family matters', finding 'a pattern only he was privileged to see' (*FM*, 136). Families can be comforting spaces, but they can also stifle with a blanket of over-protectiveness: Yezad's older sisters fiercely resent anyone vying for a share of their brother's affections; and even the well-meaning Roxana fusses over her sons, Jehangir and Murad, worrying at the slightest sign of the inevitable childhood coughs or stomach upsets. Yet, sinister examples of parental control are at work too, not only in Mr Vakeel's interdiction against Nariman marrying for love, but also towards the end of the novel when Yezad, tossed by events back to a literal and racially-based understanding of Parsi uniqueness, effectively re-enacts the same prejudicial injunctions when dealing with his eldest son's first serious relationship. Family and its expected loyalties can be as much an offensive weapon as a shield against threatening outside forces. As a counterpoint to the increasingly vehement patriarchal thunderings, a touching relationship develops between Jehangir and his incapacitated grandfather. As Nariman's body fails him, so his need for emotional and some-times physical support increases. Of all the Chenoys, Jehangir is most able to provide the sustenance Nariman requires. They are temperamentally similar – both respond readily to sensory and imaginative stimuli – and value the physical proximity which Nariman's arrival in the small flat in Pleasant Villa forces on them; Jehangir soothes his troubled grandfather at night when unbidden memories plague him, and even helps him with basic bodily functions when he lapses into an increasingly childlike helplessness as the illness progresses.

Nariman's Parkinson's disease is linked to osteoperosis. He breaks his leg when out for a walk, leading to the regime of bed rest which tests Coomy, with whom he lives at first in the inappropriately named Chateau Felicity, to her limit. Eventually, the plaster on Nariman's leg gives Coomy the idea of dislodging that other plaster, on the ceiling of their apartment, in order to keep her stepfather at the Chenoy's flat where he has been recuperating. Parkinson's and osteoperosis are only two of the many examples of what one might call bodily corruption, which mark *Family Matters*. Characters are again furnished with a full complement of ailments: Coomy's brother, Jal, is partially deaf and wrestles with a malfunctioning hearing aid; the increasingly choleric Yezad develops angina; and Jehangir has a delicate digestive system, upset by ill-prepared food and the pangs of conscience. Even the mechanical, cricket-bat-wielding Santa, erected by Yezad's employer, Mr Kapur, in his sports goods shop to celebrate Christmas and represent his inclusive view of Bombay and its communities, creaks rheumatically and shudders in its down-swing as if it too has Parkinson's. Issues of mobility versus immobility, decay and mortality are explored through Nariman's fate. From a life lived fully through the body, he comes to exist solely in the life of the mind, giving a new twist to that theme of imprisonment so popular with Mistry. As he thinks back on his blighted love for Lucy, Nariman becomes, in Yeats's terms, 'sick with desire / And fastened to a dying animal'.[6] His struggles to perform the simplest tasks become the most acute manifestation of the Sisyphian labours of other characters, such as Roxana and Yezad, struggling every day to make ends meet, or Coomy fighting vainly to hold back the tide of bitterness she feels for the old man she blames for her mother's untimely death. Jehangir's first encounter with mortality comes in the form of his grandfather's story of his now-dead best friend, who grieved so piteously over the loss of his pet dog. Yet the gallows humour and grotesquerie associated with death are on display too: for example, when Murad tells his joke about the dead Beethoven 'decomposing' (FM, 164).

Coomy and her brother-in-law, Yezad, actually share several psychologically significant traits, despite being at loggerheads over who should look after Nariman. They both baulk at the unpleasant physical realities of caring for a prostrate, paralysed relative: Coomy is sickened by his bodily effluvia, and Yezad refuses to touch the bedpan on which Nariman is now reliant. Their revulsion is of a piece with their obsessive desire to exercise control over their environments and, by extension, their destinies. Yet, in different ways, this urge is every bit as damaging for these two figures as it was for the warring women, Lucy and Yasmin, whose battle for control of Nariman sends them over the edge: literally, as, locked in struggle, they plunge to their deaths from the roof of Chateau Felicity. Thus, the corruption and breakdown of family life is inextricably linked to the physical. Yet it is also connected to that other corruption infesting the social space and political institutions of Bombay, adding urgency to what Adam Mars-Jones, in his *Observer* review of *Family Matters*, sees as one of the text's central questions: 'Do families reflect society at large, or do they act as barricades against it?'[7]

On coming to power in the 1995 elections, the Shiv Sena/ BJP administration oversaw a number of measures designed to consolidate its power and advance the cause of *Hindutva*, including abolishing the Minorities Commission, disbanding the Srikrishna Commission into the Bombay riots (which threatened to expose the active involvement of the Sena in orchestrating the violence), and withdrawing incitement charges against Bal Thackeray in relation to the same events.[8] One of the most high-profile initiatives involved the renaming of Bombay as Mumbai, seen as the first blow in a battle to expunge all 'non-Hindu' place names from a 'purified' Hindu homeland.[9] This last development impinges on the world of *Family Matters*, as it is Mr Kapur's refusal to change the name of his shop from Bombay to Mumbai Sporting Goods that attracts the attention of the murderous Shiv Sena *goondas*. Indeed the tentacular Shiv Sena has provided the 'enforcers' for many of these developments. In Mistry's novel they are also shown to have a finger in the *Matka* pie. The underground lottery helps to fund the Shiv Sena machinery. It also finances the organised crime that has infected the city and its institutions, causing the sagacious Vilas Rane to observe: 'Matka is Bombay and Bombay is Matka' (*FM*, 200). In addition to its ties with gangsters, the Shiv Sena has implemented a cultural censorship programme, much to Yezad's exasperation, and opposes a bizarre diversity of events and activities it deems corrupting to the culturally homogeneous and 'pure' nation it envisages; targets have included certain artworks, Valentine's day, men's magazines and women working in bars.[10] Top of the list, as always, are those ubiquitous 'national enemies',

Muslims. Yezad shakes his head: 'What a joke of a government. Clowns and crooks. Or clownish crooks' (*FM*, 265). Yet there is real danger in crossing them. Not only is it suggested that the Shiv Sena was implicated in the murder, during the Bombay riots, of the family of Husain, Mr Kapur's Muslim peon at the shop, but Mr Kapur himself falls victim to those representatives of the forces of sectarianism he had briefly resolved to oppose. They also beat up the radical journalist/actor Gautam for writing an article on the 'politician-criminal-police nexus' (*FM*, 199). Nowadays the enemies and 'defenders' of the state are identical and funded from the same illegal sources.

Again urban and rural oppression are drawn together, when Vilas tells the story of a pair of lovers from different castes whose relationship was felt to threaten the status quo in their village, and who were mutilated and killed as a warning to others. This sorry state of affairs provokes a discussion between Gautam and his fellow thespian, Bhaskar, over a central ethical question confronting the modern Bombayite: how does one act when faced with injustice in a situation where law and order has either broken down or is, itself, complicit with the wrong-doers? (A telling example of this is played out when, despite being an eyewitness to the murder of Mr Kapur, Husain is angrily advised by the police to stop making 'wild accusations' about Shiv Sena involvement in his employer's death.) The actors muse:

> 'Isolated incidents, they call them,' said Gautam.
> 'Exactly,' said Bhaskar. 'They say that our nation has made so much progress – satellite TV, they say, Internet, e-mail, best software designers in the world.'
> Gautam chuckled. 'Hamaara Bharat Mahaan, they repeat like that government slogan', and they laughed … 'What to do? People are afraid to accept the truth. As T. S. Eliot wrote, "Human kind cannot bear very much reality."'
> (*FM*, 202–3)

Even cricket, that watchword for probity and fair play, is now crooked, as Vilas remarks, referring to the match-fixing scandals that rocked the sport in South Asia in the late 1990s.

The moral taint that everywhere affects Bombay life also increasingly makes its presence felt in the lives of Nariman's family. The most glaring example of this is obviously Coomy's devious plan to foist her stepfather on the already financially constrained Chenoy wing of the family, and the even more underhand measures she takes to keep him there. Yet, other, less overt instances of dishonesty also typify characters' dealings with each other and, sometimes, with themselves. Jehangir's capitulation to his classmates' entreaties to turn a blind eye to their mistakes, and so earn a few much-needed extra rupees for the family's essential purchases, betrays that faith placed in him as homework monitor by his teacher, the lovely Miss Alvarez. He wholeheartedly embraces the teacher's exhortations at the beginning of the year, that moral choices made now can be carried on into adult life, and that her pupils can help to purify the befouled air of civic affairs. As for the schoolmaster Herbert Pembroke in E. M. Forster's *The Longest Journey*, who observes that 'School is the world in miniature,' so here Jehangir's classroom takes on a metonymic relationship to society and nation.[11] Although he wants to help Miss Alvarez fight corruption in his own, small way, Jehangir is eventually compromised and becomes part of it. Likewise, Yezad succumbs to temptation and removes money from the worn but neatly labelled envelopes containing savings for staple items such as 'Milk and Tea', 'Water and Electricity', to place bets on the *Matka*. (Later, he temporarily removes the envelope of money intended as payment to the Shiv Sena *goondas* in return for their turning a blind eye to the continued use of Bombay in the sports emporium's name, although he reconsiders and returns it before its absence is noticed.)

Both Yezad and Jehangir, in their different ways, violate Yezad's father's example of that scrupulous Parsi honesty for which the community is celebrated. This example was set when Mr Chenoy ensured the safe delivery of a large consignment of money to the bank for which he worked, despite the surrounding chaos and panic caused by wartime explosions. 'In gratitude for an exemplary display of courage and honesty in the course of duty' (*FM*, 224), he was presented with a commemorative clock which Yezad continues to cherish and refuses to allow Murad to wind, long after he himself has compromised the values it represents. After relating the tale of his father's heroism, Yezad, somewhat ironically, warns his sons: 'Remember, people can take everything away from you, but they cannot rob you of your decency … You alone can do that, by your actions.' However, Yezad, and the generation that comes after him, are, in a sense, victims as well as inheritors of standards set in other times, and in other contexts. The myth of Parsi honesty and integrity is an ambiguous one, both inspiration and burden. As Vilas Rane comments, such myths can become outdated and 'make misfits of men' (*FM*, 205). The complicating factor, and what prevents *Family Matters* from being simply a text lamenting moral decline, is that both Yezad and his son act as they do for the best of reasons: to secure extra funds to cover the increased cost of looking after Nariman with his expensive medicines.

In fact, moral ambiguity in motivation is at the heart of the novel. *Family Matters* repeatedly returns to questions of means and ends, and the negative outcome of the well-intended act. A number of situations lend themselves to a kind of double construction, according to the discrepancy between what characters think their actions will achieve and what the end result actually turns out to be: Roxana innocently suggests employing the incompetent handyman Edul Munshi to fix Coomy's ceiling, thus setting in train events that will lead to both their deaths; the scam to frighten Mr Kapur into running in the forthcoming municipal election is suggested by the eminently sympathetic Vilas; while Yezad suggests that real Shiv Sena *goondas* may be better equipped for the task than Vilas's verbose actor friends. Most intractable of all, perhaps – and the sequence of events that appears to initiate all the Chenoy family's subsequent troubles – is Nariman's inability to give up his relationship with Lucy Braganza, even after his marriage to Yasmin. Lucy follows him to his new family home, takes a job as an ayah with a neighbour in order to be near him, and repeatedly threatens suicide. Time and again Nariman follows her up to the roof of Chateau Felicity to dissuade her from jumping. Despite his efforts to calm his former lover, Nariman finds himself yielding to the promptings of old emotions, as well as the concern he feels for Lucy in her distressed obsession. At one point he allows himself to wonder whether Lucy's perseverance is the result of undying love or a desire for retaliation. Likewise, as readers, we are aware that, by giving way to her entreaties – albeit out of sympathy – he is hurting his wife and stepchildren: in which respect his actions can be seen as selfish rather than benevolent.

Such moral complexity gives a new twist to Mistry's perennial concern with the idea of goodness as understood in Zoroastrianism. Each of Mistry's works contains a reference to the prime requirements of the Zoroastrian faith, *'munashni, gavashni, kunashni'*: 'good thoughts, good words, good deeds'. Characters orient themselves, and to an extent are judged, according to this triple injunction. *Family Matters*, however, complicates the picture by raising the question of what exactly these good thoughts, words and deeds might consist of. How does one recognise them in a situation where everything and everyone is, to some extent, compromised? For example, whereas Gustad Noble, in *Such a Long Journey*, was able, by and large, to recognise the right path, but needed to develop the courage and will to follow it, in *Family Matters* every move seems fraught with danger, either to oneself or to others, regardless of one's designs. According to Zoroastrianism, good and evil are completely separate: the former being a positive quality emanating from the Wise Lord, and the latter being the result of the intrusion of Ahriman into the Ahuric realm.[12] Yet in the world inhabited by Yezad and his family, the notion of good is adulterated and evil is immanent in humankind. Good and bad permeate one another, partly through those ageless human proclivities, vengeance, pride and intolerance. Hence characters' motives are often grey. Coomy behaves badly towards Nariman and offloads him onto the Chenoys partly because she fears the disturbance of her carefully ordered existence and the introduction of dirt and decay, partly because she doubts her ability to cope, and partly as a belated and perhaps subconscious act of revenge for the way Nariman treated her mother. Coomy's unhealthy resentment may have festered for years, but she does have a legitimate grievance. (The father/'daughters' situation here is never as morally clear-cut as in those other dramatic tales of filial disloyalty, *King Lear* and *Père Goriot*, which provide models for Mistry's investigations.) Coomy feels guilty about what she has done, as does the younger Nariman when confronted with the proof of what his continued infatuation with Lucy is doing to his family, and Yezad spends much of the second half of the novel tortured by guilt over his covert activities until he finds that religion can conveniently be made to bear the burden of a multitude of sins. The great question of the novel, which permeates everything yet remains unasked until Jehangir's epilogue at the end, is who is to blame for Lucy and Yasmin's fatal fall? Visiting old Dr Fitter, Jehangir learns for the first time his grandmother's dying words, only half-heard by horrified bystanders, which have echoed down the years and tarred Nariman – who was on the roof at the time – and his kin with the indelible mark of scandal:

> 'all the confusion was due to one word in her sentence: did she say "he" or "we"?'
>
> 'What do you think she said?' I inquire meekly.
>
> 'Oh, I know what she said. She said, "What did we do!" But there were other people gathered around. Some of them heard, "What did he do!" and they claimed it incriminated Nariman.' (*FM*, 477)

This is significant less as some sinister plot twist than as a point about how actions have consequences which reverberate down the years, but which people – often reading backwards from their own point in time and circumstance – can interpret as they wish. Certainly, Coomy has chosen to interpret her mother's unhappy marriage and death in a certain way, as her lonely life, blighted by bitterness and an unforgiving attitude towards Nariman, make abundantly clear.

Thus, characters in *Family Matters* are seen largely to choose their own fates. Yet they do not do so arbitrarily. Each is burdened by an acute sense of duty: to family, to employer or to the city as a whole. When hearing of Mr Kapur's intention to run in the forthcoming municipal election, Yezad initially counsels that his duty lies in looking after his shop, before recognising the opportunity for an increment for himself that would accrue from the increased responsibilities. He invokes the *Bhagavad-Gita* in urging the pre-eminent claims of duty. Ironically, it is the secular-leaning Hindu, Mr Kapur, who counters this when, having decided not to run after all, he echoes Kant in justifying the decision to put family above civic duty: 'Think about it – pure duty is unconcerned with outcome. Even if I become a municipal councillor, fight the good fight, what do I have at the end? The satisfaction of knowing I've done my duty. As far as Bombay is concerned, nothing changes. Nobody can turn back the clock' (*FM*, 294).

As the pre-eminent philosopher of ethics, Kant famously proposed that the moral worth of any given action could be determined not by considering its outcome, but by identifying the intention behind it. Specifically, only actions performed in accordance with duty have genuine moral worth.[13] Although there are obvious difficulties in trying to identify whether others are acting primarily out of a sense of duty, Kant proposed some guiding principles by which the individual should orientate his or her actions. The most famous of these is his 'categorical imperative': 'I should never act except in such a way that I can also will that my maxim should become a universal law.'[14] As Roger Scruton, among others, has noted, this first formulation of the categorical imperative provides 'the philosophical basis of the famous golden rule, that we should do as we would be done by.'[15] One behaves well, according to rules one would expect everyone else to observe also, for the mutual benefit of all parties. In one respect, those of Yezad's actions which seem most questionable – taking the household savings for gambling, temporarily pocketing the protection money, setting the fake Shiv Sena thugs to frighten Mr Kapur – are all motivated by a notion of duty: the long-term duty to provide for his family. However, there is a sense in which the various duties that hem him in – to Mr Kapur as his employer as well as to his family – come into conflict with each other. Likewise, Coomy is forced to choose between the duty to look after her incapacitated stepfather, and her sense of duty to the memory of her biological mother, for whose death she holds him responsible. Of course, she decides to prioritise the latter, and lies that her ceiling has collapsed in order to absolve herself of her duties to Nariman. In neither case, however, could Yezad or Coomy wish that others would behave towards them with the same kind of deception and evasiveness as they themselves have employed. Commenting on the responsibilities imposed by Kant's categorical imperative, Warner A. Wick offers the examples of lying and gangsterism: both particularly apposite for the familial and urban politics of *Family Matters*:

> to seek credibility by lying is not a point that can be *universally* adopted! No rational agent can will that maxim as a universal law, for in its universal form it is self-contradictory. A lie can work only if enough people tell the truth to make truthfulness the normal expectation, just as the gangster can only succeed if most people are law-abiding. These miscreants act unfairly in that their maxims require that other people act differently.[16]

Extrapolating from his initial principle, Kant proposed a second formulation of the categorical imperative: 'Act in such a way that you treat humanity, whether in your own person or in the person of another, always at the same time as an end and never simply as a means.'[17] In other words, one should treat others always as self-determining agents, and never just as an instrument to be used to achieve one's own aims. Once more, Yezad and Coomy can be seen to fall short of this ideal: Yezad treats Mr Kapur and his genuine civic concern as a means to promotion; Coomy uses Nariman's illness as a way to exact revenge on him for his treatment of her mother. The point here is not to measure these characters against some impossible benchmark of good behaviour, nor to show how they fail to meet the Zoroastrian requirement of good thoughts, good words, good deeds. Rather, it is to give an indication of how the tussle of duty and inclination provides the motor which drives the action of the novel and its moral choices.

In short, *Family Matters* is concerned with causes and effects – both intended and inadvertent – and how one interprets and accounts for connections between past and present. Characteristically, the text centres on the difficulties of making sense of, narrativising, and hence controlling time and change. Many media are employed by characters in their attempts to bridge the gap between past and present. Mr Kapur's photos of Hughes Road in various stages of development (1908, 1940s, 1990) take on a sacred quality for Yezad as part of his desire to roll back the years to the uncomplicated days of childhood. The photos offer the illusion of continuity, of that elusive connection between the carefree boy he was then, and the stressed middle-aged man with responsibilities he is now.

If one cannot arrest time, can one at least exercise some mitigating power over its apparently random dispensations? Dreams seem to offer one option to Yezad in his increasingly desperate search for control over events. In particular the dreams of Villie Cardmaster, the *Matka* queen, yield arbitrary images in which she discovers those numbers that will be blessed by Chance in the weekly draw. After winning with his very first bet, a stunned Yezad reflects on Villie's accurate prediction: 'Coincidence? Or had she predicted the future? And if dreams could do that … no more worry and anxiety. The worst news, foreknown, would lose its sting' (*FM*, 196). There are other, less desperate and mercenary attempts to turn the tide of time too. Nariman's recollections of days spent with Lucy blur memories with the dreams of semi-consciousness, while snatches of old songs conjure up a wealth of submerged associations and feelings. In particular, the virtuoso violin playing of Daisy Ichhaporia offers Nariman a little heaven on earth as she serenades him with a repertoire that includes classical pieces and popular songs from his youth, including the significantly titled 'One Day When We Were Young'. Her playing acts as a restorative, effecting repairs to the ruptured skein of Nariman's ebbing life. He certainly appears to find it more congenial than his son-in-law's earnest yet aggressive bedside devotions in the disturbing scene in which Yezad's prayers and Daisy's music seem to do battle over the mute, prostrate elder (*FM*, 433–5).

Formally, the concern for past-present connections is played out through repetitions: Yezad comes to repeat Nariman's father's inflexible religious dogma; Murad's non-Parsi girlfriend threatens a repeat of the parental estrangement of the earlier generation; and, at one point, Yezad unfairly accuses Roxana of neglecting the rest of her family in favour of her father, paralleling Yasmin's earlier complaints as Nariman abandons her and the children to run after Lucy. Against these examples of family breakdown the reader can set the many types of repair attempted in *Family Matters*, only some of which are successful. Edul Munshi, the disastrous handyman, tries to repair the ceiling Coomy has vandalised, but only succeeds in bringing down a supporting beam that crushes them both to death. Dr Tavancore and the bonesetter at the hospital do their best to patch up Nariman's brittle body after his fall. Vilas's letter writing repairs families torn apart by migration. Yezad is 'touched by his employer's gentleness as he went about mending the cracks in Husain's broken life' (*FM*, 144). Finally, Dr Fitter and the father and son police combination of Superintendent and Inspector Masalavala scurry out to fix the death certificates and help tidy up after the two fatal accidents which threaten the Parsi community with scandal, viewing it as one of the 'good deeds' required of them.

A number of explanatory options are available to the Chenoys and others as they attempt to piece together the chain of events by which their family affairs have moved from initial domestic harmony to tension and hostility. In their besetting concern to find an explanation for phenomena, they sometimes resemble the characters in another of Mistry's fictional templates, Voltaire's satire *Candide*, who deliberate 'on the contingent or non-contingent events of this world … on causes and effects, on moral and physical evil, on free will and necessity …'[18] (While hospitalised, Nariman remarks on the striking physical resemblance between one of the wardboys looking after him and the great French philosopher Voltaire. The character never reappears, but in this passing reference it seems that Mistry is directing us to one of the key preoccupations of his novel.) In *Family Matters*, as in *Candide*, events are interpreted, variously, as the product of coincidence, free will, destiny or God's will. On the way to offer his condolences to Mrs Kapur after the murder of her husband, Yezad reflects on the coincidence by which Mr Kapur was visited by real Shiv Sena thugs, after the actors he had engaged to frighten his employer by playing the role of Shiv Sena *goondas* had departed: 'That was the problem, everyone dismissing the possibility of coincidence' (*FM*, 393). Later, when his newfound religiosity has taken hold and he suggests as a coincidence the fact that Nariman develops bed sores as soon as his new *ayah* arrives, Roxana reminds him: 'You say there's no such thing as coincidence … You call it another word for the Hand of God' (*FM*, 482).

The socially committed actors, Gautam and Bhaskar, have another explanation for events. Discussing the desired effect their 'performance' as Shiv Sena ruffians is to have on Mr Kapur, they rehearse the question of the role of the audience, free will and destiny. They acknowledge that their performance will be unorthodox: while an audience for the kind of street theatre they specialise in always knows it is watching a performance, Mr Kapur will be unable to distinguish between performance and reality. Unaware, he will be both actor and audience:

> 'An actor without awareness is a wooden puppet,' declared Gautam grandly, believing he had scored a decisive point.
> 'In a culture where destiny is embraced as the para-mount force, we are all puppets,' said Bhaskar with equal grandness. (*FM*, 322)

Their performance is designed to be '"a call to action for Mr Kapur, and an unstated moral: that evil must not be ignored by those able to oppose it"' (*FM*, 323).

> Basically, Mr Kapur needs to experience an epiphany. So we must convey more than just present danger to him and

his shop. We must transcend the here and now, move beyond this bank and shoal of time, and let him glimpse the horrors of a society where the best lack all conviction while the worst are full of passionate intensity. (*FM*, 323)

The actors are vehemently anti-Shiv Sena, and their street theatre has the Brechtian aim of the politicisation of the audience, moving it 'beyond catharsis' (*FM*, 324). Yet their formalist pre-occupations, symbolised by their second-hand rhetoric and abstract theorising, mean that they miss the essence of the situation. Despite their good intentions, they end up creating the same terror as the real Shiv Sena thugs, effectively paving the way for them.

The delivery of Nariman into the Chenoys' care, and the accidental death of Coomy, is ascribed to destiny in Yezad's now fatalistic outlook. Roxana reflects on the tragedy of the shattered love-match of Edul Munshi and his wife by asking, 'What is this absurd force called destiny?' to which the increasingly devout Yezad replies, 'Man proposes, God disposes' (*FM*, 398). As characters with a strong religious faith, Roxana and, latterly, Yezad, read causality in a particular way. They tend to assume the operations of cause and effect are regulated by a pre-existing entity they know as God, or *Ahura Mazda*. In effect, they hold what Kant, and indeed Voltaire, would describe as an *a priori* understanding of cause and effect. *A priori* truths are those deemed to exist independently of experience, and *a priori* knowledge is that which is not based on empirically verifiable experience. Roger Scruton gives some examples of the *a priori*:

> the following propositions seem to be true a priori: 'Every event has a cause'; 'The world consists of enduring objects which exist independently of me'; 'All discoverable objects are in space and time.' These propositions cannot be estab-lished through experience, since their truth is presupposed in the interpretation of experience.[19]

Thus, Scruton quotes Kant to show that the notion of God itself can be seen as an *a priori* regulative force: 'the ideal of a supreme being is nothing but a regulative principle of reason, which directs us to look upon all connection in the world as if it originated from an all-sufficient and necessary cause.'[20] Voltaire's *Candide* famously sends up Pangloss's unquestioning *a priori* justification of things as they are and the complacent optimism encompassed in his conviction that, regardless of how bad things appear, this is 'the best of all possible worlds'.[21] Likewise, in Mistry's novel, Roxana allows herself the luxury of a Panglossian retrospective interpretation of events working out for the best, attributing this to God's will: 'when she looked back over the events that had led them to this evening, it was almost proof of divine power in the universe, with Pappa's broken ankle the start of everything' (*FM*, 435). Doubtless, she would concur with Pangloss that 'free will is consistent with absolute necessity':[22] an outlook which can reconcile Coomy's desire to attribute the collapse of her ceiling to an act of God, with the fact that she herself has encouraged her brother to take a hammer to it.

However, religion is not simply a smokescreen or a comforting security blanket for characters here. Mr Kapur loves the heterogeneity and bustle of Bombay with the zeal of a convert, having migrated there from the Punjab at the time of Partition. He values Bombay's assimilating inclusiveness, which he links to the spirit of tolerance that historically defined Hinduism in its dealings with other faiths, before the *Hindutva-wallahs* sank their claws into it. However, there is a danger in the analogy he posits when justifying his decision not to run in the election:

> 'Hinduism has an all-accepting nature, agreed? ... Even false gods are accommodated, and turned into true ones, adding a few more deities to its existing millions.
> 'The same way, Bombay makes room for everybody. Migrants, businessmen, perverts, politicians, holy men, gamblers, beggars ... So who am I to say these people belong here and those don't? Janata Party okay, Shiv Sena not okay, secular good, communal bad, BJP unacceptable, Congress lesser of evils?' (*FM*, 351)

Mr Kapur's outlook here seems *too* relativistic, since it makes room for the Shiv Sena and BJP, forces that deny and seek to repress the very difference he cherishes. They are here depicted as a legitimate part of *Kalyug,* the Hindu age of chaos, in Kapur's now quietistic view, just another of Naipaul's 'million mutinies', characteristic of modern India.²³ (Of course, he soon discovers that, for him, it is too late too assume such studied indifference to seeping corruption and communalism.) Moreover, his visceral identification with Bombay – the desire to 'become one with the organic whole that is Bombay. That's where my redemption lies' (*FM,* 336) – is equally illusory: he tries running for the train as he has seen ordinary Bombayites do, but no one holds out a hand to help him on board, as he had hoped and believed they would. His dream of Bombay is simply that – a dream – just as Yezad's idealisation of Canada, to which he once hoped to emigrate, crumbles in the face of patronising xenophobia at the Canadian High Commission.

The religious components of identity are particularly important for the Parsi characters, especially in the context of the creeping Hindu majoritarianism that surrounds them. Other coordinates of Parsiness are once again on display, including aesthetic westernisation in the form of a preference for European classical music, and Jehangir's penchant for jigsaws and Enid Blyton books. Reference is also made to the popular farces of Adi Marzban – 'chock full of Parsi jokes and skits and songs' (*FM,* 299) – that were for many years a feature of the Parsi social calendar. Tanya Luhrmann sees Adi Marzban's plays as definitive of Parsi humour: 'They were performed in Parsi-Gujarati; you went to see them on New Year's Day, and by all accounts they were raunchy, rude and (supposedly) very, very funny.'²⁴

However, the main concern for this vulnerable community in *Family Matters* centres on issues of numerical decline and the merits or otherwise of traditional notions of ethnic purity. Luhrmann records how: 'Until 1941 the Parsi population was slowly but steadily on the rise in India. But in 1961 they were down to over 100,000; in 1971, over 90,000; in 1991 there were 76,000 Parsis in India, with around 50,000 in Greater Bombay.'²⁵ Near the end of the book, Dr Fitter and Inspector Masalavala discuss the shrinking Parsi community and what should be done to halt the diminution. They enumerate the main features accounting for decreasing numbers: a dwindling birth rate, marrying outside the community and migration to the west. Westernisation and western ideas, once seen as the lifeline of the community, are now identified as part of the problem. Inspector Masalavala's cranky suggestions to shore up the community include tying educational opportunities to an undertaking to bear a certain number of children. The more stoical prescription of Dr Fitter is for a Parsi time capsule, containing items representative of the culture, to be buried for future generations to unearth when the community has died out. That sense of loss indicative of contemporary Parsi culture in India is articulated by the inspector: 'To think that we Parsis were the ones who built this beautiful city and made it prosper. And in a few more years there won't be any of us left to tell the tale' (*FM*, 404).

For Yezad the issue is one of purity. Just as Nariman's orthodox father unwisely engaged in a fierce exchange of letters with a reformist neighbour in the pages of the *Jam-e-Jamshed* newspaper over the issue of intermarriage, so, too, Yezad comes to view 'the purity of this unique and ancient Persian community' (*FM*, 127) as being under threat from miscegenation. He speaks in almost identical terms when pondering on the ritual gestures of the *dastur* at the fire-temple, valuing 'the cumulative grace of generations and centuries ... encoded in blood and bone' (*FM*, 333). The psychological importance to the orthodox of the unique, untainted Persian blood, which is felt to distinguish Parsis from the surrounding community, should not be underestimated. The orthodox are against the mingling of this blood with any other. Biology supersedes social morality as a guarantor of worth according to this view, with a corresponding shift in that notion of the good (thought, word, or deed) fundamental to Zoroastrian ethics. As Luhrmann has noted: 'The central cosmological struggle of good against evil is described as an effort to achieve purity – that which is evil is impure, that which is impure is evil.' However, for the orthodox, a 'transformation took place with the concept of purity ... which was refigured from holiness into racial superiority.'[26]

The continuously burning fire at the temple offers that elusive past-present connection Yezad craves, and, in a way, the fire-temple replaces the family home as a sanctuary from the outside world. As he feels increasingly disempowered by events he falls back on his reawakened faith more and more. Towards the end of the novel, the focus of his piety becomes a 'holy cabinet' he has placed in a special corner of the drawing room, protected by what the sceptical Murad describes as a 'cordon sanitaire' to keep out non-Parsis or those who have not ritually purified themselves. This 'shrine' has previously contained the untouchable clockwork toys belonging to Jal and Coomy, and symbolising Coomy's attempt to hold on to something of her childhood, before death entered her world and took away first her father, then her mother. After her own demise, it comes to contain Yezad's sacred paraphernalia, which replaces the commemorative clock in his affections. Both the toys and the clock represent more of those doomed attempts to cling on to the things of the past. Yezad's new use of the cabinet merely perpetuates the same inclination, only with a different object. The cabinet holds framed pictures of Zarathustra, photographs of the remnants of the ancient Persian Empire, including the ruins at Persepolis, and a miniature plastic *afargaan* with a glowing electric flame. In a sense the cabinet is both a fire-temple in miniature and that Parsi time capsule suggested by Dr Fitter. Yet, for all his efforts to foster an atmosphere of reverence and obedience, Yezad constantly struggles to block out the music and non-Zoroastrian influences inevitable in a lively household containing two teenage sons. It seems that his attempts at sanctification have not brought him peace.

What is worse, in his new dogmatic ultra-orthodoxy, he becomes a kind of Zoroastrian fundamentalist, imposing his racial and cultural obsessions on everyone around him. He is an active member of an orthodox Zoroastrian association, attempts to inflict draconian menstruation laws on his wife and rails against Murad's non-Parsi girlfriend. The punishment he advocates for Parsis who dare to cultivate inappropriate relations with non-Parsis – excommunication and public humiliation – is different only in degree to that meted out to the two ill-fated cross-caste lovers whose story he has heard earlier. Nor does it occur to Yezad that his Parsi purism is of a piece with the exclusionary compartmentalising of those Hindu nationalist forces he has previously despised. Mistry understands the psychological and nostalgic impulses behind social and cultural conservatism as well as any other contemporary writer. But his sympathies for the consoling qualities of religion and tradition evaporate when, as so often, they become a stick with which to beat others. For him ritual and dogma is of less consequence than social morality. In a comment that sums up the choices confronting so many of his characters, Mistry has remarked, 'I'm not a practising Parsi but the ceremonies are quite beautiful. As a child I observed [them] carefully in the same way as I did my homework, but it had no profound meaning for me. Zoroastrianism is about the opposition of good and evil. For the triumph of good, we have to make a choice.'[27] It might be said that, in his reversion to a defensive, insular form of Zoroastrianism, Yezad succumbs to what Kant calls the 'fanaticism, indeed the impiety, of abandoning the guidance of a morally legislative reason in the right conduct of our lives, in order to derive guidance from the idea of the Supreme Being'.[28] Essentially, he overlooks what Richard Kearney, writing of originary cultural myths, calls the 'need to keep our mythological memories in critical dialogue with history', lest 'they engender revivalist shibboleths of fixed identity, closing off dialogue with all that is other than themselves'.[29]

Against this somewhat negative way of using narratives, Mistry shows other instances where stories offer a valuable way of orientating oneself amid the chaotic and daunting modern world. Jehangir's Enid Blyton stories may contribute to a kind of deracination – he longs to live in the sort of genteel, upper-middle-class English world enjoyed by the Famous Five, and wishes he could anglicise his name to John – but they temporarily offer him a more attractive world than the cramped and fractious environment of Pleasant Villa. This 'dream-England' – along with the jigsaw of Lake Como which is always incomplete, its promised beauty unattainable – represents for Jehangir the 'best of all possible worlds', that 'kingdom of ends', in Kantian terms, where everything is in its place and nothing contradicts the requirements of reason. It is a mark of Jehangir's development in the epilogue that he has moved on from such illusory idealism and is coming to terms with the moral complexity of things as they are, just as his father seems determined to journey in the opposite direction. The earlier, more open Yezad at one stage reflects on the need the survivors of partition seem to feel to go on telling their stories: 'like Indian authors writing about that period, whether in realist novels of corpse-filled trains or in the magic realist midnight muddles' (*FM*, 145). As with those Jews who have survived the Holocaust, there is often an urge to speak, to write, to remember: 'What choice was there, except to speak about it again and again, and yet again' (*FM*, 145). Something in the act of telling itself brings balm. In fact, religion may be simply another of those consoling fictions mitigating the loneliness and horror of life: Roxana tells the growing, and hence sceptical, Jehangir that Nariman has died and is now in heaven being feted with 'new clothes, ice cream, pudding, everything' (*FM*, 465); while Murad endures the ritual ministrations of the father with whom he is at odds during his *roj* (eighteenth) birthday 'without rolling his eyes or displaying any sign of impatience' (*FM*, 484). There is a sense in which this highly stylised language of gesture is the only level on which they can now communicate. Similarly, Jehangir restrains himself from jumping up in bed to spoil his brother's carefully planned Christmas surprise as he plays Santa, even though he no longer believes in Father Christmas: 'the Santa Claus story was like the Famous Five books. You knew none of it was real, but it let you imagine there was a better world somewhere' (*FM*, 362).

Early in his stay, Nariman tells his grandsons the story of Zuhaak and Faridoon from the *Shah-Namah*. The evil king Zuhaak murders his father, seizes his crown, and conducts a thousand-year reign of terror which includes the slaughter of young males, whose brains are scooped out to feed the two snakes sprouting from his shoulders. Eventually, Zuhaak is defeated by Faridoon – whose father had been one of the tyrant's victims – and is thrown into a bottomless pit.[30] Zuhaak is the personification of worldly evil, deployed here in another of the novel's attempts to lay hold of the roots of evil and suffering in the world. Jehangir says, 'I know there isn't any Zuhaak. It's just a story, like Santa Claus,' to which Grandpa Nariman replies, 'I think you're right Jehangir ... But even if Zuhaak were real, he wouldn't bother you, He'd be busy with diseases and famines, wars and cyclones' (*FM*, 157–8). In view of the novel's main concerns, one might wish to add corruption, brutality and communalism to the list of Zuhaak's vehicles. Against Zuhaak's feared return, Parsi folklore posits the spider, spinning the gossamer webs that are, at the same time, the chains that continue to bind Zuhaak in his subterranean captivity. Elsewhere, webs are used as images of those things which connect: Nariman and Jehangir look at a cobweb as something beautiful, while the embattled Yezad views the overhead telephone wires of Bombay as an ensnaring web. Indeed the web of stories – those which make up this novel and all like it – harmonises the discordant cacophony of difference into a single, shared human story with many variations, something Mr Kapur recognises: 'Funny thing is, in the end, all our stories – your life, my life, old Husain's life, they're the same. In fact, no matter where you go in the world, there is only one important story: of youth, and loss, and yearning for redemption. So we tell the same story, over and over. Just the details are different' (*FM*, 221).

The question 'Are you happy?' repeatedly asked of her husband and sons by the concerned Roxana, becomes almost a refrain in *Family Matters*. Characters have sought happiness, or at least stability, by following the dictates of duty as far as possible, but, as this chapter has shown, they often find that duty comes into conflict with personal inclination or immediate need. According to Kant there is no point in proclaiming happiness, in the sense of the fulfilment of one's desires, as the ultimate goal in life, because it cannot be elevated to the level of that kind of universal law his maxims demand. In fact, to try to do so would be disastrous. This is because each person's interests, and therefore definition of happiness, would be in some way different, and would actually lead to conflict: 'while everyone's interests are the same in name (happiness), they differ in fact; and this difference is almost without limit, because the specific content of happiness varies with the temperaments, circumstances, and histories of each individual.'[31] In *Family Matters*, Yezad's desires for orthodoxy and order clash with Murad's definition of happiness which includes the right to go out with whoever he wants. Thus, 'goodness' and happiness are not necessarily synonymous, so the answer to Roxana's anxious question remains, at best, hesitant and provisional.

In contrast to the notion of happiness as sensory or material gratification, Aristotle proposed the possibility of *eudaimonia*, or genuine happiness. This is to be found in the life lived not for sensations or ephemera, but for the rewards which come from that social interaction he sees as the purpose of human existence. As Simon Blackburn puts it, 'The Aristotelian alternative requires engagement with the world. It requires reasoning and activity, and engagement with others, and notably it requires real love and friendship.'[32] Hence, it is in keeping with the Zoroastrian injunction for action and against aesthetic withdrawal mentioned earlier. It is just such a life Yezad backs away from in his retreat into the penumbra of religion: a move epitomised by his decision to break with his old friend Vilas, whose letter-writing keeps just those lines of communication open. In his desire to escape from the teeming crowds of Bombay, Yezad ends the novel in a similar position to that held by Gustad Noble at the beginning of Mistry's first novel, *Such a Long Journey*. Yet, whereas for Gustad the quiet promptings of personal affection coalesce with the internalised values of his faith to bring him out of his self-imposed isolation, Yezad recoils from the mongrelisation and mixing inherent in urban life, to a space of 'purity' that is, of course, at the same time one of fantasy.

Thus, while *Family Matters* may, as Frank Kermode claims, 'lack the power and scope' of *A Fine Balance*,[33] owing to its more intrinsic concern with the Parsi community, it is nevertheless clearly continuing the investigation of the interconnected spaces of a multitudinous nation, and the intersubjective processes of storytelling that lies at the heart of Mistry's *oeuvre*. Its cast of characters includes a secular Hindu who holds out against the excesses of the zealots in his own religion, a Muslim shop worker who drinks beer with his employer, and – for a while at least – a Parsi who is determined to do his best for his family *within* a society scarred by moral turpitude and prejudice, but also exalted by small acts of generosity and kindness. Mistry is a writer for whom morality is politics and politics is morality. Dogma of any kind will not do. Only by sharing our stories can divisions be overcome and understanding promoted: 'I sometimes think there is a latent desire in all of us to be storytellers. In the best of all possible worlds, all of us would be storytellers and listeners.'[34]

Critical overview

> Peerbhoy Paanwalla had mobilized his talents ... to
> weave a tale that defied genre or description. It was not
> tragedy, comedy or history; not pastoral, tragic-comical,
> historical pastoral or tragical-historical. It was not a
> ballad or an ode, masque or anti-masque, fable or elegy,
> parody or threnody. Although a careful analysis may
> have revealed that it possessed a smattering of all these
> characteristics. (*SLJ*, 306)

CRITICAL interest in Mistry's work has thus far followed six main channels: the author's position as part of a growing body of 'ethnic' writers within 'multicultural' Canada; his writing as 'diasporic discourse', articulating a view of both Canada and India from the peripheries; the Indian subject matter he chooses and the influence of his Parsi background; the role of story-telling as both theme and technique; gender politics and the depiction of female characters; and, related to issues of reading and reception, the question of whether Mistry's style should be viewed as realist or something else. The scale and complexity of this critical engagement has, of course, grown along with the author's own output and his recognition as a postcolonial writer of stature.

The only single volume as yet devoted to Mistry's work is Jaydipsinh Dodiya's edited collection of essays entitled, *The Fiction of Rohinton Mistry: Critical Studies*.[1] This anthology brings together a diverse corpus of critics with an equally eclectic set of approaches. The essays are arranged in themed sections –

'Indian-Canadian Writing' and 'Comparative Studies' – and, thereafter, text by text. Many of the contributions are original, although some have previously appeared elsewhere. There are useful essays by Nila Shah, Vinita Dhondiyal Bhatnagar, Pramod K. Nayar and Nilufer E. Bharucha, as well as three contributions from the editor himself.[2] However, the pieces are of unequal length with the sheer quantity of essays occasionally triumphing over quality, and several offerings are rather impressionistic and superficial. This is certainly a useful text for Mistry scholars, but perhaps the editor has spared the whip a little too much in not demanding a greater consistency in the contributions. Dodiya has also contributed to, and co-edited, another collection of essays, this time in two volumes, entitled *Parsi Fiction*, which situates Mistry among his fellow contemporary Parsi scribes and analyses the themes and issues raised by his writing.[3]

Among the full length article treatments of Mistry as a Canadian writer that have appeared, Michael Thorpe, in his essay 'Canadian "Globalism": Conflicts and Contradictions', places the author's work alongside that of other incomers to Canada, such as Neil Bissoondath, Marlene Nourbese Philip and M. G. Vassanji, and argues that 'the multicultural character of contemporary Canada … offers an opportunity for an international literature in one country – and thus a broadening alternative to white nationalism'.[4] Another interesting essay along similar lines is 'Paradigms of Postcolonial and Immigrant Doubleness: Rohinton Mistry's *Tales from Firozshah Baag*' by Rocio G. Davis. This is a longer and more coherent version of his truncated piece, 'Negotiating Place/Re-Creating Home: Short Story Cycles in Naipaul, Mistry and Vassanji', in Jacqueline Bardolph's book, *Telling Stories: Postcolonial Short Fiction in English*.[5] As the title suggests, Davis is attentive to the formal mixing of 'ethnic' writing in Canada, and sees the short story cycle, with its defining generic hybridity, as a particularly pertinent model for modern Canadian literature, especially equipped to convey 'the doubleness of the between-worlds subject'.[6] Issues of migrations, multiculturalism and the contextual background to contemporary Canadian writing also preoccupy Linda Hutcheon and Marion Richmond in *Other Solitudes: Canadian Multicultural Fictions.*[7] This volume includes an interview with Mistry, conducted by Dagmar Novak, in which he expresses his reservations about the concept of multiculturalism, not so much as a state-sanctioned policy but rather because of the expectations its agenda imposes on the writer coming from a different culture: 'he must write about racism. He must write about multiculturalism. He has an area of expertise foisted on him which he may not necessarily want.'[8]

Thorpe and Davis are among several critics who have focused on the last few stories in *Tales from Firozsha Baag* which mark the protagonist's move from Bombay to Canada and his problems of assimilation there. Roshan Shahani states that, as Parsis, Mistry's characters already inhabit the periphery of the city of Bombay – and indeed India itself – while the more striking dislocation engendered by migration to North America, and their visible difference there, leaves them on the periphery of their new host society too.[9] Shahani's essay is in a collection co-edited by the single most prolific Mistry critic to date, Nilufer E. Bharucha. Bharucha is the author of several relevant articles, and, as such, someone whose benign shadow looms large over the present study. She has identified Mistry's writing as an example of that 'diasporic discourse', features of which are particularly acute in the case of Parsis. She suggests that the distinctly diasporic elements of Parsi writing include a sense of loss, nostalgia and problems in identifying with the new home.[10] Elsewhere, she situates Mistry alongside fellow Parsi writers from the 1980s and 1990s, such as Bapsi Sidhwa, Boman Desai, Farrukh Dondy and Firdaus Kanga, and declares that their work constitutes an 'assertion of ethnic identity' by a community numerically in decline.[11] In the essay '"When Old Tracks are Lost"', Bharucha notes that Mistry's position as a member of a community originally forced into exile by the Arab invasion of its homeland, coupled with his status as a migrant to Canada, means that his writing is informed by the experience of 'double displacement'[12]

The inevitable cultural hybridity attendant on the various migrations and losses described in the texts have led some critics to view Mistry's protagonists as exemplary postcolonial subjects. Ajay Heble, in his essay on storytelling techniques and framing narratives, '"A Foreign Presence in the Stall": Towards a Poetics of Cultural Hybridity in Rohinton Mistry's Migration Stories', reads the short story 'Squatter' as symptomatic of immigrant experience. For him, 'postcolonial identity is always already a hybridized formation', something Mistry's characters illustrate.[13] He maintains that Mistry's tales are full of that 'abrogation' or 'appropriation' diagnosed as symptomatic of postcolonial litera- ture by Ashcroft, Griffiths and Tiffin in *The Empire Writes Back*, and cites as examples the 'ironic continuation of certain stereotypes and clichés', such as Rustomji's lament for the passing of the British because of the disappearance of Johnnie Walker Scotch onto the black market, in 'Auspicious Occasion', and Kersi's parents' internalised ideas about the inferiority of Indians in 'Lend Me Your Light'. Such conventions are reanimated, yet their validity is simultaneously problematised and under- mined. Less convincing is the attempt to argue for Sarosh-Sid's constipation as an instance of 'resistance to hegemonic practices'. While creative and intriguing, this reading is, to coin a phrase, a little strained, and owes more to the hypotheses of minority discourse theory than to any meaning latent in the text.[14] Sarosh-Sid certainly doesn't find his predicament empowering as he perches uneasily on the toilet rim. Heble concludes that the emergence of writers of different ethnicities, such as Mistry, 'indicates the necessity of moving beyond a nationalist critical methodology ... to a cross-cultural exploration of the discourses of hybridity'.[15] Formal mongrelisation is also the focus for Amin Malak when tracing 'The Shahrazadic Tradition' in *Such A Long Journey*. As indicated earlier, I find that Malak's persuasive account of the mixing of prose narrative and oral storytelling elements in Mistry's novel can be applied equally revealingly to the structure of the later stories in *Tales from Firozsha Baag*.[16] Arguing that Mistry's first novel contains 'calculated, negotiated features, reflecting different geneses', Malak remarks: 'The epistemological and phenomenological differences separating storytelling from novel-writing make the task of a post-colonial writer like Mistry, who straddles the two traditions, quite challenging. The task of the storyteller-cum-novelist is to accommodate, reconcile and integrate the demands of both practices.'[17]

Of course, critics have not been unanimous in their praise for the writer. In particular, reservations have been voiced about Mistry's handling of gender issues and depiction of female characters. For instance, Arun Mukherjee objects to the 'sexist' humour on display in *Such a Long Journey*. In particular, 'Dinshawji's teasing of Laurie Coutino, asking her to play with his "sweet lorri" is sexual harassment, not humour, and the book, I suggest, would have been better without it.'[18] Apart from the fact that, as Michael Thorpe has observed, much male humour, especially the camaraderie of a predominantly male workspace, *is* sexist,[19] Mukherjee has here completely missed the text's insistent preoccupations with language, naming and power; Dinshawji's smirking insult to Laurie is a prime example of the abuse of the power to name. More pertinent are Mukherjee's complaints that the novel's two main female figures – Dilnavaz and Miss Kutpitia – are 'unidimensional' and portrayed as mired in superstition: although, once more, I have attempted to show how their 'superstitious' faith in eccentric cosmological systems and magical interventions is of a piece with the wider interrogation of belief systems. Mukherjee is positively restrained, however, when set beside Gita Viswanath in her comparative essay, 'Modes of Resistance in the South-Asian Novel: A Study of the Fiction of Bapsi Sidhwa, Rohinton Mistry and Yasmine Gooneratne', in the Dodiya volume. Writing of *A Fine Balance*, Viswanath laments that Dina's new-found 'economic empowerment' as the tailors' employer is short-lived, and 'the narrative (*significantly that of a male*), unable to sustain feminist individualism',[20] returns her to her brother's household. A more careful reading of the novel would presumably have made apparent the fact that the 'power' Dina temporarily enjoys is flawed and complicit with a wider network of exploitation, and even she begins to forego its trappings for a closer relationship with her employees. Viswanath is undeterred, however, bemoaning the 'defeatist end *constructed by a male writer* for Dina … [wherein she is] reduced from female individualist to feminine subject', as the author 'offers his text on the altar of realism'[21] [emphases added]. Viswanath's is a strange, essentialist reading. Needless to say, the other two authors she examines in her comparative study get a better press. This is disappointing, particularly because there *are* criticisms that can be made about Mistry's women, who often tend to be either lonely eccentrics – like Miss Kutpitia, Korshedbai, Daisy Ichaporia, and Villie Cardmaster – or domestic goddesses, like Dilnavaz, Yasmin and Roxana, whose 'power' consists in keeping the household together and putting food on the table despite the follies of their respective husbands. In fact, Dina Dalal in *A Fine Balance* escapes these fates. She is, as John Ball rightly claims, 'easily Mistry's most fully developed female character … a person of dynamic agency, possessive of a sophisticated and believable interior life.'[22]

Other legitimate criticisms include the charge of a tendency to sentimentality. In a review of *Family Matters*, Adam Mars-Jones comments that the novel 'moves to a close on a surge of pious sentiment', and accuses Mistry of differentiating between the 'significant' and 'arbitrary' fates of his characters according to whether or not they are Parsis: a charge which is perhaps a little harsh yet understandable in a text with a more intrinsic focus than the previous, expansive *tour de force*.[23] It is certainly the case that the fountain of domestic affection and comfort at which Mistry the writer often refreshes himself threatens to bubble over completely in *Family Matters*, where characters greet the signs of filial sympathy – Jehangir tenderly feeding his frail grandfather, or Yezad overcoming his aversion to help his father-in-law shave – by fighting back tears and swallowing lumps in their throats. Mistry's tender minutiae of domestic affection sometimes have the sweet simplicity found in similar scenes in Satyajit Ray's early films, but sometimes they merely cloy. In general, life's small consolations tend to be met less incontinently than by some of his characters. Amit Chaudhuri, while repeating the charge of sentimentality, this time in relation to *Such a Long Journey*, does make the interesting suggestion that the emotional surfeit connects Mistry's work to those Hindi films of which his characters are sometimes aficionados, although Mistry's quietist prose style lacks the *chutzpah* to wring the full potential out of this similarity.[24]

Writing of *A Fine Balance*, Vinita Dhondiyal Bhatnagar and Tabish Khair have both observed that Mistry deprives his characters of any radical agency in the fraught political situation of the Emergency, instead producing a bleak account at odds with popular opposition to state initiatives both at the time and since. Bhatnagar claims that 'the text highlights the elements of despair at the cost of presenting an accurate description of the forces of resistance'.[25] For her, the character of Avinash provides an embodiment of the resistant spirit abroad at the time, but is too quickly silenced. Nor is any indication given of how the lower castes were increasingly assertive in mainstream political life, becoming agents rather than mere victims: to the extent that *Dalit* (Untouchable) governments have risen to power in certain areas. Tabish Khair agrees that post-independence lower-caste gains are ignored, and states that in Mistry's novel this oversight results in 'static images' of oppression. Moreover, a lack of attention to the evolving structures of Brahminical power and the increasing sophistication of cultural and economic hegemony give the text the quality of 'a sort of eternal "epic of the victim"' and result in a 'valorization of "the poetry of poverty and suffering"'.[26] This culminates in the rather cosy bourgeois consolation that 'though Ishvar and Omprakash Darji are condemned to becoming handicapped beggars, they can still keep their sense of humour'.[27] This is all valid, although Khair betrays the perhaps unreasonably prescriptive nature of his Marxist methodology when asserting that by failing to engage with the complex dialectical, historical nature of exploitation Mistry's text 'fails to provide a plan of action to tackle it in the future'.[28] The question of whether a novelist has any obligation to such overt didacticism is rather a moot point. I have indicated that I consider the resistance in *A Fine Balance* to take place on the level of form, in the polyphonic and multilayered contestation of hegemonic and canonical discourses. Nevertheless, Bhatnagar and Khair do score palpable hits with their dissection of the actions that do, or do not, make it into the novel.

So, critics have taken issue with aspects of Mistry's work. The above debates, and my intervention in them here, also serve to prove that critics sometimes take issue with each other. In particular, the invocation of the theoretical terminology often associated with postcolonialism has exposed a bifurcation in critical responses. For example, Arun Mukherjee has objected to the responses of some western reviewers and critics to *Such a Long Journey*. She complains that the readings such critics have offered force the text into 'the good old universalist paradigm where a morally upright character goes through experience that leads to his "moral growth" or helps him achieve "a deeper sense of his own humanity"'.[29] They thereby ignore the specificity of historical and political contexts in which events take place and characters have their experiences. This is at best complacency – such reviewers need not bother themselves about the alien dynamics of such texts which might require them to transport themselves beyond their comfortable western perspectives – and at worst cultural arrogance: shown most clearly by those who objected on aesthetic grounds to the Parsi mode of disposing of their dead on the Towers of Silence, described in Mistry's novel. The compensatory practice – the 'atomising of the individual' – Mukherjee decries as a liberal humanist reading practice which, by isolating characters from their environment, promotes an apolitical (but effectively conservative) ideology. In such cases, the vague-yet-loaded epithet 'moving' 'is the highest approbation a Euro-American critic can grant to a text'.[30] Overall, Mukherjee's piece makes some excellent points about mainstream critical commonplaces and the myopia, reflected in terminology, that often descends on reviewers when confronted with books on India. However, in truth, Mukherjee's own exaggerated polemic is somewhat simplistic and collapses important distinctions of critical approach into stereotypes of cultural difference; it seems that 'Euro-American critics' (whoever they are) cannot but read 'other' texts in this blinkered, self-satisfied way, whereas those who have undergone the revelations of poststructuralism – itself arguably a 'Euro-American' benefaction – are empowered to shine a light into the cobwebbed corners of critical practice to dispel the ghosts of residual orientalism. (In fact, Michael Thorpe, perhaps possessed by the simplifying spirit of Mukherjee's approach, accuses her of an 'anti-Western diatribe'.[31])

Such problems of reception and categorisation reach their zenith in the debate around Mistry's texts as examples of realist literary practice. Drawing on the evidence of textual epigraphs – such as the quotation from Balzac at the start of *A Fine Balance* – and the attention to material detail, some critics have viewed the work as unproblematically realist whereas others have identified the presence of practices that disturb and disrupt the reflective surface. Amit Chaudhuri, in his introduction to *The Picador Book of Modern Indian Literature*, suggests that Mistry, along with Vikram Seth, has 'annexed the nineteenth-century European novel',[32] intending to indicate that the scale of the novels, and their fully-realised worlds, recalls the work of those writing at what is often taken to be the high point of the novelistic form. Similarly, in a lively and enthusiastic apprecia-tion of Mistry's *oeuvre*, Frank Kermode has noted the much-remarked affinity with Dickens, but suggests that 'the English novelist he most resembles seems to be Arnold Bennett',[33] both because, like several other Indian writers in English, he eschews extreme forms of experimentation, and because of his careful exploration of the genealogies of his main characters and interest in the legacies of the different generations of their families.

Some critics are more explicit in their identification of Mistry's writing as realist. Pico Iyer, in a review of *A Fine Balance*, deems Mistry's epic 'worthy of the nineteenth-century masters of tragic realism, from Hardy to Balzac'.[34] On the other hand, John Ball seems more hesitant when he concedes that 'realism is as good a label as any to describe his mode of representation'.[35] In a review with the telling title, 'Bombay's Balzac', Rukmini Bhaya Nair goes as far as to suggest that

Mistry has written *A Fine Balance* 'as a sort of anti-*Midnight's Children*, an anti-magic realist rewriting of substantially the same theme'.[36] This, presumably, is because Mistry offers a similar indictment of Mrs Gandhi to that famously advanced by Rushdie in the Emergency sections of his novel, although thematically the excesses of the era bear an entirely different weight and set of implications in the two books. Nair justifies this idea by charting two different literary lineages for the writers: Rushdie with his avowed indebtedness to a tradition of self-conscious fiction of which Nair feels Valéry to be the apogee; Mistry being placed within the French realist tradition epitomised by Balzac, whose motto might be that every page of his writing is 'a slice of life'. Nair observes: 'Telling it as it is, or "striking true", as Balzac puts it elsewhere, simply requires the writer to stand back and let the story tell itself without too much "artful" interference,' all of which makes Mistry, 'one of the foremost realist writers in English'.[37] Nair's is a well-written and sensitive review, and one can agree with many of its subtle observations. In the end, however, the unnuanced identification of Mistry's technique as realist accounts only for a tendency, albeit the main one, in his work. Significantly, it leaves the review unable to handle the more eccentric, 'unrealist' characters in *A Fine Balance*, such as Rajaram the hair collector or Vasantrao Valmik the allergic proof-reader. As they do not sit easily within the sturdy realist framework Nair constructs for the text, they are dismissed as 'crudely drawn, more touristy and it is not apparent that Mistry expends on them the same affection or writes of them with the same knowledge as he is able to draw on for his main quartet'.[38] As I have argued, the presence of such characters allows for a different kind of investigation of the text's key themes, taking it into the realms of satire and allegory. Ultimately, the distinction between Mistry and Rushdie, and the traditions they are said to embody, need not be as watertight or mutually exclusive as it may at first appear.

However, the most intransigent example of a reading of Mistry as simply a realist writer occurs in Hilary Mantel's review of *A Fine Balance*, entitled 'States of Emergency', in *The*

New York Review of Books. Here the conviction hamstrings the piece entirely. Beginning with a quotation from Stendhal about the realist novel being a mirror of reality, Mantel notes the praise bestowed on Mistry's 'documentary realism' in *Such a Long Journey* on the novel's appearance. (Indeed, the subsequent problems with Mantel's reading all stem from this initial misrecognition.) She says, 'we seemed to have found an author who would carry a mirror for us down the dusty highways of India, through the jostling Bombay streets, behind compound walls, and into the huts and houses where the millions sit, reinventing themselves, constantly reciting the stories of their own lives and times'.[39] She notes the prominence given to Balzac's ominous warning which forms the novel's epigraph: 'After you have read this story of great misfortunes, you will no doubt dine well ... But rest assured: this tragedy is not fiction. All is true'. This quotation is then used as support for the idea that Mistry is trying to present experiences which, if not literally factual, are at least deployed so as to create a world that is wholly believable, thereby retrieving such experiences from the oblivion of the official records. In light of this, the novel that follows appears something of a disappointment. Mantel complains of 'the cyclical pattern of disaster in which Mistry has trapped his creations', so that, in the end, 'one feels controlled, as if by a bad god'. The narrative is so 'overdetermined' that it is remarkable that the four major characters come alive at all: '"The lives of the poor are rich in symbols," Dina reflects – and again Mistry is playing with fire, for his reader may retort that all our lives are rich in symbols when we have such a determined and schematic author on our trail.'[40] 'Overdetermined'. 'Patterned'. These words should alert us to the fact that the novel is, as I have argued earlier, essentially about pattern making. After all, the Emergency is a particularly retrogressive example of an attempt to impose pattern on chaos. But for Mantel, 'Mistry's characters ... are caught in a vast, predetermined, prepatterned design which the author embroiders fiercely, glibly.'[41] To be fair, before it degenerates into rampant misreading towards the end, Mantel's review has made some interesting points about the text's moral sensibility and breadth, but also about its relentless treatment of characters such as Shankar the doomed beggar. It is thus a pity that Mantel does not recognise that, rather than being 'documentary realism', Mistry's novel is very much about the quest for pattern and the double-edged search for order in flux, in personal and social experience and on the national stage. As I have argued in *Fictions of India*:

> It uses patterns of recurrence and cyclicality and metafictional elements. It can only be read as 'over-determined' … if one accepts the dubious assertion that this is simply and solely a text in the business of holding that infamous mirror up to nature. Everything about the text's search for pattern indicates that this is not the case, and that it is fundamentally about fiction-making.[42]

These fictions often take the form of shared stories: hence the concern with that narrative patterning in which all of us engage as we attempt to understand and, as far as possible, control our own lives. At other times we are witness to the absurd moral (and sometimes physical) contortions the Emergency encourages. Perhaps the noted comparison with Dickens, whose novels are also populated by exaggerated eccentrics with implausible character 'tics', who yet rub along in a solidly realised urban world – and whom it would therefore also be difficult to categorise as unconditionally realist – would have been a profitable line to pursue.

Other, perhaps more perspicacious critics have been attentive to the way in which the skein of surface realism is persistently punctured by moments of fabulist allegory, pronounced modernist patterning and, sometimes, metafictional interventions. For instance, David Williams, who, to my knowledge, is the first critic to explore at length Mistry's concern with language and power, has remarked upon the function of the representation of the sacred wall-within-the-wall painted by the pavement artist in *Such a Long Journey*. He sees its 'infinite regress' as a challenge to the naturalism that elsewhere seems to characterise the text: 'The self-reflexive picture displays a figure founded only on itself, a sign which is wholly arbitrary and conventional', and which, thereby, partakes of 'the postrealist ideology of postcolonial writing'.[43] This phrase turns out to refer to the way in which postcolonial writing often interrogates and deconstructs legitimising hegemonic narratives, but does so in a way that retains a concern for material suffering, especially that of the body, which distinguishes it from the more internalised preoccupations with the self-referentiality of language found in postmodernism. This distinction between postcolonialism and postmodernism has generated much critical debate in recent years. For our purposes here, it is fair to say that Mistry critics have largely confined themselves to a consideration of how his works deal with actual history but move beyond the official version of the national events which form the subject matter of the first two novels, releasing narratives that run parallel to, rather than simply reflect, reality. Nilufer E. Bharucha, for example, argues that 'Mistry's fiction is fashioned in the form of alternative narratives and employs anti-realist modes of narration',[44] thereby challenging 'elitist master narratives'. Likewise, Arun Mukherjee asserts that the 'insertion of ... the stories that "everyone knew" is what differentiates Mistry's novel from the "Victorian realist novel" that it has been compared to', and that his fiction's 'total social environment ... is real, not realist ... [in its] attempts to make sense of actual historical events by narrativising them'.[45] In a sense, Mistry's position as a Parsi, marginal to hegemonic and majoritarian constructions of India, makes him acutely aware of versions other than those emanating from the sites of power, so that, as Bharucha says, 'his discourse also challenges and resists the totalization of the dominant culture within India itself'.[46] In terms of style, I have argued that in *A Fine Balance* this marginal position, along with the traditional Parsi proximity to colonial culture:

> accounts for the generically hybrid nature of the novel's tone. It is why the collapsing Mrs Gandhi cut-out scene, the Vasantrao Valmik character and so on, appear susceptible to being read *either* as an example of the fantastical, larger-than-life allegorical mode bursting through, and

exposing, the façade of social realism, *or* as idiosyncratic, quasi-Dickensian irony and exaggeration within a broad, empathetic liberal realist novel.[47]

Mistry's writing radically disturbs such neat categories.

Hence, it has not been my intention to argue that Mistry is *not* a realist writer. Rather, I have tried to show that realism only accounts for an overall tendency within his work. Another way of thinking about this is to distinguish between realism as *technique* – perhaps exemplified most famously in Ian Watt's notion of that 'formal realism' in the novel, characterised by particularity and specificity leading to verisimilitude in character, location and time, that replaced the typicality of previous modes of writing[48] – and as *effect*: in what one might call modulating apprehensions of the 'real'. In other words, as readers our sense of 'the real' can be heightened and made more vivid through the use of farce, satire and coincidence: something Dickens was keenly aware of. These non- or suprarealist elements can make a literary canvas come to life with a vivacity that takes us beyond the everyday. Thinking of the ironies, and subversions of 'official' history in Mistry's novels, one is reminded of Cedric Watts's comments on the uses of satire in Conrad's *The Secret Agent*, one of Mistry's apparent templates for *Such a Long Journey*. Watts says:

> In the satiric tradition, representations of vice and folly are heightened; the reader expects not a faithfully complex rendering of reality, but a selective and distorted rendition vindicated by the resultant intensity and magnification of some salient features of actuality. Corruption looms comically large: characters approximate caricatures … In the broad literary hinterland of *The Secret Agent* lie, for example, the harsh satires of Juvenal, the 'humours' of Jonson, the misanthropy of Swift and the eccentric and bizarre figures of Dickens.[49]

I would argue that Rohinton Mistry's work forms a postcolonial addition to this tradition.

Mistry seems to be exploring the faultlines and tensions in that characteristic of literary representation that has become known to us as mimesis.[50] However, mimesis need not mean the mechanical copying of reality. As Aristotle first observed, 'it is not the poet's function to describe what has actually happened, but the kinds of thing that might happen because they are, in the circumstances, either probable or necessary. The difference between the historian and the poet is ... that the one tells of what has happened, the other of the kinds of things that might happen.'[51] Moreover, the poet (read creative writer) has the option of presenting things in one of three ways: 'either as they were or are, or as they are said to be or seem to be, or as they ought to be':[52] a distinction that not only acknowledges the subjective nature of the reality we construct, but also makes room for variety in its representation, from Utopian writing to satire. Richard Kearney has described how Aristotle's discriminations allow for 'a creative redescription of the world such that hidden patterns and hitherto unexplored meanings can unfold. As such mimesis is essentially tied to *mythos* taken as the transformative plotting of scattered events into new paradigms ... It has little or nothing to do with the old naturalist conviction that art simply holds a mirror up to nature.'[53] Kearney's account of the inflections of mimesis could stand as a delineation of Mistry's highly original re-workings of recent Indian history: 'Far from being a passive copy of reality, *mimesis* re-enacts the real world of action by magnifying its essential traits. It remakes the world, so to speak, in the light of its *potential truths*'[54] [emphasis added].

The conjunctive qualities of such literary apprehensions of the real appear in Mistry's work in the form of a 'subtle synthesis of the available modes of novelistic writing in the post-colonial world, in its mixture of the mimetic qualities of realism (the social detail, the concern for historical verisimilitude) and the deliberate artifice and excess associated with much post-colonial Indian writing – often homogenized, somewhat misleadingly, under the heading "magic realism"'.[55] Similarly, the 'already-read' quality of some of his tropes and situations – the references to Eliot and Yeats, echoes of Dickens and Dostoyevsky, revisiting of themes and images from Anand and

Sahgal – are less reverent canonical obeisance than fore-grounded examples of that intertextuality characteristic of all literary discourses. Graham Allen neatly describes how, through intertextuality, 'Meaning becomes something which exists between a text and all the other texts to which it refers and relates, moving out from the independent text into a network of textual relations.'[56] One can imagine this idea of an ever-present patchwork of literary influences appealing to the creator of Dina Dalal's patchwork quilt of shared human stories. It alerts us to the fact that even realist texts are relational, and thereby intertextual, generating meaning – and recognisable worlds – through their interaction with pre-existing literary and cultural discourses, producing, through this melding and merging, 'reality effects', rather than reality itself. This, in turn, has implications for our reading practices.

Of course, clear-cut distinctions between realism and modernism are to a large extent invidious and impossible to sustain. Even Roland Barthes, who first codified the difference between *'scriptible'* or writerly texts – which encourage active interpretative participation by the reader in the creation of their meaning – and *'lisible'* or readerly texts – allowing a more passive response – was drawn in his own author study to the work of Balzac, one of the architects of the supposedly more passive mode of realism.[57] In the same way, debates about Mistry's literary style merely illustrate the permeable borders of critical and generic categories. Ever since his adoption of the destabilising, hybrid genre of the short story cycle in his first published volume, Mistry has performed what Ashcroft, Griffiths and Tiffin have described as a radical questioning of, 'easy assumptions about the characteristics of the genres we usually employ as structuring and categorising definitives'.[58] All such normalising critical taxonomies develop in particular historical and cultural contexts. In the case of western literary criticism they developed and solidified into virtual axioms in the era of the European empires in the late nineteenth and early twentieth centuries. Their great strength, however, has been their ability to depict themselves as universal and ahistorical. Critics such as

W. H. New have performed the service of reminding us that, when it comes to literary forms, we often internalise 'expectations that are not necessarily applicable outside the society to which they were first applied'.[59] Mistry and his writing straddle so many classifications as to form an exemplar both of the mixed Parsi inheritance, and the predicament of postcolonial culture more generally. In short, it might be concluded that the writer's hybrid techniques expose the inadequacy of such nineteenth-century European critical and taxonomical drives to the dynamic, elusive migrant literature of the present, of which Mistry's writing is a pre-eminent example.

Likewise, if his fiction is not simply realist, nor is it wholly modernist or postmodernist. There is, however, what might be described as a self-conscious impulse at work, more modest and intermittent than full-blown metafiction. This occurs in the frequent attempts by characters to transcend the piecemeal, ground-level view to which they are bound as earthly participants in their quotidian dramas, and to reach for a more holistic, pattern-making perspective: the kind of perspective usually vouchsafed only to an omniscient narrator. They seek to discover the 'whole picture', a conjunction of beginnings, middles and ends that will give meaning to their lives. Thus, we have the pavement artist in *Such a Long Journey*, with his encompassing wall of all religions: the young narrator persona experimenting with, and rejecting, conventional literary resolutions in *Tales from Firozsha Baag*; and Dina's household, with its emotional investment in the quilt which catches their experiences as they fly past, preserving them in a play of colour and shape that provides order and a sense of progression in *A Fine Balance*. Even in the more subdued *Family Matters* the same instinct is at work: Yezad and Roxana watch each other come and go from the balcony of the flat in Paradise Villas, aching to be able to supervise and put right their unravelling lives; Yezad looks out over the messy streets of Bombay from the high-rise apartment of his murdered employer, seeking some shape and meaning to events, as he also does at the Towers of Silence, high on a hill above the chaos of the city; and Jal suggests Coomy's posthumous approval for his plan for Yezad's family to move in with him: 'From up there, he said, possessed of the knowledge and wisdom which come with dying, Coomy would surely approve' (*FM*, 428). Significantly, the only character who seems to approach this omniscient ideal is the letter-writer, Vilas Rane, who is granted a kind of 'God's eye-view of the world' (*FM*, 136) even as he sits on his step, reading and transcribing his clients' innermost feelings – paradoxically, you need to be 'down to earth', in the thick of these human stories, if you want a meaningful pattern to emerge.

Of course, the author has this perspective all the time. Yet, as the multiple ironies of his characters' sometimes self-deluding search for an abstract 'meaning of life' might suggest, Mistry's narrators' own omniscient perspectives often seem imbued with a certain degree of self-consciousness. To the chagrin of reviewers like Mantel, there is always the faint but unmistakable trace of an 'author' beyond the text, *imposing* a pattern, not in any direct meddling way, but as another of the discursive consciousnesses that populate these dialogic fictions. As I have claimed above, Mistry's writing is ultimately about fiction-making, reproducing on a grand scale his characters' attempts at imposing order and meaning on the flux of experience, but, at the same time, recognising the provisional nature of all such endeavours. If this writing can be classified as realism at all it is a kind of self-conscious, 'implosive' realism: a post-colonial 'metarealism' perhaps. Beyond all the 'concrete' worlds of political intrigue and personal questing the author creates, there is always a feeling that whatever exists outside the realm of language – whether you call it God, *Ahura Mazda*, *Karma* or whatever – is uncontrollable, if not unknowable: a Joycean entity, 'invisible, refined out of existence, paring his fingernails'. In its place there is the weaver of stories, fabricating his counterpane of narrative against contingency.

Inasmuch as a critical study of this nature requires a definite resolution, Sylvia Albertazzi's comment on Mistry's style in *Tales from Firozsha Baag* may serve as an accurate overview of the author's *oeuvre*: 'In Mistry's collection, East and West, old and new, oral narration and metafiction, translation and post-modernism are fused and confused, without losing their unique characteristics.'[60] However, any reader sceptical about the fore-going argument might turn for support to Rohinton Mistry himself, a most private and craftsman-like writer who remains suspicious of critics and criticism, and who prefers to allow his fictions to speak on his behalf. In *Such a Long Journey*, the narrator follows his parodic analysis of the storyteller Peerbhoy Paanwalla's racy parables, quoted in the epigraph to this chapter, with a salutary observation for all critics. Although a study of Peerbhoy's narrative, spun for the benefit of a motley audience assembled near an overflowing drain, may reveal a smattering of many different generic forms, in the end, 'since such things as literary criticism mattered not one jot to the listeners, they were responding to Peerbhoy's narrative in the only way that made sense: with every fibre of their beings. They could see and smell and taste and feel the words that filled the dusk and conjured the tale; and it was no wonder they were oblivious to the gutter stink' (*SLJ*, 306).

Conclusion – Rohinton Mistry:
international man of stories

Twentieth-century Indians ... have voyaged widely in
search of livelihoods and ideas, and they have discovered
themselves through the clarities, oversights and
yearnings that distance induces. The exact character of
the homelands they have journeyed from has proved
elusive, and often imaginary. Where in the world is
India? (Sunil Khilnani, *The Idea of India*, p. 198)

ROHINTON Mistry has produced fictions characterised by a
style that is at once unobtrusive and apparently direct, but
which contains considerable symbolic complexity. He has
deployed this seductive yet dynamic combination of simplicity
and sophistication to analyse characters coming to terms with
social and political circumstances that often induce severe strain,
and which force them to face up to awkward questions about
morality, politics and personal responsibility. I have argued that
Tales from Firozsha Baag encodes questions of belonging,
migration and identity in a text which is, at the same time,
testing generic boundaries and mimicking and rejecting the
clichés of literary consolation. The first novel, *Such a Long
Journey*, asks questions about the trustworthiness of language
as communication in a climate of political intrigue and duplicity
and, while concluding that the consolations of friendship and
loyalty are to be recommended, also acknowledges their temporary nature. *A Fine Balance* carries these interests onto the
battlefield that is the India of Mrs Gandhi's Emergency, a
terrain populated by grimacing henchman and stoical eccentrics
whose larger-than-life qualities take the book beyond the realm

of that documentary realism sometimes seen as symptomatic of the author's writing. It also uses a variety of literary tropes and discourses as it weaves its narrative fabric, creating a quilt which sustains and supports both characters and readers as they experience the giddy fluctuations of a menacing, topsy-turvy world. Even in the ostensibly more traditional *Family Matters*, similar issues of corruption versus integrity are explored. Here, notions of the multiple and sometimes conflicting demands of duty are set alongside filial loyalty, personal vengeance and religious faith. Family certainly does matter to this author, but family-type units can materialise in unexpected ways and the ties of blood are often as onerous and oppressive as they are nurturing and supportive. At the same time, in each of his novels, Mistry, like those other influential members of the second generation of postcolonial Indian writers in English, Salman Rushdie, Bapsi Sidhwa and Amitav Ghosh, interrogates and often challenges the complacencies and orthodoxies of those secular and religious elites who run the nation and seek to shape it in their own image.

Bruce King has argued that the 'commonwealth writer in exile' has, in a sense, stolen a march on his postmodern metropolitan contemporaries in assimilating and creating literary styles to represent the fissures of a 'translated', alienated existence. He says of these writers:

> They are deconstructionists, not out of the logic that led others from structuralism to post-structuralism, but from the experience of divided, uprooted, unassimilated lives; but they are also reconstructionists in that for those genuinely threatened by chaos the logic of survival requires some new order, even if only provisional.[1]

Perhaps this explains Mistry's fascination with pattern. His characters seek patterns and shapes in the chaos of everyday lives slowly falling apart, sometimes by raiding fond memories, sometimes by reversion to the primal consolations of religious and ethnic identifications, and sometimes, more profitably, by sifting what is valuable in the past and filtering out prejudices which tie them down. The resulting patterns can be interwoven with those of contemporary lived experience to give a sense of where one has come from and, hence, where one might be going.

Mistry's Zoroastrian background informs each of his texts, providing both the subject matter and the coordinates by which his protagonists understand their encounters with the outside world. The Zoroastrian principles that inform their lives also direct their responses to the moral dilemmas they face. They can also provide interesting interpretative clues for the reader prepared to take a little time to find out more about the Parsis and their world. This ethnic identity also impacts on Mistry's style, complicating its inherent hybridity. Nilufer E. Bharucha has commented of the Parsis: 'As a diasporic people, they have perfected the art of existing in a state of liminality, partaking of different cultures yet ultimately retaining for themselves the refuge of their formative ethno-religious identity.'[2] Mistry's style appears to have evolved its characteristic features – the measured clarity of the European novel leavened by the dialogic energy of eastern storytelling traditions – to deal with the multiple interpellations of conflictual ideologies. For a writer such as Mistry then, perhaps it is the case, as Tanya Luhrmann has put it, that 'identity in a modern postcolonial context is less a self-characterising narrative with a mirroring world than a sense of command over narrative complexity'.[3] Thus, while aware of the limitations of realism, Mistry does not concede that linguistic systems are purely self-reflexive. He recognises that part of the storyteller's role is to find forms appropriate to the overlapping identities – Canadian, Zoroastrian, Indian and so on – he embodies. His philosophy regarding this necessity is straightforward: 'I don't think I have a message ... I grew up in Bombay. Now I am here [in Canada]. I'm a writer. I am determined to write good literature. This is my primary concern. But to write well, I must write about what I know best. In that way, I automatically speak for my "tribe".'[4]

Despite having lived in Canada since 1975, Mistry's fiction is imbued with the spirit of Bombay. Bombay is more than merely a location. It provides what might be described as a habitat in which characters live, breath and confront their spiritual and material demons. Indeed, Bombay is a vast treasure house of stories. In *A Fine Balance* the city is a space of shared stories: a 'story spinning mill'. For Mistry, such stories, told and retold to new acquaintances, work to mitigate the confusion of life, offering a temporary unity, and a balm to the psychic sufferings caused by time and change. In a sense, this can be seen as one of storytelling's deepest and oldest functions. Richard Kearney reminds us that 'Myths arose, as Lévi-Strauss says, as "machines for the suppression of time". Or, as Tolkien puts it, as ways of expressing our yearning for the Great Escape – from death.'[5] Likewise, Mistry has suggested that, for all his characters, the question remains essentially the same: 'Why death? Why must we struggle with life and die?'[6] The misfortunes they experience are, to an extent, determined by political forces over which they have little or no direct control. However, the essence of the domestic tragedies played out in his pages inheres in what Shomit Dutta has described as 'the interaction of external forces and personal choice'.[7] The combination of the material specificities of injustice and the spiritual apprehensions informing his world view – Zoroastrianism tinged with Platonism – at times lend Mistry's writing a similar aspect to that of the dissident writer Alexander Solzhenitsyn. There is the same tussle of pragmatism and idealism, the same preoccupation with the question of whether 'environment determines consciousness' or whether, as a character in Solzhenitsyn's *The First Circle* insists:

> Man is invested from birth with a certain ... essence. It is as it were the nucleus of his personality, his ego. The only question is – which determines which? Is man formed by life or does he, if he has a strong enough personality, shape life around him? ... because he has something against which to measure himself. Because he can look at an image of perfection, which at rare moments manifests itself to his inward ego.[8]

Bombay gives birth to Mistry's characters, but they venture forth into a wider world in both literal and literary senses.

This comparison with Solzhenitsyn calls to mind those other European, and especially Russian, writers Mistry is thought to resemble. However, it is important to recognise that Mistry is a novelist of *ethics* rather than a novelist of ideas as such. In this he more closely resembles Turgenev than Dostoyevsky or Tolstoy. Like Turgenev, he is a master of description, with an eye for those details – of dress, deportment, attitude – that mark out differences in social status. Likewise, he is not a writer who often digresses into extended social or political critiques in his work. Instead, he allows paradoxes and injustices to emerge in character and situation. How people treat one another as individuals, often in situations where exploitation and manipulation have become the norm, is more significant than whether they adhere to any particular political ideology. It might therefore be claimed – as it often is about nineteenth-century liberal novelists – that, in a subcontinent increasingly characterised by hegemonic, communalist and neo-colonial power, such liberal individualism, blind to class structures, allows the writer to diagnose contemporary ills but, at the same time, prevents him from offering any solutions. In any case, ethical considerations form a strong part of Zoroastrianism too, where the choice between good and evil is enshrined in the central moral code, 'good thoughts, good words, good deeds', and in the Persian narrative tradition; the *Shah-Namah* frequently interrupts its battle scenes and royal hunts to raise questions of moral responsibility: as in the disputation between the sage Buzurjmihr and King Naoshirvan on kingly goodness, and when Asmail and Karmail enlist as cooks to save one of every two men slain to feed the tyrant Zuhaak.[9]

Similarly, Mistry's writing raises ethical questions which, while played out through the characters, are left to the reader to resolve. In one sense all narrative does this. However, the recurring trope of the instinctive desire for communication stymied by a divisive and authoritarian political hierarchy, common to Mistry's novels, give such questions an urgent insistence. Perhaps Paul Ricoeur, quoted by Richard Kearney, indirectly provides one of the most recognisable accounts of the experience of reading a Mistry novel. He claims that the strategy of persuasion undertaken by the narrator of any given novel:

> is aimed at giving the reader a vision of the world that is never ethically neutral, but rather implicitly or explicitly induces a new evaluation of the world and of the reader as well. In this sense, narrative already belongs to the ethical field in virtue of its claim – inseparable from its narration – to ethical justice. Still, it belongs to the reader, now an agent, an initiator of action, to choose among the multiple proposals of ethical justice brought forth by the reading.[10]

In addition to the various literary prizes Mistry's writing has won, further recognition came in December 2001, when *A Fine Balance* was chosen to feature on Oprah Winfrey's television 'Book Club'. According to Mistry's Canadian agent, Bruce Westwood, 'After September 11, Oprah wanted a Book Club choice that would introduce American readers to the east'.[11] Ironically, less than a year later, this most unassuming and tolerant of writers felt compelled to abandon a promotional tour of the United States for his new novel, *Family Matters*, because of the 'humiliating' and 'unbearable' 'racial profiling' to which he was subjected at each airport along the way. It is one of those paradoxes of contemporary political history and its 'libertarian' discourses, that Mistry should have become one of the most high-profile victims of the racially-tinged institutional paranoia that has trailed in the wake of the Twin Towers attack.

Ultimately, Mistry's fiction offers the satisfactions of recognition to those familiar with the machinations of postcolonial Indian politics and the position of the Parsis as a vulnerable minority, *and* to general readers who may know little about the background, but who can identify with the characters, their experiences and life choices. Speaking of this quality in his work, Mistry has commented, 'The Parsi characters in my stories, and their dreams, ambitions and fears are as accessible to the western reader as to the Indian reader ... I don't say to myself: "This story needs three doses of universality and five doses of particularity." When I start writing it all just happens.'[12] This blend of universality and cultural and contextual specificity gives Mistry's texts their readability and seems likely to ensure their longevity too.

Of his own reasons for continuing to write, Mistry is disarmingly candid: 'I once read, I think it was by Camus, that one can redeem oneself by writing and that has stayed with me and I think that is why I began to write. I wasn't sure how redemption would come through writing, but I'm still writing.'[13]

Notes

Chapter 1

1   Walter Benjamin, *Illuminations*, trans. Harry Zohn, ed. Hannah Arendt (HarperCollins, 1992), p. 85.

2   Angela Lambert, 'Touched with Fire', *Guardian*, 27 April (2002), p. 6.

3   *Ibid.*, p. 6.

4   Salman Rushdie, *Imaginary Homelands: Essays and Criticism 1981-1991* (Granta, 1992), p. 17.

5   Stacey Gibson, 'Such a Long Journey', *University of Toronto Magazine*, 29:4, Summer (2002), p. 23.

6   Lambert, 'Touched with Fire', p. 7.

7   Eckehard Kulke, *The Parsees in India: A Minority as an Agent of Social Change* (München, Weltforum Verlag, 1974), p. 15.

8   Peter Clark, *Zoroastrianism: An Introduction to an Ancient Faith* (Brighton, Sussex Academic Press, 1998), pp. 19–21.

9   Nilufer E. Bharucha, 'Imagining the Parsi Diaspora: Narrative on the Wings of Fire', in Ralph J. Crane and Radhika Mohanram (eds), *Shifting Continents/Colliding Cultures: Diaspora Writing of the Indian Subcontinent* (Amsterdam, Rodopi, 2000), p. 57.

10 Clark, *Zoroastrianism*, pp. 4–5, 28–9.

11 See Susan Stiles Maneck, *The Death of Ahriman: Culture, Identity and Theological Change Among the Parsis of India* (Bombay, K. R. Cama Oriental Institute, 1997).

12 Clark, *Zoroastrianism*, p. 137.

13 See H. E. Eduljee (ed.), *Kisseh-i Sanjan* (Bombay, K. R. Cama Oriental Institute, 1991).

14   Andre Wink, quoted in Stiles Maneck, *Death of Ahriman*, p. 16.

15   Kulke, *The Parsees*, p. 28.

16   Nilufer E. Bharucha, '"When Old Tracks are Lost": Rohinton Mistry's Fiction as Diasporic Discourse', *Wasafiri*, 30:2 (1995), 58.

17   Kulke, *The Parsees*, p. 121.

18   Peter Childs and Patrick Williams, *An Introduction to Post-Colonial Theory* (Hemel Hempstead, Harvester Wheatsheaf, 1997), p. 15.

19   Kulke, *The Parsees*, p. 9.

20   For all these developments see, Kulke, *The Parsees*, especially pages 66, 74, 91, 122–8 and 173.

21   *Ibid.*, p. 232. See also Nilufer E. Bharucha, 'The Parsi Voice in Recent Indian English Fiction: An Assertion of Ethnic Identity', in Nilufer E. Bharucha and Vilas Sarang (eds), *Indian-English Fiction, 1980–1990: An Assessment* (New Delhi, B. R. Publishing Corporation, 1994), p. 75.

22   T. M. Luhrmann, *The Good Parsi: The Fate of a Colonial Elite in a Postcolonial Society* (Cambridge, Massachusetts, Harvard University Press, 1996), p. 17.

23   *Ibid.*, p. 16.

24   *Ibid.*, p. 126.

25   Childs and Williams, *Introduction to Post-Colonial Theory*, pp. 129–31.

26   Luhrmann, *The Good Parsi*, p. 22.

27   Stiles Maneck, *Death of Ahriman*, p. 254.

28   Roland Barthes, *Image-Music-Text*, trans. Stephen Heath (London, Collins/Fontana, 1977), p. 146.

29   Linda Hutcheon, quoted in Dipesh Chakrabarty, 'Postcoloniality and the Artifice of History: Who Speaks for Indian Pasts?', *Representations*, 37, Winter (1992), p. 2.

30   Abdul R. JanMohamed and David Lloyd (eds), *The Nature and Context of Minority Discourse* (Oxford, Oxford University Press, 1990), p. 10.

31   W. H. New, *Dreams of Speech and Violence: The Art of the Short Story in Canada and New Zealand* (Toronto, University of Toronto Press, 1987), p. x.

32   Frank Kermode, 'In the Spirit of Mayhew', *London Review of Books*, 24:8, 25 April (2002), p. 12.

33   Kulke, *The Parsees*, p. 107.

34   See Bharucha, 'Imagining the Parsi Diaspora', pp. 55–82; and 'The
     Parsi Voice in Recent Indian English Fiction', pp. 73–87. These
     newer Parsi texts include Bapsi Sidhwa, *The Crow Eaters* (1978)
     and *Ice-Candy-Man* (1988); Boman Desai, *The Memory of
     Elephants* (1988); Farrukh Dhondy, *Bombay Duck* (1990); Firdaus
     Kanga, *Trying to Grow* (1990); and Ardashir Vakil, *Beach Boy*
     (1997). For a critical overview, see Novy Kapadia, Jaydipsinh
     Dodiya and R. K. Dhawan (eds), *Parsi Fiction* (New Delhi,
     Prestige, 2001).

35   Ehsan Yarshater, 'Introduction', in Ehsan Yarshater (ed.), *Persian
     Literature* (New York, Bibliotheca Persica Press, 1988), p. 15.

36   There are various spellings of the poet's name – Firdusi, Firdausi,
     Ferdowsi – depending on translation. Despite its rather leaden-
     footed and cumbersome qualities, I have consulted Alexander
     Rogers's abridged, *The Shah-Namah of Fardusi* (Lahore, Sang-e-
     Meel Publications, 2002), as the most readily available trans-
     lation.

37   Jerome W. Clinton, 'Court Poetry at the Beginning of the Classical
     Period', in Yarshater, *Persian Literature*, p. 92.

38   Amin Banani, 'Ferdowsi and the Art of the Tragic Epic', in
     Yarshater, *Persian Literature*, p. 110.

39   *Ibid.*, p. 111.

40   See Geoff Hancock, 'An Interview with Rohinton Mistry',
     Canadian Fiction Magazine, 65 (1989), 147.

41   James Clifford, 'Diasporas', *Cultural Anthropology*, 9:3, August
     (1994), 306.

42   Elleke Boehmer, *Colonial and Postcolonial Literature* (Oxford,
     Oxford University Press, 1995), p. 234.

43   See for example, Meenakshi Mukherjee, 'The Anxiety of
     Indianness', and 'Divided by a Common Language', in *The
     Perishable Empire: Essays on Indian Writing in English* (New
     Delhi, Oxford University Press, 2000) pp. 166–86 and 187–203; G.
     N. Devy, 'The Indian-English Novel 1980–90: An Overview', in
     Bharucha and Sarang (eds), *Indian-English Fiction* pp. 9–19;
     Makarand Paranjape, 'Afterword: What About Those Who Stayed
     Back Home? Interrogating the Privileging of Diaspora Writing', in
     Crane and Mohanram (eds), *Shifting Continents/Colliding
     Cultures* pp. 225–44; Amit Chaudhuri, 'Modernity and the
     Vernacular', and 'The Construction of the Indian Novel in
     English', in Amit Chaudhuri (ed.), *The Picador Book of Modern*

Indian Literature (London, Picador, 2001) pp. xvii–xxii, and xxiii–xxxi; Aijaz Ahmad, *in Theory: Classes, Nations, Literatures* (London, Verso, 1992).

44 Vijay Mishra, 'The Diasporic Imaginary: Theorizing the Indian Diaspora', *Textual Practice*, 10:3, Winter (1996), 424; Amtav Ghosh, 'The Diaspora in Indian Culture', *Public Culture*, 2:1, Fall (1989), 78. See also Vikram Chandra, 'The Cult of Authenticity: India's Cultural Commissars Worship "Indianness" Instead of Art', *Boston Review*, February/March (2000), 42–9.

45 Amin Malak, 'From Margin to Main: Minority Discourse and "Third World" Fiction Writers in Canada', in Anna Rutherford (ed.), *From Commonwealth to Post-Colonial* (Sydney, Dangaroo Press, 1992), p. 52. For more on the nexus of narrative and nostalgia in migrant identities, see Keya Ganguly, 'Migrant Identities: Personal Memory and the Construction of Selfhood', *Cultural Studies*, 6:1 (1992), 27–50.

46 Coral Ann Howells and Lynette Hunter (eds), *Narrative Strategies in Canadian Literature: Feminism and Postcolonialism* (Milton Keynes, Open University Press, 1991), p. 1.

47 See Linda Hutcheon, 'Introduction', in Linda Hutcheon and Marion Richmond (eds), *Other Solitudes: Canadian Multicultural Fictions* (Toronto, Oxford University Press, 1990), pp. 1–15.

48 *Ibid.*, p. 2.

49 JanMohamed and Lloyd, *Minority Discourse*, p. 8. See also, Sanjay Seth, 'Liberalism and the Politics of (multi)Culture: or, Plurality is Not Difference', *Postcolonial Studies*, 4:1, 2001, 65–77.

50 See Geoff Hancock, *Canadian Fiction Magazine* (1989), 145. See also Dagmar Novak's interview with Mistry in Hutcheon and Richmond (eds), *Other Solitudes*, pp. 255–62.

51 See Sunil Khilnani, *The Idea of India* (Harmondsworth, Penguin, 1998). On page 54 Khilnani notes that 'Mrs Gandhi flirted with religious sentiments and appeals, hinting that the categories "non-Hindu" and "non-national" overlapped. It was the secular, modernist elite who dragged this language of religious affiliation into the arena of national politics.'

52 Hancock, *Canadian Fiction Magazine* (1989), 147.

53 Salman Rushdie, *Imaginary Homelands*, p. 14.

54 Firdaus Gandavia, a Bombay-based Parsee writer has claimed that Mistry is 'stuck in the groove of the 70s when he left India and went to Toronto. His concerns seem distant to anyone actually

living in Bombay; so much has happened in the meantime', in Lambert, 'Touched with Fire', p. 6.

55   Amit Chaudhuri, 'Parsi Magic', *London Review of Books*, 4 April (1991), 19.

56   Rohinton Mistry, 'The More Important Things', *Canadian Fiction Magazine*, 65 (1989), 38–55.

57   Stacey Gibson, *University of Toronto Magazine* (2002), 25.

58   Fyodor Dostoyevsky, *The Idiot*, trans. David Magarshack (Harmondsworth, Penguin, 1955), p. 378.

Chapter 2

1   Linda Hutcheon, *Splitting Images: Contemporary Canadian Ironies* (Toronto, Open University Press, 1991), p. 48.

2   Forrest L. Ingram, *Representative Short Story Cycles of the Twentieth Century: Studies in a Literary Genre* (The Hague, Paris, Mouton, 1971), pp. 15, 19.

3   *Ibid.*, p. 17. See also, J. Gerald Kennedy, 'Toward a Poetics of the Short Story Cycle', *Journal of the Short Story in English*, 11 (1988), 9–25; Gerald Lynch, 'The One and Many: English-Canadian Short Story Cycles', *Canadian Literature*, 130:3, Autumn (1990), 91–104; and Robert M. Luscher, 'The Short Story Sequence: An Open Book', in Susan Lohafer and Jo Ellen Clarey (eds), *Short Story Theory at the Crossroads* (Baton Rouge, Louisiana State University Press, 1989, pp. 148–65.

4   A baag is a Parsi housing colony. Peter Clark describes them as, 'essentially concentrated apartment blocks … [which] were set up for the most part in response to the needs of the poorer members of the Zoroastrian community … today the colonies resemble miniature villages, often with shops, including dairies and dispensaries, and invariably having a resident priest'. Peter Clark, *Zoroastrianism: An Introduction to an Ancient Faith* (Brighton, Sussex Academic Press, 1998), p. 134.

5   Lynch cites as examples of the Canadian predilection for short story cycles volumes by Duncan Campbell Scott, Stephen Leacock, Sinclair Ross, Jack Hodgins, Sheldon Currie, Margaret Laurence and Alice Munro, ranging in date from 1896 to 1979. See Lynch, *Canadian Literature*, 92.

6   Davis says, 'The fact that short story cycles exist in all the

different ethnic literatures in Canada also indicates the appropriateness of the form to the depiction of similar experiences. Rachna Mara's *Of Customs and Excise*, Shyam Selvadurai's *Funny Boy*, Dianne Maguire's *Dry Land Tourist*, M.G. Vasanji's *Uhuru Street* and Wayson Choy's *The Jade Peony* are a small sample of recent ethnic short story cycles.' Rocio G. Davis and Rosalina Baena (eds), *Tricks with a Glass: Writing Ethnicity in Canada* (Amsterdam, Rodopi, 2000), p. 77.

7 Geoff Hancock, 'An Interview with Rohinton Mistry', *Canadian Fiction Magazine*, 65 (1989), p. 146. On the same page, in response to this remark, and to the question of when he knew the volume would take this interconnected form, Mistry says, 'Only when I was halfway through ... I realised the characters could know each other and appear in each other's stories. I made small changes to the earlier stories so they could work together.'

8 Kennedy, *Journal of the Short Story in English*, pp. 16–17.

9 Tanya Luhrmann says, 'The Parsis have a religious calendar with thirty name days presided over by various spiritual forces or entities. Certain of them, like the twentieth day, Behram Roj, the *yazad*, or angel of victory, are deemed to be particularly important, and observant Parsis are likely to intensify their religious activities on such days.' T.M. Luhrmann, *The Good Parsi: the Fate of a Colonial Elite in a Postcolonial Society* (Cambridge, Massachusetts, Harvard University Press, 1996), p. 250.

10 Luhrmann, *The Good Parsi*, p. 46. Also Nilufer E. Bharucha, 'The Parsi Voice in Recent Indian English Fiction: An Assertion of Ethnic Identity', in Nilufer E. Bharucha and Vilas Sarang (eds), *Indian–English Fiction, 1980–1990: An Assessment* (Delhi, BR Publishing Corporation, 1994), p. 85.

11 Bill Ashcroft, Gareth Griffiths and Helen Tiffin, *The Empire Writes Back: Theory and Practice in Post-colonial Literatures* (London, Routledge, 1989), p. 53.

12 Sujata Patel remarks that while the population of Bombay increased by about 40 per cent between 1901 and 1931, the period encompassing Jaakaylee's arrival, the years after World War Two saw a rise of 76 per cent: 'Between 1941 and 1971, two thirds of Bombay's inhabitants had been born outside the city.' Sujata Patel, 'Bombay's Urban Predicament', in Sujata Patel and Alice Thorner (eds), *Bombay: Metaphor for Modern India* (New Delhi, Oxford University Press, 1996), p. xvi.

13 Ashcroft *et al.*, *Empire Writes Back*, p. 44.

14 Henry James, *The Turn of the Screw and Other Stories* (Harmonds-worth, Penguin, 1969).

15 Guy de Maupassant, 'Family Life', in *A Day in the Country and Other Stories*, trans. David Coward (Oxford, Oxford University Press, 1990), p. 28.

16 Alice Munro, *Lives of Girls and Women* (Harmondsworth, Penguin, 1982), p. 62.

17 Amin Malak, 'The Sharazadic Tradition: Rohinton Mistry's *Such A Long Journey* and the Art of Storytelling', *Journal of Commonwealth Literature*, 28:2 (1993), 108–18.

18 Luhrmann, *The Good Parsi*, p. 119. Luhrmann also cites a book entitled *Parsis and Sport*, by H. D. Darukhanawala, published in the 1930s, which commemorates Parsi sporting prowess and which 'reads like a believe-it-or-not encyclopedia of unsurpassed feats', p. 118.

19 See Jiri Cejpek, 'Iranian Folk Literature', in Jan Rypka (ed.) *History of Iranian Literature* (Dordrecht, D. Reidel Publishing Company, 1968), p. 642, and Ehsan Yarshater (ed.) *Encyclopaedia Iranica* (New York, Bibliotheca Persica Press, 1999), pp. 572–4.

20 Jacques Derrida, *On the Name*, David Wood, John P. Leavey and Ian McLeod trans. (Stanford, Stanford University Press, 1995), p. 119.

21 Homi K. Bhabha, *The Location of Culture* (London, Routledge, 1994), p. 92.

22 Mikhail Bakhtin, *The Dialogic Imagination*, trans. Caryl Emerson and Michael Holquist (Austin, University of Texas Press, 1981), p. 290.

23 *Ibid.*, p. 302.

24 M. Boyce quoted in Ehsan Yarshater (ed.), *Persian Literature* (New York, Bibliotheca Persica Press, 1988), p. 9.

25 Vijay Mishra, 'The Diasporic Imaginary: Theorizing the Indian Diaspora', *Textual Practice*, 10:3, Winter (1996), 422.

26 Bharati Mukherjee, 'Nostalgia', in *The Penguin Book of Modern Indian Short Stories*, ed. Stephen Alter and Wimal Dissanayake (Harmonsworth, Penguin, 1989), p. 33.

27 Rabindranath Tagore, *Gitanjali* (Macmillan India, 1976), p. 43.

28 T. S. Eliot, *Selected Poems* (London, Faber and Faber, 1961), pp. 51–75.

29 Luhrmann, *Good Parsi*, p. 174.

30 Patricia Waugh defines metafiction as 'fictional writing which self-consciously and systematically draws attention to its status as an artefact in order to pose questions about the relationship between fiction and reality'. Patricia Waugh, *Metafiction: The Theory and Practice of Self-Conscious Fiction*, p. 2.

31 V. S. Naipaul, *The Mimic Men* (Harmondsworth, Penguin, 1969).

32 Smaro Kamboureli, 'Canadian Ethnic Anthologies: Representations of Ethnicity', *ARIEL*, 25:4 (1994), 22.

33 See Ashcroft *et al.*, *Empire Writes Back*, p. 140; also, Elleke Boehmer, *Colonial and Postcolonial Literature* (Oxford, Oxford University Press, 1995), p. 214–17.

34 Hutcheon, *Splitting Images*, p. 52.

35 Craig Tapping, 'South Asia/North America: New Dwellings and the Past', in Emmanuel S. Nelson (ed.), *Reworlding: the Literature of the Indian Diaspora* (Westport CT, Greenwood Press, 1992), p. 45.

Chapter 3

1 Rukmini Bhaya Nair, 'Bombay's Balzac: *A Fine Balance* by Rohinton Mistry', *Biblio: A Review of Books*, 2:2 (1996), 14.

2 Rohinton Mistry, *Such a Long Journey* (London, Faber and Faber, 1992). Capitalising on the text's potential as a thriller, *Such a Long Journey* was made into a film in 1998, directed by Sturla Gunnarson, and starring Roshan Seth as Gustad and Om Puri as Ghulam Mohammad.

3 See Jad Adams and Phillip Whitehead, *The Dynasty: The Nehru-Gandhi Story* (Harmondsworth, Penguin/BBC Books, 1997), pp. 230–9.

4 See Nayantara Sahgal, *Indira Gandhi: Her Road to Power* (London, Macdonald and Co., 1983), p. 82.

5 Rohinton Mistry has described the Parsi reaction to the Nagarwala affair: 'Within our community the main question was "How could a Parsi have done this?"' (Angela Lambert, 'Touched with Fire', *Guardian*, 27 April 2002), p. 7.

6 *The Shah-Namah of Fardusi*, trans. Alexander Rogers (Lahore, Sang-e-Meel Publications, 2002), p. 184.

7 Rabindranath Tagore, *Gitanjali* (New Delhi, Macmillan India, 1976), XXIX, p. 17.

8   T. S. Eliot, *The Waste Land*, lines 413–14.

9   Joseph Conrad, *The Secret Agent* (London, J. M. Dent, 1997).

10 David Williams, 'Cyberwriting and the Borders of Identity: "What's in a Name" in Kroetsch's *The Puppeteer* and Mistry's *Such a Long Journey*', *Canadian Literature*, 149, Summer (1996), 59.

11 Sunil Khilnani observes that the Shiv Sena 'has internalised the nationalist faith in the magic of names so deeply that it has renamed not merely the parks and streets, but also the entire city, Mumbai'. Sunil Khilnani, *The Idea of India* (Harmondsworth, Penguin, 1998), p. 141.

12 Williams, *Canadian Literature*, 57.

13 T. S. Eliot, *The Hollow Men*, lines 72–5, 80–2.

14 John Sturrock, *Structuralism and Since: From Lévi-Strauss to Derrida* (Oxford, Oxford University Press, 1979), p. 166.

15 Fyodor Dostoyevsky, *The Idiot*, trans. David Magarshack (Harmondsworth, Penguin, 1955).

16 Plato, *The Republic* (New York, Dover Publications Inc., 2000), Book VII, pp. 177–8.

17 Clark, *Zoroastrianism*, p. 16.

18 Susan Stiles Maneck, *The Death of Ahriman: Culture, Identity and Theological Change Among the Parsis of India* (Bombay, K. R. Cama Oriental Institute, 1997), pp. 56–7.

19 Plato, *Republic*, Book VI, p. 174.

20 *Ibid.*, Book VII, p. 179.

21 Clark, *Zoroastrianism*, p. 99.

22 *Ibid.*, p. 51.

23 *Ibid.*, pp. 31–2.

24 *Ibid.*, pp. 78–9.

25 H. E. Eduljee, *Kisseh-i Sanjan* (Bombay, K. R. Cama Oriental Institute, 1991).

26 Anjana Desai, '"Was I There?" Rohinton Mistry's *Such a Long Journey*', in Nilufer E. Bharucha and Vilas Sarang (eds), *Indian-English Fiction 1980–90: An Assessment* (Delhi, BR Publishing Corporation, 1994), p. 134.

27 Arun Mukherjee, 'Narrating India', *Toronto South Asian Review*, 10:2 (1992), 87.

28 Amitav Ghosh, *The Calcutta Chromosome: A Novel of Fevers, Delirium and Discovery* (New Delhi, Ravi Dayal , 1996).

29 Plato, *Republic*, Book X, p. 254.

30 *Ibid.*, p. 258.

31 Michael Ryan, *Literary Theory: A Practical Introduction* (London, Blackwell, 1999), p. 69.

32 Mukherjee, *Toronto South Asian Review*, 84.

33 Linda Hutcheon, *A Poetics of Postmodernism: History, Theory, Fiction* (London, Routledge, 1988), pp. 105–23.

Chapter 4

1   Rohinton Mistry, *A Fine Balance* (London, Faber and Faber, 1996).

2   Gilles Deleuze and Felix Guattari, *Kafka: Toward a Minor Literature*, Dana Polan trans. (Minneapolis, University of Minnesota Press, 1986), pp. 16–17.

3   *Ibid.*, p. 17.

4   John Ball, 'Taking the Measure of India's Emergency', *Toronto Review of Contemporary Writing Abroad*, 14:2 (1996), 83–4.

5   'Rohinton Mistry talks to Robert McLay', *Wasafiri*, 23, Spring (1996), 18.

6   Franz Kafka, *The Trial*, in *Franz Kafka: The Complete Novels*, Willa and Edwin Muir trans. (London, Minerva, 1992).

7   See Tariq Ali, *The Nehrus and the Gandhis: An Indian Dynasty* (London, Picador, 1985). See also P. N. Dhar, *Indira Gandhi, the 'Emergency' and Indian Democracy* (New Delhi, Oxford University Press, 2000).

8   David Selbourne, *An Eye to India: The Unmasking of a Tyranny* (London, Pelican Books, 1977), p. 23.

9   *Ibid.*, p. 19.

10 Tariq Ali, *Nehrus*, p. 185.

11 Nayantara Sahgal, *Indira Gandhi: Her Road to Power* (London, Macdonald and Co., 1983), p. 156.

12 Jad Adams and Phillip Whitehead, *The Dynasty: The Nehru-Gandhi Story* (Harmondsworth, Penguin/BBC Books, 1997), p. 261.

13 For another story about one such victim of the ruses used to encourage sterilisation, see Salman Rushdie's story, 'The Free Radio' in *East, West* (London, Jonathan Cape, 1994).

14 'Rohinton Mistry talks to Robert McLay', *Wasafiri*, 17.

15 *Ibid.*, p. 17.

16 R. K. Narayan, *The Guide* (Harmondsworth, Penguin, 1988). For more on the Hindu life cycle see Ainslie T. Embree (ed.), *The Sources of Indian Tradition*, Volume One (New Delhi, Penguin Books India, 1992, second edition), pp. 216–17.

17 Ball, 'Taking the Measure of India's Emergency', 85.

18 Peter Morey, *Fictions of India: Narrative and Power* (Edinburgh, Edinburgh University Press, 2000), p. 183.

19 E. M. Forster, *Aspects of the Novel* (Harmondsworth, Penguin, 1990), pp. 134–53.

20 'Rohinton Mistry talks to Robert McLay', *Wasafiri*, 18.

21 Chinua Achebe, *Things Fall Apart* (London, Heinemann, 1958).

22 Dhar, *Emergency*, p. 264. See also Tariq Ali, *Nehrus*, p. 187.

23 Nayantara Sahgal, *Rich Like Us* (London, Sceptre, 1987), pp. 86–9.

24 Partha Chatterjee, *The Nation and its Fragments: Colonial and Postcolonial Histories* (Princeton, Princeton University Press, 1993), p. 194.

25 Mulk Raj Anand, *Untouchable* (Harmondsworth, Penguin, 1940).

26 Rukmini Bhaya Nair, 'Bombay's Balzac: *A Fine Balance* by Rohinton Mistry', *Biblio: A Review of Books*, 2:2 (1996), 15.

27 Honoré de Balzac, *Père Goriot*, trans. A. J. Krailsheimer (Oxford, Oxford University Press, 1991), p. 109.

28 Sunil Khilnani, *The Idea of India* (Harmondsworth, Penguin, 1998), p. 12.

29 Raymond Williams, *The Country and the City* (London, Hogarth Press 1993), p. 144.

30 Sandeep Pendse, 'Toil and Sweat in the City', in Sujata Patel and Alice Thorner (eds), *Bombay: Metaphor for Modern India* (New Delhi, Oxford University Press, 1996), pp. 6–8.

31 *Ibid.*, pp. 13–14.

32 *Ibid.*, p. 17–18.

33 Michel de Certeau, *The Practice of Everyday Life*, trans. Steven Rendall (Berkeley, University of California Press, 1988), p. 115.

34   *Ibid.*, p. 115.

35   *Ibid.*, p. 117.

36   *Ibid.*, p. 103.

37   *Ibid.*, p. 122.

38   See Adams and Whitehead, *Dynasty*, p. 260 for a true-life journalistic equivalent to Mistry's parodic deification of Sanjay.

39   J. G. Farrell, *The Siege of Krishnapur* (London, Weidenfeld and Nicolson, 1973).

40   Morey, *Fictions of India*, p. 180.

41   Mikhail Bakhtin, *Problems of Dostoevsky's Poetics*, trans. and ed. Caryl Emerson (Manchester, Manchester University Press, 1984), p. 108.

42   *Ibid.*, p. 122.

43   *Ibid.*

44   Pendse, 'Toil and Sweat', p. 16.

45   Bakhtin, *Problems*, p. 125.

46   Tabish Khair, *Babu Fictions: Alienation in Contemporary Indian English Novels* (New Delhi, Oxford University Press, 2001), p. 324.

47   *Ibid.*, p. 141.

48   See Fredric Jameson, 'Third World Literature in the Era of Multinational Capitalism', *Social Text*, 15 (1986), 65–88.

49   Amit Chaudhuri, 'The Construction of the Indian Novel in English', in Amit Chaudhuri (ed.), *The Picador Book of Modern Indian Literature* (London, Picador, 2001), p. xxiv.

50   *Ibid.*, p. xxiv.

51   Michael Sprinker, quoted in Rosemary Marangoly George, *The Politics of Home: Postcolonial Relocations and Twentieth-Century Fiction* (Cambridge, Cambridge University Press, 1996), p. 111.

52   Morey, *Fictions of India*, p. 183.

53   Homi K. Bhabha, *The Location of Culture* (London, Routledge, 1994), p. 148.

54   Paul Ricoeur quoted in Richard Kearney, *On Stories* (London and New York, Routledge, 2001), p. 189.

55   See Khilnani, *Idea of India*, pp. 50–6.

56   Salman Rushdie, 'The Assassination of Indira Gandhi', in *Imaginary Homelands: Essays and Criticism 1981–1991* (London, Granta, 1992), p. 52.

Chapter 5

1   For details see, Kalpana Sharma, 'Chronicle of a Riot Foretold', in
    Sujata Patel and Alice Thorner (eds), *Bombay: Metaphor for
    Modern India* (New Delhi, Oxford University Press, 1996), pp.
    268–86.

2   Bal Thackeray is memorably lampooned as the Mainduck, Raman
    Fielding, leader of the Mumbai Axis in Salman Rushdie's *The
    Moor's Last Sigh* (London, Jonathan Cape, 1995).

3   Novy Kapadia, 'The Politics of Survival and Domination in *A Fine
    Balance*', in Jaydipsinh Dodiya (ed.), *The Fiction of Rohinton
    Mistry: Critical Studies* (London, Sangam Books, 1998), p. 132.
    See also, Sharma, 'Chronicle', p. 274.

4   Rohinton Mistry, *Family Matters* (Faber and Faber, 2002).

5   Edward Said, 'Secular Criticism', in *The World, the Text, and the
    Critic* (Faber and Faber, 1984), pp. 1–30.

6   W. B. Yeats, 'Sailing to Byzantium', in A. Norman Jeffares (ed.),
    W. B. Yeats: Selected Poetry (London, Pan Books/Macmillan,
    1974), lines 21–2.

7   Adam Mars-Jones, 'It's all a bit of a mystery', *Observer Review*,
    21 April 2002, p. 17.

8   See Thomas Blom Hansen, 'BJP and the Politics of Hindutva in
    Maharashtra', in Thomas Blom Hansen and Christophe Jaffrelot
    (eds), *The BJP and the Compulsions of Politics in India* (New
    Delhi, Oxford University Press, 1998), pp.121–60. See also Jayant
    Lele, 'Saffronisation of the Shiv Sena: The Political Economy of
    City, State and Nation', in Thorner and Patel (eds), *Bombay*, pp.
    185–213. For *Hindutva's* impact in the realm of culture, see
    Debjani Ganguly, 'Transgressing Sacred Visions: Taslima,
    Rushdie and the Indian Subcontinent', in Ralph Crane and
    Radhika Mohanram (eds), *Shifting Continents/Colliding Cultures:
    Diaspora Writing of the Indian Subcontinent* (Amsterdam, Rodopi,
    2000), pp. 102–22.

9   Hansen, 'BJP', pp. 148–50.

10 It has also included suppression of one of the most stinging
    indictments of its ruthless style of government, Rushdie's *The
    Moor's Last Sigh*, which was temporarily banned in India at the
    behest of the communalist kingpin, Bal Thackeray. See Ganguly,
    'Transgressing', pp. 107–15.

11 E. M. Forster, *The Longest Journey* (Harmondsworth, Penguin,
    1988), p. 157.

12 Peter Clark, *Zoroastrianism: An Introduction to an Ancient Faith* (Brighton, Sussex Academic Press, 1998), p. 126.

13 Immanuel Kant, 'Grounding for the Metaphysics of Morals', in *Ethical Philosophy*, trans. James W. Ellington (Indianapolis, Hackett Publishing Company, 1994, second edition), p. 11.

14 *Ibid.*, p. 14.

15 Roger Scruton, *Kant: A Very Short Introduction* (Oxford, Oxford University Press, 2001), p. 86.

16 Warner A. Wick, 'Introduction: Kant's Moral Philosophy', in *Ethical Philosophy*, pp. xviii–xix.

17 Kant, *Ethical Philosophy*, p. 36.

18 Voltaire, *Candide and Other Tales*, trans. Tobias Smollett (London, J. M. Dent and Sons, 1937), p. 201.

19 Scruton, *Kant*, p. 30.

20 *Ibid.*, p. 69.

21 Voltaire, *Candide*, p. 108.

22 *Ibid.*, p. 120.

23 V. S. Naipaul, *India: A Million Mutinies Now* (London, Heinemann, 1990).

24 T. M. Luhrmann, *The Good Parsi: The Fate of a Colonial Elite in a Postcolonial Society* (Cambridge, Massachusetts, Harvard University Press, 1996), p. 43.

25 *Ibid.*, p. 168.

26 *Ibid.*, p. 101.

27 Angela Lambert, 'Touched with Fire', *Guardian*, 27 April (2002), p. 7.

28 Scruton, *Kant*, p. 96.

29 Richard Kearney, *On Stories* (London, Routledge, 2002), p. 90.

30 *The Shah-Namah of Fardusi*, trans. Alexander Rogers (Lahore, Sang-e-Meel Publications, 2002), pp. 21–60.

31 Wick, in *Ethical Philosophy*, p. xxviii.

32 Simon Blackburn, *Being Good: A Short Introduction to Ethics* (Oxford, Oxford University Press, 2001), p. 85.

33 Frank Kermode, 'In the Spirit of Mayhew', *London Review of Books*, 24:8, 25 April 2002, p. 12.

34 Geoff Hancock, 'An Interview with Rohinton Mistry', *Canadian Fiction Magazine*, 65 (1989), 150.

Chapter 6

1   Jaydipsinh Dodiya (ed.), *The Fiction of Rohinton Mistry: Critical Studies* (London and New Delhi, Sangam Books, 1998).

2   Nila Shah, 'Novel as History: A Study of *Such a Long Journey* and *A Fine Balance*', pp. 96–101; Vinita Dhondiyal Bhatnagar, '"And Everything Ends Badly": A Reading of *A Fine Balance*', pp. 102–9; Pramod K. Nayar, 'The Text of Cruelty: Power and Violence in *A Fine Balance*', pp. 119–26; Nilufer E. Bharucha, '"When Old Tracks are Lost": Rohinton Mistry's Fiction as Diasporic Discourse', pp. 23–31, and 'From Behind a Fine Veil: A Feminist Reading of Three Parsi Novels', pp. 44–53; Jaydipsinh Dodiya, 'Literature of the Indian Diaspora in Canada', pp. 11–13; '*Such a Long Journey*: A Critical Study', pp. 70–2; and 'The Parsi Community in *Such a Long Journey*', pp. 93–6; all in Dodiya (ed.) *Rohinton Mistry*.

3   Novy Kapadia, Jaydipsinh Dodiya and R. K. Dhawan (eds), *Parsi Fiction*, 2 vols (New Delhi, Prestige, 2001).

4   Michael Thorpe, 'Canadian "Globalism": Conflicts and Contradictions', in Wolfgang Zach and Ken L. Goodwin (eds), *Nationalism v Internationalism: (Inter)National Dimensions of Literatures in English* (Tubingen, Stauffenburg Verlag, 1996), p. 293.

5   Rocio G. Davis, 'Paradigms of Postcolonial and Immigrant Doubleness: Rohinton Mistry's *Tales from Firozsha Baag*', in Rocio G. Davis and Rosalina Baena (eds), *Tricks with a Glass: Writing Ethnicity in Canada* (Amsterdam, Rodopi, 2000); and 'Negotiating Place/Re-Creating Home: Short Story Cycles by Naipaul, Mistry and Vassanji', in Jacqueline Bardolph (ed.), *Telling Stories: Postcolonial Short Fiction in English* (Amsterdam, Rodopi, 2001).

6   Davis, 'Paradigms', p. 71.

7   Linda Hutcheon and Marion Richmond (eds), *Other Solitudes: Canadian Multicultural Fictions* (Toronto, Oxford University Press, 1990).

8   *Ibid.*, p. 259.

9   Roshan Shahani, 'On the Periphery of the City', in Nilufer E. Bharucha and Vilas Sarang (eds) *Indian-English Fiction, 1980–1990: An Assessment* (Delhi, BR Publishing, 1994), pp. 33–6.

10 Nilufer E. Bharucha, 'Reflections in Broken Mirrors: Diverse Diasporas in Recent Parsi Fiction', *Wasafiri*, 21, Spring (1995), 32–5.

11   Nilufer E. Bharucha, 'The Parsi Voice in Recent Indian English Fiction: An Assertion of Ethnic Identity', in Bharucha and Sarang (eds), *Indian-English Fiction*, pp. 73–87.

12   Nilufer E. Bharucha, '"When Old Tracks are Lost": Rohinton Mistry's Fiction as Diasporic Discourse', *Journal of Commonwealth Literature*, 30:2 (1995), 57.

13   Ajay Heble, '"A Foreign Presence in the Stall": Towards a Poetics of Cultural Hybridity in Rohinton Mistry's Migration Stories', *Canadian Literature*, 137, Summer (1993), 53.

14   *Ibid.*, pp. 54–6.

15   *Ibid.*, p. 60.

16   See my observations on 'Squatter' in Chapter 2.

17   Amin Malak, 'The Shahrazadic Tradition: Rohinton Mistry's *Such a Long Journey* and the Art of Storytelling', *Journal of Commonwealth Literature*, 28:2 (1993), 114.

18   Arun Mukherjee, 'Narrating India', *Toronto South Asian Review*, 10:2 (1992), 87.

19   Thorpe, 'Canadian "Globalism"', p. 296.

20   Gita Viswanath, 'Modes of Resistance in the South-Asian Novel: A Study of the Fiction of Bapsi Sidhwa, Rohinton Mistry and Yasmine Gooneratne', in Dodiya (ed.) *Fiction of Rohinton Mistry*, p. 41.

21   *Ibid.*, pp. 41–2.

22   John Ball, 'Taking the Measure of India's Emergency', *Toronto Review of Contemporary Writing Abroad*, 14:2 (1996), p. 84.

23   Adam Mars-Jones, 'It's all a bit of a mystery', *Observer Review*, 21 April 2002, p. 17.

24   Amit Chaudhuri, 'Parsi Magic', *London Review of Books*, 4 April 1991, p. 19.

25   Bhatnagar, '"Everything ends badly"', p. 102.

26   Tabish Khair, *Babu Fictions: Alienation in Contemporary Indian English Novels* (New Delhi, Oxford University Press, 2001), p. 144.

27   *Ibid.*, p. 325.

28   *Ibid.*, p. 148.

29   Arun Mukherjee, 'Narrating India', p. 85. Mukherjee is here quoting the reviewer Philip Marchand in *The Toronto Star*, 4 May 1991.

30   *Ibid.*, p. 86.

31   Thorpe, 'Canadian "Globalism"', p. 296.

32   Amit Chaudhuri (ed.) *The Picador Book of Modern Indian Literature* (London, Picador, 2001), p. xxiv.

33   Frank Kermode, 'In the Spirit of Mayhew', *London Review of Books*, 24:8, 25 April (2002), 11.

34   Pico Iyer, 'Down and Really Out', *Time Magazine*, 147:17, 6 May 1996, p. 61

35   Ball, 'Taking the Measure of India's Emergency', p. 87.

36   Rukmini Bhaya Nair, 'Bombay's Balzac: *A Fine Balance* by Rohinton Mistry', *Biblio: A Review of Books*, 2:2, March (1996), 14.

37   *Ibid.*, pp. 14–15.

38   *Ibid.*, p. 15.

39   Hilary Mantel, 'States of Emergency', *New York Review of Books*, 43:8, 20 June 1996, 4.

40   *Ibid.*, p. 6.

41   *Ibid.*

42   Peter Morey, *Fictions of India: Narrative and Power* (Edinburgh, Edinburgh University Press, 2000) pp. 183–4.

43   Williams, 'Cyberwriting', p. 67.

44   Bharucha, '"When Old Tracks are Lost"', p. 59.

45   Mukherjee, 'Narrating India', p. 83.

46   Bharucha, '"When Old Tracks are Lost"', p. 59.

47   Morey, *Fictions of India*, p. 183.

48   Ian Watt, *The Rise of the Novel* (London, Hogarth Press, 1987), pp. 9–34.

49   Cedric Watts, 'Introduction', in Joseph Conrad, *The Secret Agent: A Simple Tale*, (London, J. M. Dent, 1997), p. xx.

50   The classic account of mimesis in western culture remains Eric Auerbach's *Mimesis: the Representation of Reality in Western Literature*, trans. Willard R. Trask (Princeton, Princeton University Press, 1953).

51   Aristotle, *Poetics*, Chapter 9, in *Classical Literary Criticism*, trans. Penelope Murray and T. S. Dorsch (Harmondsworth, Penguin, 2000), p. 68.

52   *Ibid.*, Chapter 25, p. 92.

53   Richard Kearney, *On Stories* (London and New York, Routledge, 2002) p. 12.

54   *Ibid.*, p. 131.

55   Morey, *Fictions of India*, p. 183.

56   Graham Allen, *Intertextuality* (London and New York, Routledge, 2000), p. 1.

57   See Roland Barthes, *S/Z*, trans. Richard Miller (London, Jonathan Cape, 1975). See also Barthes's 'The Death of the Author' and 'From Work to Text' in *Image-Music-Text*, trans. Stephen Heath (London, Fontana, 1977).

58   Bill Ashcroft, Gareth Griffiths and Helen Tiffin, *The Empire Writes Back: Theory and Practice in Post-Colonial Literatures* (London and New York, Routledge, 1989), p. 181.

59   W. H. New, *Dreams of Speech and Violence: The Art of the Short Story in Canada and New Zealand* (Toronto, University of Toronto Press, 1987), p. x. See also, Helen Tiffin, 'Post-Colonialism, Post-Modernism and the Rehabilitation of Post-Colonial History', *Journal of Commonwealth Literature*, 10:1 (1988), 172.

60   Sylvia Albertazzi, 'Passages: the "Indian Connection" from Sara Jeanette Duncan to Rohinton Mistry', in M-T Bindella and G. V. Davis (eds), *Imagination and the Creative Impulse in the New Literatures in English* (Amsterdam, Rodopi, 1993), p. 66.

Chapter 7

1   Bruce King, 'The Commonwealth Writer in Exile', in Anna Rutherford (ed.), *From Commonwealth to Postcolonial* (Aarhus, Dangaroo Press, 1992), p. 42.

2   Nilufer E. Bharucha, 'Imagining the Parsi Diaspora: Narrative on the wings of fire', in Ralph Crane and Radhika Mohanram (eds), *Shifting Continents/Colliding Cultures: Diasporic Writing of the Indian Subcontinent* (Amsterdam, Rodopi, 2000), p. 82.

3   Tanya Luhrmann, *The Good Parsi: The Fate of a Colonial Elite in a Postcolonial Society* (Cambridge, Massachusetts, Harvard University Press, 1996), pp. 210–11.

4   Geoff Hancock, 'An Interview with Rohinton Mistry', *Canadian Fiction Magazine*, 65 (1989), 145.

5   Richard Kearney, *On Stories* (London and New York, Routledge, 2002), p. 6.

6   Hancock, 'Interview', p. 148.

7   Shomit Dutta, 'Midnight Muddles', *Daily Telegraph*, Saturday 4 May 2002, p. A3.

8   Alexander Solzhenitsyn, *The First Circle* (London, Collins/Fontana, 1970), p. 312.

9   For Buzurjmihr and Naoshirvan's debates see *The Shah-Namah of Fardusi*, trans. Alexander Rogers (Lahore, Sang-e-Meel Publications, 2002), pp. 457–70; for Asmail and Karmail see pp. 31–2.

10 Ricoeur quoted in Kearney, *On Stories*, p. 190.

11 See Angela Lambert, 'Touched with Fire', *Guardian*, Saturday April 27, 2002, p. 7.

12 Hancock, 'Interview', pp. 147–8.

13 'Rohinton Mistry talks to Robert McLay', *Wasafiri*, 23, Spring (1996), 18.

Select bibliography

Primary sources

BOOKS BY MISTRY

Tales From Firozsha Baag, London, Faber and Faber, 1987.
Such a Long Journey, London, Faber and Faber, 1991.
A Fine Balance, London, Faber and Faber, [1995] 1996.
Family Matters, London, Faber and Faber, 2002.

SELECTED INTERVIEWS BY MISTRY

Interview with Geoff Hancock, *Canadian Fiction Magazine*, 65 (1989), 144–50.

Interview with Dagmar Novak, in Linda Hutcheon and Marian Richmond (eds), *Other Solitudes: Canadian Multicultural Fictions*, Toronto, Oxford University Press, 1990, pp. 255–62.

'Rohinton Mistry talks to Robert McLay', *Wasafiri*, 23 (1996), 16–18.

'Touched with Fire', interview with Angela Lambert, *Guardian*, 27 April 2002, pp. 6–7.

'Such a Long Journey', interview with Stacey Gibson, *University of Toronto Magazine*, Summer 2002, pp. 20–5.

Secondary sources

SELECTED MISTRY CRITICISM AND REVIEWS

Albertazzi, S., 'Passages: The "Indian Connection", from Sara Jeanette Duncan to Rohinton Mistry', in M-T. Bindella and G. V. Davis (eds), *Imagination and the Creative Impulse in the New Literatures in English*, Amsterdam, Rodopi, 1993, pp. 62–6.

Ball, J., 'Taking the Measure of India's Emergency', *Toronto Review of Contemporary Writing Abroad*, 14:2 (1996), 83–7.

Bharucha, N. E., 'Imaging the Parsi Diaspora: Narrative on the Wings of Fire', in Ralph J. Crane and Radhika Mohanram (eds), *Shifting Continents/Colliding Cultures: Diaspora Writing of the Indian Subcontinent*, Amsterdam, Rodopi, 2000, pp. 55–82.

Bharucha, N. E., 'The Parsi Voice in Recent Indian English Fiction', in N. E. Bharucha and V. Sarang (eds), *Indian-English Fiction, 1980–1990: An Assessment*, Delhi, BR Publishing, 1994.

Bharucha, N. E., 'Reflections in Broken Mirrors: Diverse Diasporas in Recent Parsi Fiction', *Wasafiri*, 21 (1995), 32–5.

Bharucha N. E., '"When Old Tracks are Lost": Rohinton Mistry's Fiction as Diasporic Discourse', *Journal of Commonwealth Literature*, 30:2 (1995), 57–64.

Chaudhuri, A., 'Parsi Magic', *London Review of Books*, 4 April 1991, p. 19.

Davis, R. G., 'Negotiating Place/Re-Creating Home: Short Story Cycles by Naipaul, Mistry and Vassanji', in J. Bardolph (ed.), *Telling Stories: Postcolonial Short Fiction in English*, Amsterdam, Rodopi, 2001, pp. 323–30.

Davis, R. G., 'Paradigms of Postcolonial and Immigrant Doubleness: Rohinton Mistry's *Tales from Firozsha Baag*', in R. G. Davis and R. Baena (eds), *Tricks with a Glass: Writing Ethnicity in Canada*, Amsterdam, Rodopi, 2000, pp. 71–90.

Desai, A., '"Was I There?" Rohinton Mistry's *Such a Long Journey*, in N. E. Bharucha and V. Sarang (eds), *Indian-English Fiction, 1980–1990: An Assessment*, Delhi, BR Publishing, 1994.

Dodiya, J. (ed.), *The Fiction of Rohinton Mistry: Critical Studies*, London, Sangam, 1998.

Dutta, S., 'Midnight Muddles', *Daily Telegraph*, 4 May 2002, p. 3.

Freely, M., 'Ken Loach in Bollywood: *Family Matters* by Rohinton Mistry', *New Statesman*, 8 April 2002, pp. 56–7.

Garebian, K., 'In the Aftermath of Empire: Identities in the Commonwealth of Literature', *Canadian Forum*, April 1989, 25–33.

Heble, A., '"A Foreign Presence in the Stall": Towards a Poetics of Cultural Hybridity in Rohinton Mistry's Migration Stories', *Canadian Literature*, 137 (1993), 51–61.

Iyer, P., 'Down and Really Out', *Time Magazine*, 6 May 1996, p. 61.

Kain, G., 'The Enigma of Departure: The Dynamics of Cultural Ambiguity in Rohinton Mistry's *Swimming Lessons and Other Stories from Firozsha Baag*', in G. Kain, *Ideas of Home: Literature of Asian Migration*, East Lansing, Michigan State University Press, 1997, pp. 63–73.

Kapadia, N., Dodiya, J., and Dhawan, R. K. (eds), *Parsi Fiction*, 2 vols, New Delhi, Prestige, 2001.

Kermode, F., 'In the Spirit of Mayhew', *London Review of Books*, 25 April 2002, pp. 11–12.

Khair, T., *Babu Fictions: Alienation in Contemporary Indian English Novels*, New Delhi, Oxford University Press, 2001.

Malak, A., 'Insider/Outsider Views on Belonging: The Short Stories of Bharati Mukherjee and Rohinton Mistry', in J. Bardolph (ed.), *Short Fiction in the New Literatures in English: Proceedings of the Nice Conference of the European Association for Commonwealth Literature and Language Studies*, Nice, Faculté des Lettres et Science Humaine, 1989, pp. 189–95.

Malak, A., 'The Shahrazadic Tradition: Rohinton Mistry's *Such a Long Journey* and the Art of Storytelling', *Journal of Commonwealth Literature*, 28:2 (1993), 108–18.

Mantel, H., 'States of Emergency', *New York Review of Books*, 43:8 (1996), 4–6.

Marchand, P., 'A Tale of Moral Conflict in Bombay', *Toronto Star*, 4 May 1991, p. 13.

Mars-Jones, A., 'It's All a Bit of a Mystery', *Observer Review*, 21 April 2002, p. 17.

McClaren, J., 'From Raj to Republics: State and Nation in Fiction from the Subcontinent', *World Literature Written in English*, 36:1 (1997), 39–56.

Morey, P., *Fictions of India: Narrative and Power*, Edinburgh, Edinburgh University Press, 2000.

Mukherjee, A., 'Narrating India', *Toronto South Asian Review*, 10:2 (1992), 82–91.

Nair, R. B., 'Bombay's Balzac: *A Fine Balance* by Rohinton Mistry', *Biblio: A Review of Books*, 2:2 (1996), 14–15.

Shahani, R., 'On the Periphery of the City', in N. E. Bharucha and V. Sarang (eds), *Indian English Fiction, 1980–1990: An Assessment*, Delhi, BR Publishing, 1994, pp. 33–44.

Sunwani, V. K., 'Rohinton Mistry's *A Fine Balance*: A Critique', *Journal of Indian Writing in English*, 25:1–2 (1997), 107–12.

Tapping, C., 'South Asia/North America: New Dwellings and the Past', in E. S. Nelson (ed.), *Reworlding: The Literature of the Indian Diaspora*, Connecticut, Greenwood Press, 1992, pp. 35–46.

Thorpe, M., 'Canadian "Globalism": Conflicts and Contradictions', in W. Zach and K. L. Goodwin (eds), *Nationalism v Internationalism: (Inter)National Dimensions of Literatures in English*, Tübingen, Stauffenburg, 1996, pp. 293–7.

Williams, D., 'Cyberwriting and the Borders of Identity: "What's in a Name" in Kroetsch's *The Puppeteer* and Mistry's *Such a Long Journey*', *Canadian Literature*, 137 (1993), 51–61.

OTHER WORKS

Adams, J. and Whitehead, P., *The Dynasty: The Nehru-Gandhi Story*, Harmondsworth, Penguin, 1997.

Ali, T., *The Nehrus and the Gandhis: An Indian Dynasty*, London, Picador, 1985.

Allen, G., *Intertextuality*, London and New York, Routledge, 2000.

Ashcroft, B., Griffiths, G. and Tiffin, H., *The Empire Writes Back: Theory and Practice in Post-Colonial Literatures*, London and New York, Routledge, 1989.

Balzac, H. de, *Père Goriot*, trans. A. J. Krailsheimer, Oxford, Oxford University Press, 1991.

Bardolph, J. (ed.), *Telling Stories: Postcolonial Short Fiction in English*, Amsterdam, Rodopi, 2001.

Barthes, R., *Image-Music-Text*, trans. S. Heath, London, Collins/Fontana, 1977.

Barthes, R., *S/Z*, trans. R. Miller, London, Jonathan Cape, 1975.

Blackburn, S., *Being Good: A Short Introduction to Ethics*, Oxford, Oxford University Press, 2001.

Certeau, M. de, *The Practice of Everyday Life*, trans. S. Rendall, Berkeley, University of California Press, 1988.

Chakrabarty, D., 'Postcoloniality and the Artifice of History: Who Speaks for "Indian" Pasts?', *Representations*, 37 (1992), 2–23.

Chatterjee, P., *Nationalist Thought in the Colonial World: A Derivative Discourse?*, London, Zed Books, 1986.

Chatterjee, P., *The Nation and its Fragments: Colonial and Postcolonial Histories*, Princeton, Princeton University Press, 1993.

Chaudhuri, A., *The Picador Book of Modern Indian Literature*, London, Picador, 2001.

Childs, P. and Williams, P., *An Introduction to Post-colonial Theory*, Hemel Hempstead, Prentice Hall/Harvester Wheatsheaf, 1997.

Clark, P. *Zoroastrianism: An Introduction to an Ancient Faith*, Brighton, Sussex Academic Press, 1998.

Clifford, J., 'Diasporas', *Cultural Anthropology*, 9:3 (1994), 302–38.

Conrad, J., *The Secret Agent: A Simple Tale*, London, J. M. Dent, 1997.

Davis, R. and Baena, R. (eds), *Tricks with a Glass: Writing Ethnicity in Canada*, Amsterdam, Rodopi, 2000.

Deleuze, G. and Guattari, F., *Kafka: Toward a Minor Literature*, trans. Dana Polan, Minneapolis and London, University of Minnesota Press, 1986.

Derrida, J., *On the Name*, trans. D. Wood, J. P. Leavey jr. and I. McLeod, Stanford, Stanford University Press, 1995.

Desai, B. *The Memory of Elephants*, New Delhi, HarperCollins, 2000.

Dhar, P. N., *Indira Gandhi, the 'Emergency' and Indian Democracy*, New Delhi, Oxford University Press, 2000.

Dostoyevsky, F., *The Idiot*, trans. D. Magarshack, Harmondsworth, Penguin, 1955.

Eduljee, H. E., *Kisseh-i Sanjan*, Bombay, K. R. Cama Oriental Institute, 1991.

Eliot, T. S., *Selected Poems*, London, Faber and Faber, 1961.

Ford, R. (ed.), *The Essential Tales of Chekhov*, London, Granta, 1999.

Ganguly, K., 'Migrant Identities: Personal Memory and the Construction of Selfhood', *Cultural Studies*, 6:1 (1992), 27–50.

George, R. M., *The Politics of Home: Postcolonial relocations and twentieth-century fiction*, Cambridge, Cambridge University Press, 1996.

Ghosh, A., 'The Diaspora in Indian Culture', *Public Culture*, 2:1 (1989), 73–8.

Howells, C. A. and Hunter, L. (eds), *Narrative Strategies in Canadian Literature: Feminism and Postcolonialism*, Oxford, Oxford University Press, 1991.

Hutcheon, L., *Splitting Images: Contemporary Canadian Ironies*, Toronto, Oxford University Press, 1991.

Hutcheon, L. and Richmond, M. (eds), *Other Solitudes: Canadian Multicultural Fictions*, Toronto, Oxford University Press, 1990.

Ingram, F. L., *Representative Short Story Cycles of the Twentieth Century: Studies in a Literary Genre*, Paris, Mouton, 1971.

Jaffrelot, C. and Hansen, T. B. (eds), *The BJP and the Compulsions of Politics in India*, New Delhi, Oxford University Press, 1998.

JanMohamed, A. and Lloyd, D. (eds), *The Nature and Context of Minority Discourse*, Oxford, Oxford University Press, 1990.

Joyce, J., *Dubliners*, London, Grafton, 1977.

Kafka, F., *The Complete Novels*, trans. W. and E. Muir, London, Minerva, 1992.

Kamboureli, S., 'Canadian Ethnic Anthologies: Representations of Ethnicity', *ARIEL*, 25:4 (1994), 11–52.

Kant, I., *Ethical Philosophy*, trans. J. W. Ellington, Indianapolis, Hackett Publishing, 1994, second edition.

Kearney, R., *On Stories*, London and New York, Routledge, 2002.

Kennedy, J. G., 'Toward a Poetics of the Short Story Cycle', *Journal of the Short Story in English*, 11 (1989), 9–25.

Khilnani, S., *The Idea of India*, Harmondsworth, Penguin, 1998.

Kriwaczek, P., *In Search of Zarathustra: The First Prophet and the Ideas that Changed the World*, London, Weidenfeld and Nicholson, 2002.

Kulke, E., *The Parsis in India: A Minority as an Agent of Social Change*, München, Weltforum, 1974.

Luhrmann, T. M., *The Good Parsi: The Fate of a Colonial Elite in a Postcolonial Society*, Massachusetts, Harvard University Press, 1996.

Luscher, R. M., 'The Short Story Sequence: An Open Book', in S. Lohafer and J. E. Clary (eds), *Short Story Theory at the Crossroads*, Baton Rouge, Louisiana University Press, 1989.

Lynch, G., 'The One and the Many: English-Canadian Short Story Cycles', *Canadian Literature*, 130:3 (1990), 91–104.

Maupassant, G. de, *A Day in the Country and Other Stories*, trans. D. Coward, Oxford, Oxford University Press, 1990.

Mishra, V., 'The Diasporic Imaginary: Theorising the Indian Diaspora', *Textual Practice*, 10:3 (1996), 421–36.

Mukherjee, M., *The Perishable Empire: Essays on Indian Writing in English*, New Delhi, Oxford University Press, 2000.

Munro, A., *Lives of Girls and Women*, Harmondsworth, Penguin, 1982.

Murray, P. and Dorsch, T. S., eds and trans., *Classical Literary Criticism*, Harmondsworth, Penguin, 2000.

Naipaul, V. S., *Miguel Street*, Harmondsworth, Penguin, 1971.

Narayan, R. K., *The Guide*, Harmondsworth, Penguin, 1988.

New, W. H., *Dreams of Speech and Violence: The Art of the Short Story in Canada and New Zealand*, Toronto, University of Toronto Press, 1987.

Patel, S. and Thorner, A. (eds), *Bombay: Metaphor for Modern India*, New Delhi, Oxford University Press, 1996.

Plato, *The Republic*, trans. Benjamin Jowett, New York, Dover Publications, 2000.

Rushdie, S., *East, West*, London, Jonathan Cape, 1994.

Rushdie, S., *Imaginary Homelands: Essays and Criticism 1981–1991*, London, Granta, 1992.

Rushdie, S., *The Moor's Last Sigh*, London, Vintage, 1996.

Rutherford, A. (ed.), *From Commonwealth to Post-colonial*, Dangaroo, 1992.

Ryan, M., *Literary Theory: A Practical Introduction*, London, Blackwell, 1999.

Rylance, R. (ed.), *Debating Texts: A Reader in Twentieth-Century Literary Theory and Method*, Milton Keynes, Open University Press, 1987.

Rypka, J. et al., *History of Iranian Literature*, Dordrecht, D. Reidel Publishing, 1968.

Safran, W., 'Diasporas in Modern Societies: Myths of Homeland and Return', *Diaspora*, 1:1 (1991), 83–99.

Sahgal, N., *Indira Gandhi: Her Road to Power*, London, Macdonald, 1983.

Sahgal, N., *Rich Like Us*, London, Sceptre, 1987.

Scruton, R., *Kant: A Very Short Introduction*, Oxford, Oxford University Press, 2001.

Selbourne, D., *An Eye to India: The Unmasking of a Tyranny*, London, Pelican, 1977.

Shah-Namah of Fardusi, trans. A. Rogers, Lahore, Sang-e-Meel, 2000.

Sidhwa, B., *The Crow Eaters*, London, Jonathan Cape, 1980.

Solzhenitsyn, A., *The First Circle*, trans. M. Guybon, London, Collins, 1970.

Stiles Maneck, S., *The Death of Ahriman: Culture, Identity and Theological Change Among the Parsis of India*, Bombay, K. R. Cama Oriental Institute, 1997.

Sturrock, J. (ed.), *Structuralism and Since: From Lévi-Strauss to Derrida*, Oxford, Oxford University Press, 1979.

Tagore, R., *Gitanjali*, Delhi, Macmillan India, 1976.

Tolstoy, L., *Anna Karenina*, trans. R. Pevear and L. Volokhonsky, Harmondsworth, Penguin, 2000.

Turgenev, I., *Fathers and Sons*, trans. R. Edmonds, Harmondsworth, Penguin, 1965.

Turgenev, I., *Sketches from a Hunter's Album*, trans. Richard Freeborn, Harmondsworth, Penguin, 1990.

Voltaire, *Candide and Other Tales*, trans. T. Smollett, London, J. M. Dent, 1971.

Williams, P. and Chrisman, L. (eds), *Colonial Discourse and Post-Colonial Theory: A Reader*, Hemel Hempstead, Harvester Wheatsheaf, 1993.

Yarshater, E. (ed.), *Persian Literature*, New York, Persian Heritage Foundation, 1988.

Yarshater, E. et al. (eds), *Encyclopaedia Iranica*, Bibliotheca Persica Press, 1999.

Yeats, W. B., *Selected Poetry*, ed. A. N. Jeffares, London, Pan and Macmillan, 1974.

Zach, W. and Goodwin, K. L. (eds), *Nationalism vs Internationalism: (Inter)National Dimensions of Literatures in English*, Tübingen, Stauffenburg, 1996.

Index

abrogation, 155
Abul Kavim-i-Mansur *see*
    Fardusi
Achebe, Chinua, 109
Ahura Mazda (Ohrmazd), 7, 86
Albertazzi, Sylvia, 169
Allen, Graham, 167
Anand, Mulk Raj, 17, 98, 111
Angra Mainyu (Ahriman), 7
a priori truths, 142
Aristotle, 90, 150, 166
asceticism, 86–7
Ashcroft, B., 40, 167
Atash Bahram, 7
autobiographical fiction, 4
Ayodhya, 125

Babri Mosque, 125
Bahujan Samaj, 123
Bakhtin, M., 55–6, 119–20
balance in writing, 106
Ball, John, 95, 106, 157, 160
Balzac, Honoré de, 17, 112, 160–
    1, 167
Banani, Amin, 17
Bardolph, Jacqueline, 153
Barthes, Roland, 167
Beckett, Samuel, 81
Benjamin, Walter, 2
Bennett, Arnold, 160
Bhabha, Homi K., 12, 55, 64, 123

Bharucha, Nilufer E., 9–10, 15,
    153–4, 164
Bhatnagar, Vinita Dhondiyal,
    153, 158–9
Bhutto, Zulfikar Ali, 72
Bissoondath, Neil, 20
BJP (Bharatiya Janata Party),
    126, 131, 143
Blackburn, Simon, 150
Blyton, Enid, 2, 144, 147–8
Boccaccio, Giovanni, 20
Boehmer, Elleke, 18
Bombay, 10–11, 23–5, 33, 35, 39,
    55, 70, 75–8, 97, 113, 122–
    3, 125–6, 131–3, 143–4,
    154, 162, 168
Boyce, M., 56

Cama, K. R., 11
Camus, Albert, 17
caste, 95, 109–11, 121, 158
categorical imperative, 137–8
Certeau, Michel de, 115
Charteris, Leslie, 2
Chatterjee, Partha, 111
Chaucer, Geoffrey, 29
Chaudhuri, Amit, 24, 122, 158,
    160
Chekhov, Anton, 17
Childs, P., 12–13
Christie, Agatha, 2

Clark, P., 86
Clifford, James, 18
Cole, Nat King, 81
colonial identity, 12–13
Congress Party, 11, 22, 98–9
Conrad, Joseph, 77, 82–3, 165
Crompton, Richmal, 2

Dabydeen, Cyril, 20
dastan, 54
Davis, Rocio G., 30, 153–4
Deleuze, G., 94–5
Derrida, Jacques, 54–5, 78, 80, 85
Desai, Anjana, 87
Desai, Boman, 15, 154
Dhondy, Farukh, 15
diasporic discourse, 18–19, 154
Dickens, Charles, 3, 17, 29, 77,
    122, 160, 163, 165–6
Dodiya, Jaydipsinh, 152–3
Dondy, Farrukh, 154
Dostoyevsky, F., 17, 25–6, 82, 166

Elavia, Freny, 3
Eliot, T. S., 17, 59–62, 69–70, 77,
    79, 87, 166
eudaimonia, 150
exile, 1–2, 58, 64–5

Fardusi (Abul Kavim-i-Mansur),
    16, 125
Farrell, J. G., 118
Faulkner, William, 30
Firdausi *see* Fardusi
Fire Temple, 7
Forster, E. M., 108–9, 133
Franck, Cesar, 81

Gandhi, Feroze, 93
Gandhi, Indira, 5, 22–3, 70–4, 80,
    84–5, 93, 95–100, 103,
    109–10, 117, 122–3, 161
Gandhi, Mahatma, 99–100
Gandhi, Rajiv, 108

Gandhi, Sanjay, 22, 71, 93, 100,
    118
gender issues, 156
Ghosh, Amitav, 19, 89
Gibson, Stacey, 25
Griffiths, G., 40, 155, 167
Guattari, F., 94–5
Gujarat, 9–10

happiness, 149–50
Hardy, Thomas, 160
Hart House literary competition,
    3–4, 27
Heble, Ajay, 155
Homer, 29
Hunter, Lynette, 20
Hutcheon, Linda, 13, 20–1, 28–9,
    66, 92, 154

Ingram, Forrest L., 29
intertextuality, 167
irony, 29
Iyer, Pico, 160

Jadi Rana, 9
James, Henry, 41
JanMohamed, Abdul, 14, 21
Jeejeebhoy, Sir Jamset, 11
Jonson, Ben, 165
Joyce, James, 17, 30, 169
Juvenal, 165

Kafka, Franz, 97, 122
Kaikobad, Bahman, 9
Kamboureli, Smaro, 64–5
Kanga, Firdaus, 15, 154
Kant, Immanuel, 137–8, 142,
    147–9
Kapadia, Novy, 126
Karaka, D. F., 11, 15
Kearney, Richard, 166
Kennedy, Gerald, 32
Kermode, Frank, 15, 150, 160
Khair, Tabish, 121, 158–9

Khilnani, Sunil, 23
Khodadad Building, 75–6, 91
Kisseh-i Sanjan, 9, 87
Kulke, Eckehard, 6, 10

Lamming, George, 32
Lloyd, David, 14, 21
logocentrism, 80, 85
Luhmann, Tanya, 12–13, 35, 61,
    144–5
Lynch, Gerald, 30

Mahmud, Sultan of Ghazna, 16
Malabari, Behramji, 11, 15
Malak, Amin, 19–20, 155–6
Mantel, Hilary, 161–3, 169
Mars-Jones, Adam, 131, 157
Marxism, 158
Marzban, Adi, 144
Maupassant, Guy de, 43–4
Mehta, Pherozeshah, 11
mimesis, 165–6
Minorities Commission, 131
minor literatures, 94
Mistry, Rohinton
    Life:
    birth and family background, 2
    critical interest in, 152, 158
    criticisms of, 156–7
    earliest writing, 3–4
    education, 2–4, 14
    emigration to Canada, 3
    literary prizes, 3–4
    marriage, 3
    religious writing, 7–8
    Works:
    'Auspicious Occasion', 4, 8,
        27, 31–7, 155
    'The Collectors', 8, 25, 33, 42,
        44–7, 61
    'Condolence Visit', 31, 33,
        42–4
    'Exercisers', 30–1, 33, 46, 60
    Family Matters, 7–8, 23, 61,
        66, 124, 126–45, 148–50,
        157, 168–9
    A Fine Balance, 23, 59, 70,
        75, 93–106, 109–23, 128,
        150, 156–61, 164, 168
    'The Ghost of Firozsha Baag',
        32–3, 38–42
    'Lend Me Your Light', 18, 20,
        30, 32–3, 56–7, 59–60, 63,
        155
    'The More Important Things',
        24–5
    'One Sunday', 3–4, 27, 32–3,
        36–8, 43
    'The Paying Guests', 32–3,
        49–50
    'Squatter', 18, 22, 30, 32–3,
        51–6, 91, 155
    Such a Long Journey, 4, 8, 22,
        25, 39, 49, 51, 70–2, 77–
        95, 119, 135, 150, 152–70
    'Swimming Lessons', 27, 30,
        33, 54, 63–7
    Tales from Firozsha Baag, 1–
        2, 4–5, 15, 19–20, 23, 25,
        27–38, 67–8, 70, 74, 90,
        154–5, 168–9
    'Of White Hairs and Cricket',
        33, 42, 48, 67
Mukherjee, Arun, 89, 156, 159–
    60, 164
Mukherjee, Bharati, 5, 19, 58
multiculturalism, 5, 22, 154
Multiculturalism Act (1988), 21
Munro, Alice, 47

Nabokov, Vladimir, 17
Nagarwala, Sohrab Rustom, 72–
    3
Naipaul, V. S., 17, 19, 63–4, 144
Nair, Rukmini Bhaya, 69, 111,
    160–1
Namjoshi, Suniti, 20
Naoroji, Dadabhai, 11

Narayan, R. K., 17, 98, 105
Naxalite insurgency, 99
Nayar, Pramod K., 153
Nehru, Jawaharlal, 71, 99–100
New, W. H., 15, 167–8
Novak, Dagmar, 154

Ohrmazd see Ahura Mazda
Ondaatje, Michael, 20
Othello, 55–6

Pakistan, 71–2, 90, 102–3
Parsi community, 8–19, 24, 31–7, 42, 49, 52, 57–8, 61, 66, 79, 87, 94–5, 122–3, 127, 134, 144–51, 153–4, 157, 159, 164, 168
Partition, 102–3
pavement art, 87–92
Pendse, Sandeep, 97, 113–14, 119
Petit, Sir Dinshaw, 11
Picador Book of Modern Indian Literature, 160
Pinter, Harold, 81
Plato and Platonism, 54, 84–90
poetry, 166
postcolonialism, 14–15, 30, 40, 152, 159, 164–6, 168
postmodernism, 164
poststructuralism, 160

Ray, Satyajit, 157
readerly texts, 167
Readymoney, Sir Cowasjee, 11
realism, 161, 163, 165, 167
Richmond, Marion, 154
Ricoeur, Paul, 123
Rushdie, Salman, 1, 3, 5, 13, 19, 22–4, 44, 123–4, 161
Ryan, Michael, 92

Sahgal, Nayantara, 17, 98
Sassanians, 6–7, 9
Scruton, Roger, 137, 142

Selbourne, David, 99
Seth, Vikram, 160
Shah, Nila, 153
Shahani, Roshan, 154
Shah-Namah, 15–16, 52, 54, 56
Shakespeare, William, 3, 55–6, 106
Shastri, Lal Bahadur, 71, 93
Shiv Sena, 23, 70, 116, 125–6, 131–4, 142–3
short story cycles, 29–32, 153, 167
Sidhwa, Bapsi, 15, 154
Solzhenitsyn, Alexander, 94
Sorabji, Cornelia, 11, 15
Spark, Muriel, 17
Sprinker, Michael, 122
Srikrishna Commission, 131
Stendhal, 162
Stiles Maneck, Susan, 13, 85
Suhrawadi, 85
Swift, Jonathan, 165

Tagore, R., 17, 76
Tapping, Craig, 67
Tata, J. N., 10
Thackeray, Bal, 126, 131
Thoreau, Henry David, 32
Thorpe, Michael, 153–4, 156, 160
Thousand and One Nights, The, 29, 54
Tiffin, H., 40, 155, 167
Tolstoy, Leo, 17, 101
Toynbee, A., 10
Turgenev, Ivan, 17, 29

Vakil, Ardashir, 15
Vassanji, M. G., 20
Viswanath, Gita, 156–7
Voltaire, 140–3

Wacha, D. E., 11
Wadia, N. M., 11
Watt, Ian, 165
Watts, Cedric, 165

westernization, 144–5
Wick, Warner A., 138
Williams, David, 78–9, 163
Williams, P., 12–13
Williams, Raymond, 113
writerly texts, 167

xenophobia, 144

Yasna ceremony, 86
Yeats, W. B., 17, 98, 109, 130,
    166

Zarathustra, 6, 16, 86, 146
Zoroastrianism, 6–9, 14–16, 25,
    59, 61, 70–1, 74, 85–8,
    101, 127, 135, 145–7, 150